Thomas Macdonough

Additional titles in the Library of Naval Biography series, edited by James C. Bradford

Confederate Admiral: The Life and Wars of Franklin Buchanan
by Craig L. Symonds

Andrew Foote: Civil War Admiral on Western Waters
by Spencer C. Tucker

Thomas ap Catesby Jones: Commodore of Manifest Destiny
by Gene A. Smith

Joshua Barney: Hero of the Revolution and 1812
by Louis Arthur Norton

Matthew Calbraith Perry: Antebellum Sailor and Diplomat
by John H. Schroeder

Mad Jack Percival: Legend of the Old Navy
by James H. Ellis

Commodore Ellsworth P. Bertholf: First Commandant of the Coast Guard
by C. Douglas Kroll

LIBRARY OF NAVAL BIOGRAPHY

Thomas Macdonough by Gilbert Stuart
National Gallery of Art, Washington, D.C.

Thomas Macdonough

MASTER OF COMMAND IN THE EARLY U.S. NAVY

David Curtis Skaggs

Naval Institute Press
Annapolis, Maryland

Naval Institute Press
291 Wood Road
Annapolis, MD 21402

Library of Congress Cataloging-in-Publication Data
Skaggs, David Curtis.
    Thomas Macdonough : master of command in the early U.S. Navy / David
Curtis Skaggs.
    p. cm. — (Library of naval biography)
    ISBN 1-55750-839-9 (acid-free paper)
    1. Macdonough, Thomas, 1783–1825. 2. Admirals—United States—Biography. 3.
United States. Navy—Biography. 4. United States—History—War of 1812—
Naval operations. 5. United States—History, Military—19th century. I. Title. II. Series.
    E353.1.M2 S53 2002
    973.5'25'092—dc21

                                                          2002004610

Printed in the United States of America on acid-free paper ∞
10 09 08 07 06 05 04 03 9 8 7 6 5 4 3 2
First printing

For Margo, with love

CONTENTS

AT NO TIME in American history was naval policy and strategy as hotly contested as during the era of the early Republic, a time when leaders of the young nation believed the very existence of the United States to be in peril. During its first two decades, the United States Navy fought an undeclared naval war with France, grappled with Barbary corsairs in the Mediterranean Sea, and inflicted strategic defeats on the Royal Navy of Great Britain during the War of 1812. Indeed, in no other war has naval power been as vital to the survival of the nation as it was during the War of 1812. Naval victories near Put-in-Bay on Lake Erie and at Plattsburgh on Lake Champlain secured the territorial integrity of the United States, turned back a British invasion, and convinced the British cabinet to seek peace without victory in 1815.

The career of Thomas Macdonough spanned this era. He entered the young U.S. Navy during the Quasi-War with France, fought for three years in the Mediterranean, and directed the construction of gunboats after the Jefferson administration adopted a strategy of coastal defense rather than defense through a blue-water Navy. During the War of 1812 Macdonough drew upon experience gained building gunboats to construct a squadron of sailing vessels on Lake Champlain, then led that squadron to victory against superior British naval forces in the Battle of Plattsburgh.

A shortage of personal papers has deterred previous historians from attempting a biography of Macdonough, but David Skaggs has succeeded masterfully where others have feared to write. He possesses the perfect combination of experience and knowledge to write the first scholarly biography of Thomas Macdonough. An award-winning scholar and teacher of both early American and military history, Skaggs is the coeditor of *The Sixty Years' War for the Great Lakes, 1754–1814* and the coauthor of *A Signal Victory: The Lake Erie Campaign, 1812–1813*. The first book provides the context for the warfare in which Macdonough achieved immortal fame, and the second explores the art of commanding a vessel of war during battle, analyzing the leadership qualities of Oliver Hazard Perry. In this biography he subjects Thomas Macdonough to similar scrutiny. Skaggs finds

Macdonough a worthy subject, one whose technical and tactical proficiency, personal conduct, quest for self-improvement, personal courage, and training of subordinates placed under him made him an exemplary American naval officer of the Age of Sail. John Paul Jones, Stephen Decatur, and Oliver Hazard Perry shared Macdonough's courage under fire and command presence, and Thomas Truxtun and Edward Preble were as professionally proficient as Macdonough, but in none of these individuals were as many commendable qualities combined without corresponding weaknesses. At the center of Skaggs's study is a detailed analysis of the characteristics of sound naval leadership that is as applicable today as it was in the early nineteenth century. In this fine biography, Thomas Macdonough belatedly receives the attention due him.

The Library of Naval Biography provides accurate, informative, and interpretive biographies of influential naval figures—men and women who have shaped or reflected the naval affairs of their time. Each volume will explain the forces that acted upon its subjects as well as the significance of that person in history. Some volumes will explore the lives of individuals who have not previously been the subject of a modern, full-scale biography, while others will reexamine the lives of better-known individuals adding new information, a differing perspective, or a fresh interpretation. The series is international in scope and includes individuals from several centuries. All volumes are based on solid research and written to be of interest to general readers as well as specialists.

With these goals in mind, the length of each volume has been limited, the notes have been placed at the end of the text, and a brief essay on "Further Reading" has been provided to assess previous biographies of the subject and to direct the reader to the most important studies of the era and events in which the person participated.

It is the intention that this combination of clear writing, fresh interpretations, and solid historical context will result in volumes that restore the all-important human dimension to naval history and are enjoyable to read.

JAMES C. BRADFORD
Series Editor

ON 11 SEPTEMBER 1814 the United States Navy won a squadron action against elements of the Royal Navy on Lake Champlain, one of the first successful fleet encounters for the young American navy. It set a tradition of seeking combat and of determined fighting that characterizes that service to this day. Although this triumph was the most important tactical and strategic naval victory for the United States in the War of 1812, its commander, Thomas Macdonough, is virtually unknown. In his popularized account of the engagement, Charles G. Muller argues that Macdonough's "light has burned long enough under a bushel." This book lifts that bushel a little higher and illuminates Macdonough's whole life, personal and professional.

Thomas Macdonough's life story characterizes a generation of young men who helped in the refounding of the United States Navy, 1794–1820. This generation fought an undeclared war against the French navy, waged another war against the Barbary States of North Africa, and took on the armed might of the Royal Navy in the War of 1812. It confronted a serious strategic policy dilemma of how to counter much larger naval forces in an era of constrained budgets and conflicting visions of the United States' role on the salt and freshwater seas. Macdonough died before the technological change brought about by steam power and high-powered rifled artillery seriously compromised the skills he developed with wind, sail, and smoothbore cannons. His forte was not national diplomacy, strategic policy, or technological innovation; rather, it was tactical leadership. Here he excelled and inspired; his efforts were epitomized in one pungent phrase from the pen of his colleague Oliver Hazard Perry: "We have met the enemy, and they are ours." Commodore Macdonough was a commander, a leader of men in that most awesome and awful of human encounters—combat. He learned the profession of arms from some of its finest practitioners, and he taught that profession to many who served with him.

Macdonough described his triumph on Lake Champlain as a "signal" victory, and that it was. It signaled the emergence of successful squadron operations in the history of the U.S. Navy. It signaled the rise of a professional officer corps that dominates the naval forces of the United States to this day. It signaled the continued development of a fighting tradition in the navy of the young Republic that idealized the combat commander. And it signaled determination and perseverance in the face of great odds.

In a recent novel Diana Gabaldon wrote that historians' "greatest crime is that they presume to know what happened, how things came about, when they have only what the past chose to leave behind—for the most part, they think what they were meant to think, and it's a rare one that sees what really happened, behind the smokescreen of artifacts and paper." This is the great difficulty of writing history: seeing through the smokescreen of what the past has left behind. In the case of Macdonough it is a very thick layer of smoke. Aside from his official letters in naval archives, little of his personal correspondence survives, and that which does is scattered in a variety of institutions in the eastern half of the United States. Yet this biography seeks to find some of the familial characteristics of the commodore. Moreover, it devotes extensive space to his career after the battle that made him famous. The focus is on naval leadership during the Age of Fighting Sail. The art of command can be partially taught, but successful command requires a character that goes beyond the status conferred by rank and position. We can never fully penetrate the smokescreen of artifacts and paper, but we can attempt to see, however dimly, the individual that lies hidden in the midst of a wooden world we have lost.

ACKNOWLEDGMENTS

No SCHOLARLY endeavor can be successful without the collaboration of countless individuals. Among those persons and institutions to whom considerable indebtedness is owed are the following: Kausala Padmaraj, Mary Beth Zachary, and the staff of Jerome Library, and Bob Graham of the Historical Collection of the Great Lakes, Bowling Green State University, Bowling Green, Ohio; Wayne Miller, Special Collections, Feinberg Library, State University of New York, Plattsburgh; Shirley Koester, Clinton County Historical Association and Museum, Plattsburgh, New York; Karen Campbell, Elizabeth H. Dow, and Jeffrey D. Marshall, Special Collections, Bailey-Howe Library, University of Vermont, Burlington; Cinda May and the staff of the Lilly Library, Indiana University, Bloomington; Barbara DeWolfe, John Harrison, and Brian Leigh Dunnigan, William L. Clements Library, University of Michigan, Ann Arbor; Mary Rose Catalfamo, Special Collections, Nimitz Library, U.S. Naval Academy, and Scott Harmon and James Cheevers, U.S. Naval Academy Museum, Annapolis, Maryland; Glenn Helm, Naval Department Library, Naval Historical Center, Washington, D.C.; Frederick Bauman and the Manuscripts Division staff at the Library of Congress, Washington, D.C.; Raymond Teichman and Nancy Snedeker, Franklin Delano Roosevelt Library, Hyde Park, New York; Nancy Rucker, the Sheldon Museum, Middlebury, Vermont; Rick Stattler, Rhode Island Historical Society, Providence; Karen Quinn, Corbit-Calloway Memorial Library, Odessa, Delaware; Constance Cooper, Historical Society of Delaware, Wilmington; Dione Longley, Middlesex County Historical Society, Middletown, Connecticut; and J. C. A. Stagg and his staff, Papers of James Madison, University of Virginia, Charlottesville. The staffs of the Russell Library, Middletown, Connecticut, the National Archives in Washington, D.C., the Naval War College Library in Newport, Rhode Island, the Air University Library at Maxwell AFB, Alabama, the John Carter Brown Library and the John Hay Library at Brown University, Providence, Rhode Island, and the Vermont Historical Society, Montpelier, all aided me with my unusual demands on their busy schedules.

Special assistance came from unexpected sources. Professor Christopher McKee gave sound guidance and wise counsel that assisted greatly throughout the research and writing of this book. Quality advice came from Timothy Dubé, military archivist with the National Archives of Canada. Captain Frank Pabst, Lake Towing and Salvage, Plattsburgh, New York, and Art Cohn, David Robinson, and Chris Sabick of the Lake Champlain Maritime Museum, Vergennes, Vermont, provided information on the recently discovered *Confiance* anchor. Donald Petrie of Wainscott, New York, informed me on prize monies. The staff of the Middletown Probate Court, Middletown, Connecticut, patiently allowed me to examine the Macdonough probate records. Jackie Gorn of the Church of the Holy Trinity in Middletown graciously searched the parish records for data. John Hutto, M.D., my summertime neighbor in Brutus, Michigan, and Kenneth Kiple, Ph.D., my former colleague at Bowling Green State University, expanded my understanding of yellow fever and tuberculosis. Philander D. Chase, editor of the Papers of George Washington, University of Virginia, guided me to the papers of the Rev. Philander Chase Jr. at Kenyon College, Gambier, Ohio, where I received a warm welcome from Professor Reed Browning and the library's staff. Professor Emerita Shirley Pipes Thomas of Adrian College translated the Tuché paper on French participation in the battle of Lake Champlain. Cdr. Tyrone Martin (Ret.), former commander of and the leading authority on the USS *Constitution*, assisted this landsman on a number of naval matters. Rendering gracious hospitality to perfect strangers during our visit to Plattsburgh were Bill and Bunny Rowe of Peru, New York. There we also met Thomas Macdonough Russell III, his wife Peggy, and Thomas Macdonough Russell IV, who provided entrée to a number of Macdonough family sources of information and a look at some of the silver awarded the commodore by the state of Delaware. No university-based scholar can operate without the cooperation and support of the department within which he serves. Particular thanks must go to three departmental chairs, Donald Nieman and Fujiya Kawashima of Bowling Green State University and Michael Palmer of East Carolina University, who opened their budgets and the services of their staffs in support of this study.

Karen Mulcahy of East Carolina University's Geography Department produced the maps of Lake Champlain and the Mediterranean. Special permission for reproducing materials in their respective collections has been granted by the Smithsonian Institution and the National Gallery of Art, Washington, D.C.; the Delaware Public Archives, Dover; the

Middlesex County Historical Society, Middletown, Connecticut; the United States Naval Academy Museum, Annapolis, Maryland; and the Lake Champlain Maritime Museum, Vergennes, Vermont. Cathy Williamson and Martha Randolph "Randy" Wyatt of The Mariners' Museum, Newport News, Virginia, provided last-minute assistance in identifying an illustration.

Travel expenses for this study were generously supported by the award of a Vice Admiral Edwin B. Hooper Research Grant from the Naval Historical Center in Washington and of a John Nicholas Brown Research Fellowship by the John Nicholas Brown Center for the Study of American Civilization at Brown University. William S. Dudley and Joyce M. Botelho, directors of each of these institutions, graciously provided assistance to me during research trips to Washington and Rhode Island. In particular, Michael Crawford, Christine Hughes, and Carolyn Stallings of the staff of the Early History Division, Naval Historical Center, allowed me access to the vast resources they have gathered for the production of *The Naval War of 1812: A Documentary History*. I cannot express too strongly my appreciation to Charles Brodine of the Early History Division, not only for his excellent advice and aid during my stay in Washington but also for scurrying all over the District in search of documents I missed when in the nation's capital.

My onetime Air War College visiting professor colleague, James C. Bradford of Texas A&M University, the editor of the Library of Naval Biography series, has been most helpful and understanding. He even allowed me to change completely the original focus of this volume.

Finally, but really first, is my wife Margo, whose wise counsel, research assistance, and editing have helped to make this as thorough and readable a biography as we could make it. Our forty years of marriage has been a cruise over mostly smooth waters, where the wind has been usually on our quarter and shallow waters and lee shores have been avoided. My CINCFAM rates a hearty "well done."

31 Dec. 1783	Born in New Castle County, Delaware
5 Feb. 1800	Receives warrant as midshipman, U.S. Navy
1800–1801	Service on USS *Ganges* in Caribbean
1802–3	Service on frigate *Constellation* in Mediterranean
1803	Service on frigate *Philadelphia* in Mediterranean
1804–5	Service on schooner *Enterprise* in Mediterranean
16 Feb. 1804	Helps destroy the *Philadelphia* at Tripoli
3 Aug. 1804	Fights in gunboat battle in Tripoli Harbor
6 Sept. 1804	Promoted to acting lieutenant on *Enterprise*
1805–6	First lieutenant on brig *Syren*
1807	Gunboat construction duty, Middletown, Connecticut
6 Feb. 1807	Promoted to lieutenant
1807–8	First lieutenant of sloop-of-war *Wasp* in Atlantic
1808	First lieutenant on frigate *Essex*
1809–10	Gunboat commander, Middletown
1810–11	On furlough, captain of commercial brig *Gulliver* to India
1812	Resigns first lieutenancy of *Constellation;* assigned to Portland, Maine; reassigned to Lake Champlain
1812–14	Commodore, U.S. Navy squadron, Lake Champlain
12 Dec. 1812	Marries Lucy Ann Shaler, Middletown
24 July 1813	Promoted to master commandant
11 Sept. 1814	Commander of U.S. naval forces in battle of Lake Champlain; promoted to captain
1815	Captain of steam frigate *Fulton First*
1815–18	Commander of Navy Yard, Portsmouth, Maine
1818–19	Captain of frigate *Guerrière* in Baltic and Mediterranean
8 July 1819	Relieved of command of *Guerrière*
1820–24	Commander of ship-of-the-line *Ohio*, New York Navy Yard
1824–25	Commander of *Constitution* and commodore of U.S. Mediterranean Squadron
9 Aug. 1825	Lucy Ann (Shaler) Macdonough dies in Middletown; five of ten children survive
10 Nov. 1825	Dies at sea on the *Edwin;* buried in Middletown

Thomas Macdonough

Chapter One

Naval Heritage

Roll on, thou deep and dark blue Ocean—roll!
Ten thousand fleets sweep over thee in vain;
Man marks the earth with ruin—his control
Stops with the shore;—upon the watery plain
The wrecks are all they deed, nor doth remain
A shadow of man's ravage, save his own,
When for a moment, like a drop of rain,
He sinks into thy depths with bubbling groan,
Without a grave, unknell'd, uncoffin'd, and unknown.

Lord Byron, *Childe Harold's Pilgrimage*

THOMAS MACDONOUGH's triumph on Lake Champlain was the product of a tradition in the American navy that dated back to the War for Independence. Despite the victories of such luminaries as John Barry, John Paul Jones, and Lambert Wickes during that war, the Continental Navy made little contribution to the conflict's final outcome. One authority has called it "a rather drab and unimportant sideshow of the Revolution."[1] Some argue that it was American privateers and state navies, like those of Pennsylvania and South Carolina, that constituted the more important naval contributions of the rebelling colonies. Others contend that it was the French and Spanish navies that kept the Royal Navy at bay and incapable of effectively blockading the North American coasts. Certainly it was the French navy that won the decisive naval engagement for United States independence: the battle off the Chesapeake capes, 5–9 September 1781.[2]

Yet men like Barry, Jones, and Wickes left a tradition of daring and a willingness to engage the enemy that was not forgotten. Even after Congress abolished the Continental Navy in the 1780s, the legacy of combat symbolized by these men's gallantry inspired those who followed them. And the loss of protection to American maritime commerce once provided by the Royal Navy meant the young Republic's merchantmen were vulnerable to attack from the Barbary coast nations along the Mediterranean's south shore. Such attacks began as early as 1784 and continued for a decade before the nation decided it had had enough. On 27 March 1794 Congress reconstituted the navy to combat "the depredations committed by the Algerine corsairs on the commerce of the United States."[3] From this temporary mission the United States Navy was reborn. Congress directed the constructions of six frigates to conduct operations against the Barbary States.

Building Stoddert's Navy

In the following decade the young navy reconstituted itself and waged two conflicts that trained, tested, and culled the young officers who would lead the country in its second war with Great Britain. While several men were responsible for the rebirth of the American navy, perhaps one dominated: Benjamin Stoddert. The 1794 law creating the navy placed it within the War Department, making it, in effect, a Department of Defense. However administratively logical this might appear, the early overseers of national security were little acquainted with or interested in naval affairs. Henry Knox served only briefly in this dual capacity as secretary of war in 1794, when Timothy Pickering succeeded him as the cabinet officer in charge of the army and navy. Pickering served from 1795 to 1796, when James McHenry assumed the post. Construction of the navy's first three frigates proceeded at a crawl, and McHenry halted work on the other three. At the same time relations with France and Great Britain deteriorated and the Barbary corsairs seized American merchantmen in the Mediterranean. By 1798 McHenry was a political liability to the John Adams administration. Yet he had a powerful ally—Alexander Hamilton, an important figure in the Federalist Party. Other Federalists sought McHenry's replacement, but President Adams hesitated. Instead, he followed the suggestion of Capt. John Barry, USN, and established a separate naval department. Congress followed suit on 30 April 1798, creating the Department of the Navy. McHenry would remain as secretary of war until May 1800.[4]

When Adams's first choice as the naval secretary declined the appointment, the president proposed Benjamin Stoddert (1751–1813) of Georgetown, Maryland (now the District of Columbia). Stoddert's apprenticeship as a merchant ended when the War for American Independence broke out and he accepted an appointment as a captain in a Continental Army regiment being raised in Maryland by James Wilkinson. Wounded at the battle of Brandywine, Stoddert used his Wilkinson connection (by now Wilkinson was a brigadier general) to become acquainted with the Board of War's leading general officers. Disappointed in a quest for a staff officer assignment and discouraged when regimental consolidation ruined his chances for promotion in the infantry, Stoddert resigned his commission in 1779. This did not terminate his services to the Continental Army, however. He served briefly as a deputy forage master general under the supervision of Wilkinson's father-in-law, a civilian position that entitled him to be called "major," an appellation by which he was often called thereafter. All his efforts brought him in close connection with senior military officers and with the critical problem of all military operations, logistics.

Stoddert may have had a reason other than a desire for public service for accepting the president's offer. The declining trade from Georgetown's port adversely affected his economic welfare, and his dabbling in District of Columbia land schemes brought more debt than profits. The government's annual salary of three thousand dollars was not substantial, but it might tide him over what he hoped were temporarily straitened circumstances. Although reluctant to accept the position, he was energetic in his performance of his duties, strict in his management of the department's finances, and imaginative in his conception of the American strategic situation. Stoddert proved a wise choice for the new cabinet post.

After relocating his large family to Philadelphia, the nation's temporary capital, Stoddert immersed himself in the administrative detail of the department and confronted deteriorating foreign relations with France following the XYZ scandal. When three American envoys went to Paris in 1796 to settle issues revolving around the seizure of our neutral vessels and their crews, they found themselves facing three French agents (designated Mr. X, Mr. Y, and Mr. Z in the published version of the meetings) who demanded a large bribe before negotiations began. Publication of the official report on the affair aroused public indignation and forced the Adams administration to take strong measures against the French. This led to what is known as the Quasi-War, the first undeclared military conflict in American history. To protect commercial shipping and patrol American shores, McHenry hastily acquired a West Indian merchant vessel, *Ganges*, armed it, and sent it out with the mission of protecting the coast from New York to Norfolk. Because the biggest threat came from the French West Indies, Capt. Thomas Truxtun sailed the first of the new frigates, the *Constellation*, to cruise from the Chesapeake to the border of Spanish Florida.

Stoddert found that the *Constellation* was the only completed vessel of the six ordered in 1794 and that only two of the remaining five were even under construction. This caused him to rely on more converted merchantmen like the *Ganges*. Soon two more frigates joined the fleet, the *United*

States and *Constitution*. Naval historian Michael Palmer notes that "while the frigates proved the backbone of the navy, the converted ships furnished the muscle."[5] The privateers added more sinews to the American effort. Using a combination of frigates, converted merchantmen, and privateers, Stoddert sought to demonstrate national will and naval power by inserting U.S. vessels in the Caribbean where the French were most vulnerable. On 11 July 1798 he ordered Capt. John Barry of the newly commissioned *United States* to lead a squadron of three other vessels on a two-month cruise off the Lesser Antilles, the object of which was "to do as much injury to the armed vessels . . . of France, & to make as many captures as possible, consistently with a due Regard . . . to the security of our own" vessels. Stoddert also wanted to establish an American naval character that imbued "a Love of Country and Jealousy of it's honor" in all his sailors. Thus began the conflict with France.

Eventually Stoddert evolved a three-pronged American naval strategy. A small force operated off Cuba to protect merchantmen engaged in trade with that Spanish colony. Another squadron operated in the Windward Passage between Cuba and Haiti, scene of the most American losses in 1797. Finally, Stoddert concentrated most of his strength against the Lesser Antilles, especially off Guadeloupe, from which most of the French privateers operated.[6] The Caribbean theater would be the initial training ground for Thomas Macdonough and a generation of young naval personnel who would come to leadership positions a decade and a half later.

The conflict with France allowed Stoddert to build the navy during the remainder of the Adams administration. Though in 1797 McHenry reported that only the *Constellation* was "in great forwardness," by 1798 Stoddert noted that the federal government had built the frigates *United States, Constitution,* and *Constellation,* and by 1801 he had nine large, fast frigates. Three of them were of 1,576 tons, forty-four guns each (the *Constitution, United States,* and *President*), and five were of 1,265 tons, thirty-six guns (the *Chesapeake, Congress, Constellation, New York,* and *Philadelphia*). These vessels constituted the pride of the navy. In addition, the government built the thirty-two-gun frigate *Essex* and the twenty-eight-gun frigates *Adams, Boston, General Greene,* and *John Adams.* To meet the emergency of the Quasi-War, the navy purchased the ships *George Washington, Ganges, Delaware, Montezuma, Baltimore,* and *Herald,* which were between 279 and 624 tons and carried between eighteen and twenty-four guns. By gift the government received the ship *Merrimack* and the brig *Richmond,* and there were several more being built in 1797. In 1801, however, Stoddert knew that the incoming Jefferson administration was unlikely to continue such a large fleet, and he recommended that the navy's size be diminished. After noting the end of the Quasi-War, he suggested the reduction of the navy to thirteen vessels: the *United States, President, Constitution, Chesapeake, Philadelphia, New York, Constellation, Congress, Essex, Boston, John Adams, Adams,* and *General Greene.* "The rest," he concluded, "were either built of materials which do not promise long duration, or are too small to form a part of the national defence." With amazing exactitude, he claimed all this could be done for a cost of $1,225,048.73—a major reduction from the previous year's cost of $2,434,261.10.[7] Still, the budgetary axe of the Jeffersonians was likely to be far more severe than this. But before the axe fell, Macdonough began his career in the United States Navy.

Life at Sea

Learning the routine of naval life was at the core of the first cruises of Midshipman Macdonough. No matter how many the instructions, how much the advice of his older brother, nothing could have prepared him fully for the reality of shipboard life in the wooden world he now confronted. Foremost, it was a world of seemingly chaotic running and noise that underlay the ordered routine of the ship's daily life. One soon became used to the constant movement of the deck under one's feet. Hazardous skills involved becoming a topman, climbing the ratlines, holding on to the shrouds, and waiting for the roll of the ship as one ascended to the foretop. Landsmen mounted the top through the lubber's hole, a square cut in the platform that allowed one to mount safely and easily. But experienced sailors demonstrated their courage and dexterity by going the awkward and risky way via the futtock shrouds, which required one to hang backward while mounting the swaying platform from the outside.

Then there was the monotony of the menu, in which the same food appeared the same day of the week, month after month. It provided sufficient calories for the physical labor involved in handling a sailing vessel, but it was plain and very restricted in range. Prominently featured were salted beef, pork, and fish, along with a hard biscuit that often contained weevils or maggots. There were few vegetables and fruits aboard ships. The absence of the latter contributed significantly to the common presence of scurvy among seamen. While the daily ration of grog—three parts water to one of whiskey or rum—kept a sailor warm when climbing the rigging in cold weather, it also contributed to drunkenness, common among many sailors.[8]

The provisions allocated for the USS *United States* in 1798 illustrate naval diet:

55248 Pounds of Bread
28392 — ditto Beef
23392 — ditto Pork
14196 Pints of Peas or Beans
9464 — ditto of Rice
7089 pounds of Cheese
18928 — ditto of Potatoes or Turnips
9465 — ditto of Salt Fish
4732 — ditto — Flour
3549 — ditto — Molasses
33124 pints Rum
1183 pounds Butter.[9]

As bad and monotonous as this diet may seem, it was considerably better than that enjoyed by many urban poor of the day and constituted a reason for enlistments from this segment of the population.

Early on, the novice midshipmen and the landsmen had to master the strange language of the sea and the complicated nomenclature of the ship. One learned that "tackle" is pronounced "tay-kel," "trenail" is "trunnel," "forecastle" is "folks'l," and "boatswain" is "bo'sun," for instance. Terms like "catted" involved weighing the anchor, "hogging" concerned the tendency of a ship to arch in the middle when overloaded, a "tompion" was a wooden plug used to keep moisture out of the muzzle of a gun, and a "yard" was the horizontal spar to which a sail was attached. A ship's rigging contained miles of cordage and dozens of blocks that supported the masts and controlled the sails, each having names the seaman needed to know. Among the sails there were flying jibs, jibs, staysails, mainsails, topsails, topgallants, and spankers, each of which could be designated for the bowsprit, foremast, main mast, and mizzenmast from which they were hung. Soon one could identify a variety of ship designs denoted by their size and rigging that included first- through sixth-rate men-of-war, brigs, ketches, snows, schooners, and sloops.

Most of the ship's company served on one of two divisions or watches, starboard or larboard (port). The twenty-four hours of the day were divided into seven watches:

Noon to 4:00 P.M., afternoon watch
4:00 P.M. to 6:00 P.M., first dogwatch
6:00 P.M. to 8:00 P.M., last dogwatch

8:00 P.M. to midnight, first watch
Midnight to 4:00 A.M., middle watch
4:00 A.M. to 8:00 A.M., morning watch
8:00 A.M. to noon, forenoon watch

Each watch lasted four hours, except for the two two-hour dogwatches in the late afternoon and early evening. This system allowed night duty to be fairly shared between each watch since the larboard watch turned out at midnight one day, the starboard watch the next. By the same token, most of the men never had more than four hours of sleep. On the other hand, in calm weather, those crewmen not at the wheel or on watch could catch sleep when nothing else was being done. The dogwatches found the off-duty division relaxing by singing, dancing, playing an instrument, or carving pieces of ivory into scrimshaw. As long as the weather remained calm, little interrupted the routine. But when things turned foul, the boatswain's pipe called the off-duty division to their posts to assist during the bad weather. The true test, the one that determined the acceptance of naval life, came when the wind blew strong and the waves rolled over the main deck. The seamen knew how each midshipman behaved under such circumstances.

Because the officer's day was divided into three watches, they could sleep longer at any one time, but they were never allowed to sleep on duty. Typically, a ship had at least three lieutenants, one of which commanded during his watch. One or more of the midshipmen would assist the lieutenant. The captain was on call at any time.

Besides its elegant simplicity, the genius of the divisional system was that it placed responsibility upon the junior officers, midshipmen, and warrant officers for the operation of the ship during their watches. To be successful they had to be concerned about the welfare of the men serving under them, to know them as individuals.

The ship's bell notified the crew of the passage of time on board ship. On each half-hour of a watch the ship's bell received an additional stroke, so that the end of a four-hour watch was at eight bells; the dogwatches ended at four bells. The quartermaster, or his mate, watched the last grains of sand run into the bottom of the watch glass, turned it, and struck the bell. At every hour on the hour, the officer of the watch recorded the ship's speed and the wind direction and marked the ship's course in chalk on the log board. He could add any events since the last entry.

Officially the duty day began at noon, not midnight. All this undoubtedly confused the typical landsman, who found that the morning of 25 May was followed by the afternoon of the twenty-sixth, which after midnight became the morning of the twenty-sixth. Each day at noon the officers took observations on the sun to determine the ship's position. For the midshipmen this was the critical hour of the day. Here their navigational skills received a daily test. How close were their observations to those of the ship's sailing master? After the calculations were compared, the sailing master took the log board and retired to a quiet place where he recorded the previous twenty-four hours' activities of the vessel. These were then presented to the captain for his approval.

Central to the naval world was the hierarchical nature of shipboard life. Reigning supreme over the vessel was its master and commander, known as the captain, regardless of his actual rank. In the U.S. Navy of 1801 there were only nine captains to command its six frigates and various dockyards. For them the rank and title were the same. Contemporaries called them "post captains." For those commanding the many small craft, the senior officer was not a captain in rank but merely in title. Most commonly the master commandants commanded vessels smaller than twenty guns, and at times senior lieutenants received command of vessels smaller than those given master commandants, for example, schooners, sloops, and gunboats.

Regardless of pay grade, the master and commander of a man-of-war held a most autocratic office. Much more than contemporary ground commanders, the captain of a naval vessel was singularly powerful and isolated from his rank equivalents. He was under constant pressure to preserve his vessel and his crew from other vessels, fire, rocks, shoals, winds, rain, snow, and icebergs. He had to navigate his ship to the designated location on the globe, exit and enter strange harbors, secure necessary water and provisions, prosecute and punish wrongdoers among his crew, and conduct diplomatic negotiations with foreign governments. The situation was even more delicate, controversial, and important when he found himself in contact with a probable enemy. Every day he had to make dozens of critical and rapid decisions.

Because according to *Naval Regulations* the captain was "responsible for the whole conduct and good government of the ship, and for the due execution of all regulations which concern the several duties of the officers and company of the ship," personnel were "to obey him in all things which he shall direct them for the service of the United States." A squadron commander received the power to "suspend from their stations the captains of vessels, or any other officers under his command, who, for bad conduct or incapacity, he shall think deserving of such punishment." Command was a lonely job. The successful captain always maintained his dignity and never appeared unduly partial or friendly toward members of the crew. He constantly kept a distance between himself and the officers and men under his command and saw that the rules and customs of the service were observed.[10]

Limiting the autocracy of command was the interdependence of the captain and the crew; they worked together to achieve a smooth functioning vessel in what was a very hazardous profession. Whatever troubles the officers and men got into when ashore, on board ship there existed a mutual need to cooperate. Because American crews were all volunteers—there were no impressed sailors on U.S. vessels—the relationship between officers and men had to be close and respectful. The growing sense of egalitarianism in the United States affected military command in the navy. Captain Truxtun reflected this outlook when he wrote that his officers "shou'd be Civil and polite to everyone . . . for [this] does not interfer[e] with discipline." An officer was responsible to prevent "Sculking and Loitering about" among the enlisted men while at the same time never losing "sight of that humanity and Care that is due to those who may be really Sick, or otherwise Stand in need of his assistance and attention."

There remained, however, an etiquette of subordination and custom that dominated the conduct of officers and men toward one another. When an officer came on board or left the ship, stepped on the quarterdeck, addressed another officer or enlisted man when on duty, or passed another officer when on or off duty, he saluted by lifting his hat. When petty officers, seamen, or marines spoke to an officer, they held their hats in hand. Captain Truxtun cautioned his officers that "improper familiarity" between themselves and enlisted men lessened the "authority and respect due" an officer and gentleman. On the other hand, Truxtun felt "free[,] open [and] polite Conduct" among the officers of a mess was considered proper. Moreover, when invited to the captain's table, junior officers were expected to set aside the deference shown on duty and to "be at ease" so their commander might "better able to judge the Capacities of each, as to men and things and employ them on Certain Occasions accordingly."[11]

The first lieutenant was critically important to the success of any vessel. He saw that the warrant and petty officers' tasks were performed, that the watch, station, gun, and berthing assignments were made, that the crew practiced gunnery, and that the vessel itself and the sailors uniforms and equipment were clean and ready for the captain's inspection. Occupying the post of a modern executive officer, the first lieutenant commanded the vessel if the captain was sick, wounded, or absent. Depending on the size of the crew, each of the remaining lieutenants was assigned duties as the captain saw fit; usually the second and third lieutenants commanded the two watches. The junior lieutenant's duties included exercising the men in small arms and leading boarding parties.[12]

A select few officers, warrant officers, petty officers, and men were not assigned normal watch duty. Such specialists were designated "idlers." They included warrant officers such as the carpenter, purser, surgeon, chaplain, and their subordinates, and petty officers such as the sailmaker, yeoman of the powder room, armorer, gunner, master at arms, captain's clerk, cook, schoolmaster, and any mates of these. The distinction between the idlers, who worked during the day and slept at night, and the seamen, who stood watches, divided the ship's company into two unequal parts.

Most aspiring officers began their careers as midshipmen. The post was an ambiguous one, being somewhere between the officers and the petty officers. According to U.S. *Naval Regulations* midshipmen were "promptly and faithfully to execute all orders for the public service, of their commanding officers," but they were not to be assigned "particular duties." They were to "keep regular journals" and were to "employ a due portion of their time in the study of naval tactics, and in acquiring a thorough and extensive knowledge of all the various duties to be performed on board of a ship of war." The captain had a special responsibility toward these young men, usually teenagers, because they were "a class of officers, meriting in an especial degree, the fostering care of their government." Captains, therefore, were to see that "schoolmasters perform their duty towards them, by diligently and faithfully instructing them in those sciences appertaining to their department; that they use their utmost care, to render them proficients [*sic*] therein." In terms of pay, midshipmen received nineteen dollars per month, placing them below the sailing master, master's mates, purser, surgeon, surgeon's mate, chaplain, clerk, carpenter, boatswain, gunner, and sailmaker. Receiving the same pay were carpenter's mates and boatswain's mates.[13]

Patrick O'Brian, the famous British novelist of the Royal Navy, perhaps best described the midshipman's place in the naval hierarchy:

> A midshipman is an officer only by courtesy; he has no commission until he is made a lieutenant. His legal status is that of a man appointed, or rated, by the captain—he is rated a midshipman on the ship's books, just as he might be rated a sailmaker or a butcher, and he is in fact no more than a petty officer. He is below the warrant officers such as the gunner, the carpenter or the bo'sun . . .

and he can be disrated, or transformed into an ordinary seaman, at the captain's pleasure. And once he has been turned before the mast he can be flogged or punished in the same way as the rest of the lower-deck—a terrifying threat in a captain's mouth at any time, and even more so when there is the prospect of a very long voyage still to come.[14]

Knowledge of the sea and of seamanship was not a requirement for entering midshipmen. Secretary Stoddert and his successors preferred "sprightly young men of good education, good character, and good connections" for the position. Macdonough possessed all these attributes. The navy would teach him the art of sailing and the profession of arms. Naval service weeded out many of the unfit, unsuitable, and insubordinate while they were still midshipmen: two-fifths of them were gone within thirty months of service, and another fifth failed to complete the five years normally expected for promotion to lieutenant. It was this attrition process that first confronted Macdonough as he entered the service as a teenage midshipman.[15]

On board most men-of-war were three noncombatant officers: the surgeon, the chaplain, and the purser. These men could become particular confidants of the captain because their duties were technically specialized and did not conflict with the ship's operations either in navigation or combat. Moreover, these officers were more likely to be of an age close to that of the commanding officer.

The purser was the ship's accountant and bookkeeper, responsible for victualing the ship and purchasing consumable supplies. He maintained the ship's books for both commodities and pay, and he often operated the ship's store, providing officers and sailors with sundry items, called slops, which were charged against their pay. It was a highly risky business and one subject to severe censure by crewmen who felt themselves cheated by the purser's books.[16]

The duties of surgeons and their assistants, known as surgeon's mates, are obvious. Most surgeons in the early U.S. Navy had formal medical training and entered the navy as a surgeon's mate. After a number of years of such service they received promotion to the rank of surgeon. For instance, Usher Parsons, who served with Oliver Hazard Perry as a surgeon's mate during the War of 1812 and with Macdonough as a surgeon afterward, enjoyed an extensive and important naval career before setting up private practice in Providence and becoming a professor of surgery at Brown University.[17]

A chaplain's duties are not as obvious as the title might indicate. In the early navy few chaplains were ordained clergy, although they might have some clerical training. The chaplain had three duties: read the Sunday service (usually morning prayer from the Book of Common Prayer of the Episcopal Church), perform funerals for those dying at sea, and serve as the ship's schoolmaster for the midshipmen and sailors. Many small vessels had no chaplain at all, and these duties had to be performed by other officers. Sometimes the chaplain served as the captain's clerk, as Philander Chase Jr. did with Macdonough on the *Guerrière*.[18]

Possessing neither a commission nor a warrant was the captain's clerk. A clerk wore a midshipman's uniform, though he was a young man hired by the captain to assist with his correspondence. He served at the captain's pleasure. A capable clerk might find a captain to support his pursuit of a chaplaincy or a pursership. Sometimes a clerk received a midshipman's warrant and found himself on the promotion track.

Between the "gentlemen" officers and the ordinary sailors were the warrant and petty officers. Their status roughly corresponded to the distinctions between "gentlemen" and clerks and artisans that existed in the community as a whole. That warrant officers received warrants rather than commissions symbolized the social and professional distinctions involved. Commissioned officers traditionally represented the educated governing elite of the community, whereas the warrant officers held positions as specialists. Some of these positions required literacy and mathematical skills traditionally associated with gentlemen. Most warrant officers rose through the ranks of seamen to their status.

The most important warrant officers were the sailing master, gunner, carpenter, and cook. The sailing master navigated the ship under the captain's direction, kept the log book, maintained the ship's trim, and saw that the ship's rigging and stores were preserved. Most sailing masters were experienced merchant seamen who desired the security of a naval berth. A few of them became lieutenants. Because they often aspired to be commissioned officers, they, along with the midshipmen, were allowed on the quarterdeck.

Of the petty officers, the boatswain was in charge of the ship's cordage, anchors, rigging, cables, sails, and boats. The master sailmaker and his mates were in charge of the repair, maintenance, and conversion of sails. The gunner was in charge of the ship's ordnance, ammunition, small arms, and powder. An armorer and gunsmith assisted him. In the wooden world of sailing ships the carpenter was a critical individual. In charge of "the care and preservation of the ship's hull, masts, &c," he was particularly concerned with caulking, pumping, and repair of combat damage. The cook prepared the food. Each of these petty officers had assistants, called mates, who were apprentices in their various crafts and skills.[19]

Seamen, divided into able seamen, ordinary seamen, and landsmen, were the largest percentage of the crew. Normally it took a year at sea to advance from landsman to ordinary seaman and another year to advance to able seaman. Each of the watches was divided into "parts of the ship" to which these sailors were assigned. British scholar N. A. M. Rodger succinctly describes the distribution of these enlisted men:

> The least experienced, and the most troublesome, joined the after guard on the quarterdeck, and the waisters in the waist. Here, under the immediate eye of the officers, they hauled on sheets, halliards and braces, work which called for collective strength and co-ordination, but little individual skill. The smart young seamen worked aloft as topmen, handling and loosing sail. Upper yardmen, the youngest of the topmen, often no more than older boys, worked on the topgallant and royal yards, the highest of all, whose sails and gear were lightest. Older seamen, no longer agile enough to work aloft, joined the forecastlemen under the boatswain, where they handled the headsails, and dealt with the vital and tricky work of clearing away the anchors to let go, and catting and fishing them when unmooring.[20]

One other component of a ship's company cannot be ignored—the marines. In the tradition of the Royal Navy, American marines were aboard ship to protect the naval officers from a mutinous crew. In short, they were the ship's police, enforcing regulations about fires, thievery, and misconduct by sailors. In battle they provided musket and rifle fire from the quarterdeck and fighting tops against closely engaged enemy ships. They joined sailors in landing parties ashore. The rivalries between the men of the two services were intense. Sailors detested the policing activities of the marines and regarded them as inferior beings who could not make able seamen. Marines disliked sailors and looked upon them with disdain.[21]

Living conditions on board a man-of-war were necessarily confining. Ships were crowded with men, animals, guns, and cargo. Sailors slept and dined on the gun deck, where they ate in messes of six men each. This deck was dark since the gunports, which were less than six feet from the waterline, had to be kept closed when the ship was at sea. The only light came down the main hatch. The stuffy atmosphere was alleviated somewhat by windsails directing air into a draft below the main deck. Life before the mast reeked of human odor despite attempts to fumigate the hammocks with regular scrubbings and dryings. Were all this not enough, one often found sleep interrupted by rainwater or salt spray leaking through the deck onto a hammock. Clothing often went wet for days without any means of drying it out.

Each man received fourteen inches of width for his hammock, although in reality, because of the divisional system, he had twenty-eight. When their hammocks were not in use, sailors rolled them into a sausage shape and stowed them in netting troughs lining the main deck. In battle these hammock rolls provided modest concealment and cover from enemy small-arms fire.

The Ladder of Promotion

Once the initial appointments in the navy had been made after the reestablishment in 1794, most officers were promoted from one grade to another by seniority. Thus the most senior lieutenant could expect the next promotion to master commandant when a vacancy occurred. The same applied to promotion from master commandant to captain. During the War of 1812, Secretary of the Navy William Jones deplored the fact that "commanders of talents, local knowledge, influence, and distinguished courage" in civilian life could not be commissioned in the navy, as they could in the army, without following the rule of promotion by "regular graduation." The navy had no such tradition corresponding to brevet (temporary) rank or militia rank that allowed the army some flexibility in the seniority rule.

However, there were exceptions to the seniority rule. Foremost were "special promotions for signal service" due to combat heroism. Macdonough received his post captaincy after his victory at Lake Champlain and thereby leaped over several senior master commandants to this exalted position. Other promotions came with particular assignments. A number of sailing masters received commissions as lieutenants and thereby moved onto the promotion ladder. Lieutenant Macdonough jumped several places on the navy list by being assigned to the Lake Champlain fleet—a post that needed at least a master commandant to command. Undoubtedly this was a belated recognition of his distinguished service as a midshipman during the Barbary Wars. One of his seniors on the 1812 lieutenant's list, Robert Henley, would serve under Master Commandant Macdonough at Lake Champlain. Undoubtedly this early promotion contributed to Henley's problems with Macdonough.

Most officers kept close records of just where everyone stood on the navy list. Each year the Navy Department published it for all to see. For instance, Capt. John Shaw's 1822 *Register of the Commission and Warrant*

Officers of the Navy of the United States carefully crossed out the names of those who resigned, died, or were otherwise unable to serve in each grade. You can be sure that each officer knew precisely where he stood and the status of everyone above him on the list. Promotions outside the seniority list elicited controversy. When someone received a promotion others thought undeserved, the secretary of the navy was bombarded with complaints from those passed over.[22]

The despair over slow promotion and the lockstep nature of the seniority list caused Midn. William L. Madison to resign his navy warrant and request an army commission. He wrote his uncle, the president, "In the Army, promotion is comparatively quick, in the Navy it must necessarily be slow. Let the merit of a Midshipman be what it may, he is compelled to serve at least three years before he can be qualifyed for promotion," and it was highly likely that it would be "five or six years" before he received a lieutenant's commission.[23] This pessimism caused many resignations and requests for furloughs in the years following the end of the Barbary Wars. A naval lieutenancy corresponded to four grades in the army: second lieutenant, first lieutenant, captain, and major. When one went from a high-numbered lieutenant to first lieutenant aboard ship, one did not receive any obvious promotion in insignia or pay.

Macdonough missed some of this despair. The Peace Establishment Act of 1801 reduced the U.S. Navy's officer corps to 6 captains, 36 lieutenants and 150 midshipmen. It said nothing of the rank of master commandant, which stood between lieutenant and captain. The navy never achieved this reduction goal because the Barbary War required more officers than this. By 1805 there were 10 captains, 8 master commandants, 73 lieutenants, and 150 midshipmen, and Secretary of the Navy Robert Smith wanted even more officers.[24] The expanding number of lieutenancies in the early years of the Jefferson administration meant that young midshipmen who survived the reduction of 1801 would enjoy considerable opportunity for promotion because of the increase in demand for experienced officers. This increased requirement for more officers during their early naval years greatly influenced Macdonough's career. It was the men who entered the navy after 1801, like Midshipman Madison, who endured the excessive slowness of promotion before 1812.

Naval Strategy and Tactics

Secretary Stoddert's orders to Captain Truxtun of the *Constellation* in 1798 set the fundamental naval strategy of the United States for most of the next century. The navy engaged in what was known as a *guerre de course,* a war against commerce, for most of this period. With fast ships and bold captains, the navy built warships "designed to hit and run, to attack enemy merchant vessels and small warships and flee if faced with a stronger naval opponent." It was not until the late nineteenth century that the United States Navy adopted a strategy of *guerre d'escadre,* a war against squadrons, with large warships designed to fight fleet engagements. It was for the protection of American commerce that Stoddert sent Truxtun and others into the Caribbean to escort merchant vessels flying our flag and to attack French warships and privateers preying on them. Similarly, the Barbary Wars concerned the right of merchant vessels to sail the seas without molestation. In no way could the United States afford to match the great sailing leviathans of the British, French, or Spanish navies of the late eighteenth century. Instead of ships-of-the-line, it was the fast frigate that excited the interest of the early proponents of an American naval presence on the high seas.[25]

From time to time big navy advocates sought to build the period's equivalent of a pocket battleship. In 1798 Stoddert requested twelve seventy-four-gun ships-of-the-line. Seventy-fours were classed as a third-rate vessel, below first rates of one hundred guns or more and second rates of between ninety and ninety-nine guns. Third rates had between sixty-four and eighty guns. Congressional opposition, led by Albert Gallatin of Pennsylvania, reduced the number to six, and these were never built. In 1801, the Jefferson administration, of which the frugal Gallatin was now the secretary of the treasury, canceled their procurement. The most Stoddert could secure were the final three thirty-two-gun frigates (fifth-rate ships) authorized in 1794 plus a few smaller auxiliary vessels.

It was the *guerre de course* strategy and its tactics to which Macdonough would be introduced during the Barbary Wars. To be sure, there were operations involving vessels in concert during the Caribbean and Mediterranean operations, 1798–1805, but never did the U.S. Navy confront squadron actions from either the French or Barbary corsairs. Nor did the United States have a tradition of naval maneuvers in which fleet tactics might be practiced for the edification of officers and men of all grades. Nor was there any military education system by which officers could contemplate and debate such situations. Only self-education and shipboard conversations allowed the officers of the early navy an opportunity to contemplate the manner by which a *guerre d'escadre* might be fought. Certainly the commentary in British naval journals such as the *Naval Chronicle* and other naval literature of the day provided examples of what should and should not be done. Such book learning hardly substituted for practical experience or formal study in naval operations. Also American officers also observed Royal Navy squadron maneuvers when their vessels sailed to such ports as Gibraltar during the Barbary Wars.

It was at ship-to-ship operations that the Americans learned to excel. The officers honed their all-volunteer crews in the art of sailing and practiced regularly in gunnery. It was the gunnery skills of American seamen that distinguished them in most engagements. *Naval Regulations* required captains "frequently to exercise the ship's company in the use of the great guns and small arms."[26] A perusal of the logs of early navy ships indicates that gunnery and small-arms exercises received considerable attention.

In duels between two ships of relatively equal armament, seamanship and accurate gunnery could be decisive. During the War of 1812, the Americans' fast frigates designed in the 1790s provided that margin of speed and armament that allowed many of them to engage successfully equivalently armed British vessels. However, after these initial defeats of the Royal Navy in single-ship actions, the British required multiship squadrons to blockade American ports with ships-of-the-line, thereby forcing many United States vessels to stay in port for extended periods. The *Constellation*, for instance, never exited the Chesapeake Bay during that conflict due to the Royal Navy blockade.

Squadron actions required the commander to have a disciplined fleet capable of obeying instructions from the flagship via a system of signals. Flexibility was a key to combat success since rapid alterations in formation were necessary to meet fluid situations created by both enemy maneuvers and wind and sea changes. The Royal Navy, which frequently faced an enemy with equal or superior squadrons, exercised fleet maneuvers regularly and created a degree of cooperation among its senior commanders epitomized by Horatio Nelson's felicitous phrase calling his captains a "band of brothers." In closely engaged fleet-to-fleet encounters, aimed gunnery and maneuvers were not nearly as important as ship coordination and rapidity of fire.[27]

As naval tactics evolved in the age of fighting sail, the basic fleet-to-fleet encounter involved the vessels sailing on parallel lines firing broadside after broadside into the opponent's warships. Fundamental to this tactic was that the squadron must keep in line and not engage in individual ship-to-ship encounters. It was Nelson, a subordinate captain, who took responsibility to modify the continual attention to maintaining the line by attacking the Spanish van at Cape St. Vincent and engaging in a pell-mell battle that separated the van from the rest of the Spanish line. Men like Nelson proved willing to take a calculated risk of ship-to-ship encounters and to depend upon his more experienced officers and crews to win.

The rigidity of the line also received an impetus to change when Adm. Alan Duncan fought the battle of Camperdown and anticipated Nelson's tactics at Trafalgar by sending his ships vertical to the Dutch line, breaking the line at several points, and thereby allowing his artillery to rake the length of the enemy vessels. From that time on, "crossing the T" was a critical maneuver in battles at sea.

Naval encounters sometimes involved attacks against ships at anchor. Two such engagements, the battles of the Nile and Copenhagen, saw the Royal Navy destroy anchored vessels of their opponents. In both, Nelson's audacity overcame a supposed advantage of his foe's position. In all these aspects of fleet-to-fleet operations, junior officers such as Macdonough learned from the discussions of them in the journals of the day, especially the *Naval Chronicle*.

The continuous success of the British in naval encounters during the age of Nelson also imbued too many of His Majesty's officers with an expectation of victory and an arrogance when confronting the infant U.S. Navy. A generation of officers and men used to triumphs like the Glorious First of June (1794), Cape St. Vincent (14 February 1797), Camperdown (11 October 1797), the Nile (1 August 1798), Copenhagen (2 April 1801), and Trafalgar (21 October 1805) can be excused for being presumptuous when confronting a nation with virtually no combat naval experience.

Professional Development

To counter Royal Navy experience in operations, the Americans copied the British system of career development. The desired design required midshipmen to learn professional duties, values, and naval culture on board one of the large frigates, where they experienced daily contact with their seniors who demonstrated such skills. The era of the Quasi-War and the Barbary Wars, 1794–1805, provided ample opportunity for midshipmen to demonstrate their talents in front of their seniors, men who would influence their careers for years to come. The favored young gentlemen who exhibited the best in naval talent found themselves almost continually at sea during this decade. Their cruises to the Caribbean and Mediterranean and across the North Atlantic provided a spectrum of sea conditions, role models, and discipline modes that influenced the midshipman's outlook on naval leadership.

The first experience a midshipman faced required his learning the skills of the various enlisted positions. This partially met the two principles of successful leadership: to be technically and tactically proficient and to set the example for subordinates. Captain Truxtun ably expressed the desire of senior officers for this training of their young charges when he wrote that midshipmen ought to mix with the sailors "in the exercise of extending or reducing the sails in the tops." This required him to accomplish these tasks in the worst weather. He should fear the "dreadful consequences . . . of being stigmatized with the opprobrious epithet of *lubber*" by not ascending to the tops during a whistling storm. "An ignorance of this practical knowledge will . . . necessarily be thought an unpardonable deficiency by those who are to follow his directions."[28]

This quest for practical experience must not allow one to cross the line of excessive familiarity between the apprentice officer and the enlisted men, however. Truxtun admonished the midshipmen "resolutely to guard against this contagion with which the morals of [some] of his inferiors may be infected." While excellence in seamanship skills, even superiority in their execution, was to be admired in the midshipman, he must also maintain the gulf between officers and men necessary for a ship's discipline. This he did by setting the example of personal conduct to his subordinates. Historian Christopher McKee argues that critical to the establishment of this distinction was social and ethical conduct as a gentleman: "*Behavior of a gentleman* was a broad umbrella, embracing ethical conduct, internalized discipline, avoidance of indulgence or self-destructive excess, courteous and harmonious relationships with one's peers, manners, personal cleanliness, neatness in one's belongings and surroundings, refined personal interests, and the habit of associating with, and emulating those who were one's social equals or—better yet—those of superior social standing."[29] Both in personal conduct and language, the junior officer needed to maintain the distinction between himself and his subordinates or the necessary coordination and discipline aboard a sailing vessel might collapse.

Competence in seamanship skills and gentlemanly behavior must be accompanied by obedience to orders and attention to duty. Setting an example required the young officer to develop what McKee calls an "ingrained habit of obedience" to the lawful orders of one's superiors, even if one might question their utility or necessity. Obedience to a superior's directions was "the cement that held the social order of the ship together under whatever strains—battle, deprivation, disease, life-threatening storm—might be placed upon it."[30] Such obedience required the midshipman to make sound and timely decisions. Teenage boys commanding men years older and more mature than themselves had to demonstrate this principle early in their career on what might seem the simplest of tasks. As they moved up the ladder of seniority, successful candidates for lieutenancies sought responsibility and took responsibility for their actions regardless of the outcome. Installation in young officers of a desire for command, for leadership—for power, if you may—was the objective of a training period involving increased responsibility. Senior officers sought to create a desire for rank, not for personal gratification, to develop an emotionally mature "socialized power" quest which exercised command for organizational and national needs. This was a critical professional value and one which superiors noted among the aspiring midshipmen.

Inherent in this leadership trait was the development of a sense of responsibility among one's subordinates. Subordinate development required each officer to keep enlisted personnel informed about the situation and to encourage all crewmembers to offer suggestions for the improvement of ship operations. All this had to be accomplished without excessive familiarity between officers and men. The young leader had to build bonds of mutual respect, trust, confidence, and understanding between himself and his subordinates that created a sense of unit cohesion and confidence. The objective was to create a crew that performed its tasks as a unit, each man accomplishing his designated job with competence and in coordination with other crewmembers.

One principle of leadership that constantly affected officers in their career was learning to know oneself and seeking self-improvement. Industriousness, devotion to the service, dependability, objectivity, and ambition coupled with a professional studiousness demonstrated a positive attitude toward the navy that contributed to one's advancement. In an era without formal naval education, the junior officer educated himself by reading, listening, observing, and following the example of those he admired.

A peculiarly military attribute of naval leadership demanded physical and moral courage. Such courage required more than the willingness to face the dangers of an ever-temperamental sea; it meant risking one's life and the lives of the crew in battle against dangerous enemies for causes higher than the preservation of life. In its physical sense, courage involved bravery, willingness to conquer fear, apprehension, and the unknown. "Courage," says the U.S. Naval Academy's textbook on leadership, "is not being without fear; it is suppressing fear and carrying out assigned duties despite the recognition of manifest danger."[31] Courage assumes risk taking, but it also requires prudence. One does not engage a ship when the probability of defeat is high unless there is a larger strategic objective to be accomplished. To risk one's life, the lives of the crew, and the nation's ships in vain bravado is not an example of leadership excellence. The line between courage and recklessness is a thin one; but it is a distinction that naval training sought to create among its officer candidates.

During the years that Thomas Macdonough progressed from midshipman to lieutenant, he immersed himself in the values, characteristics, and customs of the early U.S. Navy. In the next chapter we will examine how his professional career demonstrated the acquisition of the leadership traits outlined above. The requirements of a good leader cannot be placed in a strict order of importance or in particular molds. They vary with circumstance, personality, and opportunity. The U.S. Navy wished its junior officers to have practical experience in ship operation and navigation, command experience in a variety of situations, shore and ship duty, felicity of written and oral expression, moral character, courage, and patriotism. As we examine Macdonough's life, we also determine how he stood up to that ideal.

Preparation for Command

Thou are not dead,
Though housed in Hades, while thy children live,
For children are as echoes that prolong
Their parents' fame; the floating cork are they
That buoyant bear the net deep sunk in the sea.

Æschylus, *Chephoræ*

On 27 May 1800, sixteen-year-old midshipman Thomas Macdonough Jr. reported to the USS *Ganges* in New Castle, Delaware. While the small port town was only a few miles from his home, the *Ganges* was a world away from the Trap, the farm on which he had been raised. When he first saluted Lt. John Mullowney, the captain of his first naval vessel, the young midshipman entered a world totally alien to that with which he was accustomed. That night, swaying in a hammock in the cramped midshipmen's berth, he listened to the strange sounds of his new profession—the tolling of the bell each half hour, the lapping of the waves against the hull, the creaking blocks, and the gentle straining of cordage and sailcloth. Just over fourteen years later Commo. Thomas Macdonough would achieve national acclaim and international stature as the commander of an outgunned squadron that won a victory over experienced sailors from the Royal Navy. This chapter explores the factors that contributed to this Delaware boy's evolution into the successful commander of a small U.S. squadron on Lake Champlain.

The development of successful military and naval leaders has been examined for centuries by those interested in analyzing the achievements of famous captains. While command success is much like windward and leeward—it varies with time, wind direction, and latitude—there are a few recognized features among the victorious that merit special consideration. Among these features are moral character, professionalism, experience, and opportunity. We will examine each of these as they apply to young Macdonough's career before he assumed command on Lake Champlain.

Moral Character

Psychologists tell us that family and environment shape our character. Around 1730 the Macdonoughs of County Kildare, Ireland, sent three sons to the New World. One of these, James Macdonough (d. 1792) settled in southern New Castle County, Delaware. It appears that James was a man of some prominence in a region of modest wealth. Family traditions hold that he was a physician, but no documentary proof of this exists. In 1746 he married seventeen-year-old Lydia Laroux, daughter of a local Huguenot family. She bore seven children—Thomas, Bridget, John, James, Patrick, Mary, and Micah—before her death at thirty-five in 1764. The cycle of pregnancy, childbirth, lactation, and pregnancy was typical of women at this time. How much her early death was due to the constant strain on her body of these cycles is unknown. Undoubtedly her death had a decided impact on the lives and outlook of her children, the eldest of whom, Thomas, was just seventeen at her death. Lydia Macdonough's life had an unusual impact on her husband. Though he lived nearly thirty years longer than she did, he never remarried, something rare in his day. Her name would be perpetuated for generations in the Macdonough family.[1]

Assuredly a large amount of the supervision of both his younger siblings and of the family farm fell upon the eldest son. Somehow Thomas apprenticed as a physician (under his father?) and practiced in and around the southern township of the county (known as St. Georges Hundred) until the War for Independence broke out in 1775. Just twenty-eight years old, Thomas did not immediately join the Continental Army, but his younger brother James went off to war and died early in the conflict. But when Maj. John Macpherson of the Delaware Continentals died in the siege of Quebec, the Delaware General Assembly named Thomas, a lieutenant colonel in the militia, to replace him in March 1776. Nothing says more of the family's stature in the community and of Macdonough's devotion to the patriot cause than his willingness to serve as a combat officer rather than a medical one.

The Delmarva Peninsula, of which Delaware was a part, along with the Eastern Shore counties of Maryland and Virginia was a hotbed of Loyalist sentiment. The suppression of this dissent to growing movement toward independence required military force. In the first months of his commissioned service, Major Macdonough commanded about two hundred Continental Army soldiers in Sussex County.[2]

As the British threat to New York became apparent, Major Macdonough and his troops received orders to join Maj. Gen. George Washington in defense of that critical port. The Delaware Continentals were about to achieve the reputation as one of the best fighting regiments in the Continental Army. Although Col. John Haslet commanded the regiment, Major Macdonough was in command at the battle of Long Island, 27 August 1776, because his superior was on detached duty. In this battle, the Delaware Continentals distinguished themselves, holding the far right of the American line against a much greater force and withdrawing in good order to fortifications at the heights of Brooklyn. Major Macdonough received special commendation in the dispatches of the commanding general, an honor that was the eighteenth-century equivalent of a decoration for valor.

The Delaware Continentals participated in the withdrawal to Manhattan and the retreat up that island to the Bronx and Westchester County. On 22 October Colonel Haslet and his men conducted a bold night raid on the Queen's American Rangers, Maj. Robert Rogers's Loyalist unit. During the battle of White Plains, on 28 October, the Delaware Blues again covered the American withdrawal with distinction. Wounded in this battle, Major Macdonough returned home and did not participate in the battles of Trenton and Princeton. Having served its allotted time, the Delaware regiment disbanded in January 1777. With that Major Macdonough's obligation to national service ended.[3]

When a replacement regiment was organized in Delaware, the state government offered its command to Macdonough, but he declined. Yet that did not end his revolutionary war service. The 1776 Delaware Constitution provided for a president (governor), privy council (cabinet), and bicameral general assembly. Unable to secure his services in the Continental Army, the legislature elected the major one of the first members of the four-man privy council in February 1777. This office placed him in close contact with Caesar Rodney, the state's first president, and his nephew, Caesar Augustus Rodney. These political connections would prove useful to his children later in life.

After serving his two-year term in the privy council, Macdonough accepted a commission as the colonel commanding the Seventh Regiment of the Delaware militia, a post he held from 1779 to 1782. Although he would not command the regiment during what was probably the most critical time of Delaware's defense—the 1777 British attack against Philadelphia—he was nonetheless commander of a regiment central to the state's defense in New Castle County during most of the war. Moreover, there is little doubt that his service as privy councilor during the British invasion involved numerous instances of military advice.

Few states were more vulnerable to British amphibious attack and few had more potential internal threats of loyalism than Delaware. When American fortunes were at their nadir, Dr. Macdonough accepted election again for the privy council in October 1780. He served in that capacity for most of the time until June 1788. Twice his colleagues elected him speaker of the council. From 1788 until his death in 1795, Macdonough served as a justice on the Court of Common Pleas and Orphans' Court of New Castle County. As colonel and councilor, he proved his patriotism at critical times in the national history. His willingness to risk life, limb, and property in the defense of the fledgling nation provided an example of devoted national service that inspired his two eldest sons.

In 1770, Macdonough married Mary, the daughter of Samuel Vance, a local farmer of English extraction who served as a captain in the colonial militia. Thomas and Mary lived the first fourteen years of their married life in a small, story-and-a-half log house with weatherboard siding about three-quarters of a mile south of his father's home at the Trap. Here were born their first six children, Lydia, Hannah, James, Mary, Hester, and Thomas Jr. (the eventual commodore).

In 1784 Justice Macdonough moved to a substantial brick house on a knoll at the Trap farm.[4] Here were born four more children, Samuel, Jane, John, and Joseph. At the Trap, Thomas Jr. (born in 31 December 1783) spent a fondly remembered childhood wandering in the woods and fields on some of the richest soil in the new state. The farm's produce easily went to market via Drawyer's Creek to the village of Cantwell's Bridge (now Odessa) and hence to the world market down Appoquinimick Creek.

This idyll ended when a series of disasters struck the family. The children's grandfather, James Macdonough, and their mother, Mary Vance Macdonough, died in 1792. Mary had undergone ten births in twenty-two years of marriage. Three years later their father followed them to the grave. The ten Macdonough children were orphans. The family was not impoverished; they had a larger-than-average farm for the region and three slaves. But the family's capacity to train and educate these children in their most critical developmental years was severely impaired.[5]

We do not know how relatives and the elder sisters in the family assisted during this critical period, but it is clear that Thomas was strongly attached to his eldest sister, Lydia, and that attachment lasted until the end of his life.[6] By 1800 Lydia and her sisters Hannah and Mary were married, leaving Hester—only a few months older than Thomas—the senior member of the household. As youths, the elder Macdonough boys gained a reputation as being somewhat wild and fond of practical jokes.[7]

It may be that around the family fire stories were told of devoted service, not only by the patriarch but also by uncles John, who died in the Revolutionary War, and Patrick, who fought at the battle of the Wabash in Ohio in 1791, where the Miami chief Little Turtle destroyed a U.S. Army expedition led by Gen. Arthur St. Clair.[8] One suspects that the good doctor, like most veterans, did not extol his own adventures, but the extended Macdonough family and neighbors probably did. The Macdonoughs' connections to the political leadership of the state meant the councilor-colonel-justice's family could expect some political patronage reward for services rendered.

With the death of Thomas Macdonough Sr., the welfare of the large Macdonough family was a serious problem. While the daughters married and established their own families, the sons had to find employment befitting their social status and their precarious economic straits.

Neither James nor Thomas seems to have considered farming as an occupation. Nor do they appear to have contemplated following their father into the medical profession. Was the lack of a proper education or financial backing a factor in this? They did not venture to northern New Castle County and join in the development of flour milling and other milling activities along Brandywine River.[9] Nor did they migrate to the rapidly growing cities of Baltimore and Philadelphia. Maybe Thomas received enough of an unfavorable indoctrination to the commercial life as a clerk in a Middletown store. Instead, using their political connections, governmental service beckoned the two oldest sons. The navy offered a tempting prospect for the Macdonough boys because it cost little in initial capital (only uniforms and equipment) and it provided one with a technical education and responsibility which, if one resigned from the service, could be put to good use in either the merchant marine or a commercial career. Moreover, there was always the prospect of gaining considerable wealth if one were to be fortunate enough to secure prize money. Then there was the lure of adventure in exotic places otherwise known only in books and tales. And unlike many of their contemporaries, the older brothers Macdonough did not have to face parental opposition to their hazarding their lives at sea.

Political influence assisted the eldest son of the family in securing a midshipman's berth in the newly created United States Navy and receiving an assignment to the illustrious Baltimore-built frigate *Constellation*, Capt. Thomas Truxtun commanding, and John Rodgers, first lieutenant. However, Midn. James Macdonough II's naval career was short. During the Quasi-War with France the *Constellation* fought a memorable duel with *L'Insurgente* on 9 February 1799. The American victory came at a small price, only one dead and two wounded among the crew. Unfortunately, one of the wounded was young James, who lost a foot. Unable to perform naval duties, he retired to Delaware with a small pension. This particular engagement made Truxtun and his first lieutenant, Rodgers, national heroes. They would not forget young James Macdonough's bravery, and they would be patrons of his younger brother for years to come.[10]

James Macdonough's peg leg forced his return to the Trap. Despite his wound, he told stories of the sea that inspired Thomas to follow in a naval career. Years later the *Delaware Gazette* described how Thomas caught "the Soldier's flame" from his older brother.[11] Moreover, James's presence reduced any obligation Thomas may have felt to continue supporting his younger siblings. Using the family's connections with Caesar A. Rodney and U.S. senator Henry Latimer, a physician and prominent revolutionary leader, young Thomas secured a midshipman's warrant in the U.S. Navy on 5 February 1800. For one so young to receive a warrant was somewhat unusual and demonstrated the importance of his family connections. Most boys his age began as a "young gentlemen" (cabin boys).

If the fires of patriotism and public service had been nourished in Thomas Macdonough's early life, another influence impacted upon his intellectual development: religion. The Macdonoughs of Delaware developed a devotion to the Church of England. In all probability Lydia Laroux's Huguenot and Mary Vance's English traditions contributed to this religious inclination. The combination of Scottish-Irish, French, and English ancestry was not unknown in colonial British North America, but it was somewhat unusual. The Macdonoughs were members of St. Ann's Parish, Middletown. Dr. Thomas Macdonough served as warden of the parish in 1793–94. Unfortunately, the incomplete parish records do not provide evidence of earlier roles the family's members may have played in its establishment and development.

The Church of England was a major denomination in colonial Delaware, probably the largest before the Revolution. But there were several problems adversely affecting the church. First, unlike in neighboring Maryland, it was not the established church in the colony, so it had to depend upon voluntary contributions and missionary support to provide clergy and buildings. Two Anglican missionary societies, the Society for the Propagation of the Gospel and the Society for the Promotion of Christian Knowledge, assisted in these efforts, although the amount of support sought by churchmen throughout the British Empire exceeded the ability to provide it. Second, although it was episcopal in its governance, there was no bishop in the New World. American-born colonials seeking holy orders had to go to England for ordination. These restrictions meant that there were never enough clergy to satisfy the demand for them. In fact, the maximum number at any one time in colonial Delaware was five.

This situation required lay leadership for the denomination's survival. Fortunately, the Anglican tradition allowed for such direction. A group of laymen called the vestry and wardens provided parish governance. When a rector was present, he presided over the vestry, but in his absence the senior warden was in charge. Thus, during periods of clerical vacancy these lay leaders maintained the church property and conducted services. Fortunately for them, eighteenth-century churchmanship did not involve frequent reliance on the Holy Eucharist, which had to be performed by an ordained minister. Most services were either morning or evening prayer, and laymen could lead them. The Book of Common Prayer provided an orderly and satisfactory ritual for church attendees. Published sermons by distinguished Anglican clergy could be read in place of an original homily.

The Church of England was particularly active in New Castle County throughout the colonial and revolutionary eras. St. Ann's Parish of Middletown was blessed with the presence of an Anglican minister, the Reverend Mr. Philip Reading, whose service continued through the war years and afterward. How much influence Reverend Reading had over the development of young Thomas Macdonough Jr. is unknown, but the devout churchmanship that characterized Macdonough's life provides significant testimony to this rector's importance. We do know that Reading's life story provided an example of confronting moral dilemmas that had to impact on the Macdonoughs. The rector of St. Ann's was a Loyalist who remained at his post throughout the Revolution even though one of his leading parishioners was a prominent Patriot. Both Reading and Thomas Macdonough Sr. kept their faith while disagreeing on their politics. For the younger Thomas, the Bible and the Book of Common Prayer were to play important roles in his adult life.[12]

Somehow, Thomas Macdonough Jr. received a competent elementary education during his years at Trap farm. Did a family member—his mother or father or elder siblings—educate him, or was a traveling schoolmaster or Reading his early teacher? We may never know. However, he achieved skills in writing and mathematical calculations which, honed in studies aboard ship, were to serve him throughout his life.

Shaped by a warm family, educated to be a gentleman, tested by the loss of his parents at a young age, and devoted to Christ, the teenager who came aboard the *Ganges* that spring day in 1800 carried in his intellectual baggage the moral character of a loving, industrious, committed individual. These characteristics dominated his career. Eighteen years later a young midshipman described Commodore Macdonough as "a moral and religious Man of high tone and character . . . abstemious and very correct in his deportment."[13] When he boarded the *Ganges*, however, Macdonough knew nothing of the sea and of life on it. The navy would provide him with the professionalism that would be a necessary component in his leadership development.

Professionalism

Into the young Republic's navy, 1794–1815, there came 885 young midshipmen, candidates for officership. In many ways, Thomas Macdonough was typical of this group. He came from a coastal community which was not prospering in the aftermath of the Revolution, his father served in the War for Independence and provided an example of sacrificial patriotism to his children, his father was deceased, he was middle class in his background and had local gentry connections, and he possessed the modest formal education expected of young gentlemen.[14]

Like any other profession, the profession of arms developed its own expertise through specialized knowledge, its own sense of social responsibility (in this case to the nation), and a sense of corporateness among its officers that they constituted an important subculture within the larger society.[15]

Before he ever reported to Lieutenant Mullowney, Thomas acquired the peculiar dress and personal accouterments of his new trade. Probably utilizing some of his older brother's clothing and equipment, he filled his sea chest with such items as uniform coats; a round jacket suit; a surtout and a watch-coat; several hats; white jean and nankeen trousers; jean and kerseymere waistcoats; linen and calico shirts; wool stockings and several pairs of shoes; a mattress, blankets, and coverlet; combs and brushes for teeth, shoes, and clothes; towels, sheets, and pillowcases; a knife, fork, tablespoon, and teaspoon; a pewter wash basin and cup; and a pocket knife and pen knives. For his new profession he acquired a quadrant, a small day and night glass, a logbook and journal, pens and ink, a sword, and the requisite books on navigation and tables.[16] Finally, he inserted a Bible and prayer book.

From the moment he stepped on board the *Ganges*, Thomas Macdonough began the long process by which the U.S. Navy taught him the profession of arms by organizing his life around a specialized body of terminology and conduct that would dominate the rest of his life. Foremost among the topics he had to learn was the rank and status of personnel on board.

Central to the naval world was the hierarchical nature of shipboard life. For those commanding small craft like the *Ganges*, the senior officer was not a captain in rank but merely in name. Lieutenant Mullowney was its third commander; on its two previous cruises the captains were Richard Dale and Thomas Tingey, both of whom subsequently had distinguished naval careers. Reputedly once the youngest drummer boy at Valley Forge, Mullowney was an old soldier turned sailor. He had a reputation of operating a tight ship with little corporal punishment and minute attention to detail.

The *Ganges* was a converted merchantman laid down in 1795 and acquired by the navy three years later. One of eight merchantmen purchased to build an instant squadron following the reconstitution of an American navy in 1794, it was the first operational warship of the reborn U.S. Navy. It was a three-masted ship of 504 tons displacement and carried a crew of 220. Armed with twenty-four 9- and 6-pounder long guns, the Navy Department ordered it into West Indian waters to patrol against French privateers attacking American shipping in the vicinity of the former French colony of St. Domingue, modern Haiti.[17]

Before his vessel even left the Delaware River port, Mullowney's tolerance would be sorely tested. Six *Ganges* midshipmen—Bill Blaine, Joel Calkins, Chet Clark, Rex Otis, Joseph Robbins, and Thomas Macdonough—were typical mischievous teenagers. They found New Castle a quiet town—too quiet, in fact. In the middle of the night, one of them climbed to the top of the local Episcopal Church and lowered the bell rope to the others below. All of them pulled on the rope, creating a ringing that awakened the whole town. The stress the six put on the rope was more than the bell's supports could tolerate and they broke, causing the bell to come crashing down. The young men quickly ran to the ship, but many villagers recognized them and Mullowney soon learned of their escapade.

One can only imagine Mullowney's outrage at his midshipmen's misconduct. He hauled them before him and demanded they pay for the bell's restoration to its proper place. As president of the midshipmen's mess (a job going to the junior member thereof), Thomas Macdonough collected the money from his compatriots and wrote an unsigned apology to the rector. This was not a very auspicious beginning to a naval career.

Young Macdonough began learning his new profession when in late May 1800 the *Ganges* began its cruise by escorting a convoy of merchant ships into West Indian waters. Secretary of the Navy Benjamin Stoddert ordered Mullowney to "pay them all the attention in your power." The cruise portended an excellent opportunity for Midshipman Macdonough to learn the customs of the service, the strange nomenclature and functioning of the ship's component parts, the intricacies of navigation and gunnery, and the experience of limited combat. But he also entered a crowded ship in a tropical world filled with biological challenges to survival. It was this epidemiological challenge that would prove the most formidable for the teenage midshipman.

The *Ganges* was a motherly ship, broad of beam, built to carry cargo at a prudent pace, not as a sleek man-of-war. It was a good vessel upon which to learn the art of sailing on the high seas, and on it, Macdonough began to the study of seamanship that would distinguish his career. We may assume it was on this cruise that he began collecting the volumes of navigational literature described in his final library. But it is doubtful he found time or money for the works on literature, travel, history, and Christian homiletics that eventually filled the same collection.[18]

The one maritime task peculiar to naval vessels was that of gunnery. Its artillery skill was one in which the U.S. Navy took great pride. Mullowney scheduled the exercising of his crew in the intricacies and routine of handling the ship's long guns, and the *Ganges*'s first lieutenant directed the exercising. Nine-pounders normally required a seven-man crew headed by a gun captain. Two guns, commanded by a midshipman, made a division. As has been so often in the history of navies, the education in military arts of a junior member of the crew required the support of the petty officers and gun crew. A novice like Midshipman Macdonough needed enlisted men's cooperation for his division to perform efficiently and effectively.

There was no prescribed gun drill in the navy of this period, but certain procedures were common to most vessels. A drumbeat called all hands to quarters. They quickly stowed hammocks and furniture and stood beside their respective piece. They cleared their guns for action after the command "Cut loose the battery," at which time the lashings that held the guns in place were released. "Take out—tompions" caused the extraction of the wooden plugs which covered the muzzle. Since guns were always ready to fire while at sea, the normal procedure for loading powder and shot was not required for the first round to be fired. The command "Prick and prime" necessitated inserting a wire into the vent and pricking the cartridge holding the power in the muzzle followed by pouring powder into the vent. Now the piece was ready to be aimed. One of several commands directed the crowbar and handspike men to heave the breech of the gun toward the bow or stern and to elevate or depress the barrel. With the gun now ready, the order to fire resulted in either the match being applied to the priming powder at the vent or the lanyard being pulled on a flintlock that ignited the priming powder. Subsequent commands required the crew to serve the vent, sponge the bore, load a new cartridge, load the shot, and run out the gun. After this, the routine began all over again until the order to secure the guns.

Midshipman Macdonough learned that there were two types of fire, ricochet and direct. The latter sought to hit the target without grazing, while ricochet fire bounced a round off the water's surface toward its target. Ricochet fire was used at long ranges, but it had less impact since the shot lost its force when it hit the water. Naval gunners employed three firing methods: independent firing (firing at will), firing in succession, and broadside firing. Difficult to execute once combat began, the latter impacted enormously when several rounds hit on an opponent simultaneously. Firing in succession was often used when a vessel's guns could reach their target only as the ship slowly approached its opponent. Once closely engaged, most fire was done independently of a common command as each crew fired as fast as it could. Because rapidity of fire was more critical in close-range engagements than accuracy, Mullowney concentrated on the speed by which his gun crews exercised the guns.[19] Before the *Ganges* reached the Caribbean combat zone, he knew his crew was far better prepared for the exigencies of warfare than when they left Delaware Bay. Macdonough learned by doing and his confidence in successfully performing his tasks undoubtedly rose after several such drills.

Another task Macdonough had to learn was the computation of the ship's position on the earth's surface. At seven bells in the forenoon watch the midshipmen began assembling on the gangway with their quadrants or sextants. When the sun approached the meridian half an hour later they began their calculations. The young gentlemen tested their knowledge of sine, cosine, tangent, cotangent, secant, and cosecant in a frantic effort to locate their position. They hurried to their *Requisite Tables* and *Nautical Almanac* in search of the right numbers. The ability to achieve trigonometric accuracy was the key to their promotion. It was this skill above all that divided the officers from the enlisted men. Fellow midshipman John Wood bragged that with his good quadrant he expected to become "a good navigator and not a bad seaman" by the time the *Ganges* returned home. For Thomas Macdonough the calculations probably came slowly at first, but gradually he could follow the location of the *Ganges* as it moved southward: 38° 29' North off Cape Henlopen, Delaware, on 4 June, to 20° 26' North off Cap Français, Haiti, on the twenty-sixth.[20]

Concurrently he learned the tragic consequences of a misstep on board a ship at sea. On 26 July, William McMullen, a landsman on the *Ganges* crew, fell over board and drowned "notwithstanding every exertions being made" to rescue him.[21]

The voyage to the Caribbean was not a peacetime cruise; the United States was engaged in its first undeclared war—this one with France. Mullowney returned to Delaware Bay from one cruise in those waters on 3 May and left a few weeks later for another. Near the end of June *Ganges* would lay off Cap Français, where Midshipman Macdonough first caught sight of what would be his last command, the U.S. frigate *Constitution*, Silas Talbot commanding. Here he learned another of the courtesies of his new profession when Captain Talbot entertained Captain Mullowney on board his vessel. He learned about similar maritime gestures when the *Ganges* encountered the sloop *Supply* with several sick on board and Mullowney sent his surgeon and medicines to assist.[22]

The *Ganges'* principal mission was the protection of American merchantmen from French men-of-war and privateers. On 19 July it intercepted the slave ship *Prudent,* and the following day it retook the brig *Dispatch,* which had been taken by a French privateer a few days earlier. Mullowney ordered Midn. R. B. Robins and Midn. Jacob Jones to serve as prize masters of these vessels and sent them to Philadelphia. That junior crewmen could be given such responsible commands must have impressed the young midshipman.[23]

Macdonough was not at sea for two months before he saw his first combat. Cruising off the Straits of Florida was the French privateer *La Fortune* with six 6-pounders and a crew of seventy. In the darkness of the morning of 28 July the ship tried to sneak out of Mantanzas Harbor in Cuba. Spotted that afternoon, the *Ganges* gave chase and at the range of six hundred yards began firing vigorously. Caught between the American vessel

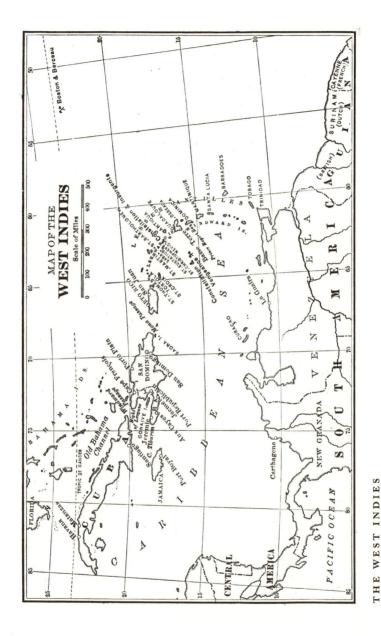

THE WEST INDIES

Reprinted from Gardener W. Allen, *Our Naval War with France* (Boston: Houghton Mifflin Company, 1909)

and the shore, *La Fortune*'s captain ran the ship aground and its crew escaped, swimming to shore. Mullowney sent his third lieutenant, John Love, two midshipmen (one of whom was Macdonough), and a small prize crew to board the ship. They brought it off the shore, and subsequently it was taken to Havana, then sent as a prize to Philadelphia. Mullowney proudly reported that his success had rid the Florida Straits of any privateering threat. Thomas Macdonough was now entitled to his first prize money.[24]

But the young midshipman was about to meet a more formidable foe than a French privateer. On the morning of 18 August 1800, Mullowney unmoored the *Ganges* from its anchorage off Mantanzas and entered into the log the brief notice, "Crew very sickly." He sailed to Havana, where he sent ashore to the local "hospital" Midns. Ephraim Blaine, Robert McConnell, and Macdonough, Surgeons Mate Gershom Jacques, and five seamen. They were infected with that most fatal of tropical diseases, yellow fever. Characteristics of this acute viral disease are a sudden onset of moderately high fever, a slow pulse rate, jaundice (from which the ailment acquired its name), and in severe cases the vomiting of blood. The virus is transmitted to man via the mosquito, and after an incubation period of from three to six days there occurs a period of infection for about three days. After a short remission, there is a period of intoxication which is either fatal by about the ninth day or the patient slowly recovers. With convalescence there is normally a rapid recovery, and a lifelong immunity results.

It would be nearly a century before the source of the disease would be found and preventive measures taken. Mullowney knew that it could spread throughout his crew and lead to fatal consequences. He headed the *Ganges* toward the Delaware River, hoping to arrive before the disease cut down so many of his crew that they could not sail her. His log recorded the deadly toll: "Departed this life Mr. John Wood, Midshipman, . . . Edward Moore, Landsman, . . . Thomas Derrick, Seaman, . . . Peter Lynn, Seaman—and Mr. John Wetherspoon, Midshipman." Before it was all over the Grim Reaper added nineteen names to his ledger, including three from the midshipmen's mess. For the nine men left behind in Havana, hospitalization seemed a death sentence. All the enlisted men died, as did Midshipman McConnell. The latter's death particularly touched Mullowney, who wrote a friend that the young midshipman "lived and died a favorite, and would have been a bright ornament to our navy. Thus, as is often the case, the best are taken off first."[25]

Macdonough and Blaine, along with Surgeons Mate Jacques, survived what Macdonough recalled was a "dirty Spanish hospital" from which the dead "were taken out in carts as so many hogs would have been." The American consul in Havana supplied the three with clothing and passage money. The British captured their American merchant vessel off the Delaware Capes because it carried Spanish cargo and the British and Spanish were at war. Put ashore at Norfolk, Virginia, Macdonough worked his way back to New Castle, stopping off at the Trap, where his family was astonished to learn that he was still alive. He appeared at home with a "straw hat, canvas shoes and in other respects poor enough."[26]

In 1801, Macdonough sailed with Captain Mullowney and the *Ganges* for one short Caribbean cruise. A storm severely damaged the ship, and it put into Basseterre Roads, St. Christopher. Commo. John Barry surveyed it and found it "unfit for sea." The *Ganges* remained on Guadeloupe station until May, when it proceeded north with a convoy and reached Philadelphia in June. The end of the Quasi-War and the advent of the Thomas Jefferson administration signaled the end of Macdonough's cruises on this former East Indiaman. The *Ganges* would soon be decommissioned and the navy would undergo a major reduction in ships and personnel. The next few months were critical to Macdonough's naval career. Would he remain on the navy list? For the rest of his life he credited his survival to the influence of Caesar Augustus Rodney. But Macdonough demonstrated a degree of professionalism during his short career that may have made him eligible for retention without political influence. He acquired considerable skill as a navigator and seaman during his *Ganges* cruises. Certainly he established a reputation for devotion to duty during the various activities on board the ship, including the seizure of *La Fortune*, and in his return to duty after surviving the horrors of yellow fever. While there would never be a band of "Mullowney's boys" to match to the cult that surrounded Capt. Edward Preble, Macdonough acquired the basic skills of his profession under the former drummer boy's tutelage.[27]

Experience

The Peace Establishment Act of 1801 reduced the U.S. Navy's officer corps. But the Barbary Wars required more officers than this act allowed.[28] A dramatic increase in the number of lieutenants in the early years of the Jefferson administration meant that young midshipmen who survived the reduction of 1801 would enjoy considerable opportunity for promotion because of the increase in demand for experienced officers. Promotion required the third component in Macdonough's preparation for command:

experience. While he learned the basic ingredients of professionalism from Mullowney, he needed the opportunity to serve on larger and more important vessels of the young navy to become a responsible commander himself. The decade following his departure from the *Ganges* in 1801 was critical in providing him this experience.

In January 1802 Macdonough received orders to report to the U.S. frigate *Constellation,* Capt. Alexander Murray commanding.[29] James Macdonough must have been overjoyed that his brother Thomas was now on the very vessel he had served on just a few years earlier. Midshipman Macdonough boarded one of the world's finest naval vessels of its class in the world.

Built in Baltimore in 1797, *Constellation* was 1,278 tons burden, 162 feet, 10 inches long, with a beam of 40 feet, 6 inches. Its full crew complement was 340 officers and men. The ship was ornately carved and carried a figurehead of a female representing Nature. Technically rated a thirty-eight-gun vessel with two decks, *Constellation* carried twenty 32-pounder carronades on the upper deck and twenty-eight 18-pounder long guns on the gun deck. It also carried long chase guns on the forecastle and cohorns on the rail. Because of their great length, the ships were subject to hogging (the straining of a vessel's frame caused when the midship section is supported by a wave but the bow and stern are poised over the trough between waves), a condition exaggerated by the tendency of captains to overload their ships with heavy ordnance. In 1801 the *Constellation* capsized in the Delaware River after running aground and it took five weeks to right it. It required complete replacement of its waterlogged running rigging, and sections of its planking were removed so it could be cleansed inside. Secretary of the Navy Robert Smith kept pushing Murray to speed up the repairs since he wanted the vessel to sail for the Mediterranean in early 1802.[30]

In the midst of the effort to bring the *Constellation* into active service, Secretary Smith issued a series of directives that were to materially affect Thomas Macdonough's career. One circular to all commanders dated 19 August 1801 carefully laid out the distinction between sailors and marines and their respective duties on board a vessel. Two particular clauses were to be important to Macdonough: (1) "Marines as well as Seamen, shall cheerfully, promptly and without any appearance of hesitation, obey every order given by the Captain or commanding Officer: and no person shall on board presume to object to or in any manner or form question the Propriety of any such order," and (2) "No Gentleman worthy of the honor of commanding a Ship in the navy of the United States, will ever be capable of an Act so abhorrent to the Principles of an Officer as to abuse this great and important Authority."[31] These two criteria, obedience and gentlemanly conduct, were to dominate Macdonough's behavior throughout his career.

Of more immediate significance were the *Naval Regulations* issued by Smith on 25 January 1802. These bore the authority of President Jefferson and provided a concise list of duties for each officer, petty officer, and crewman. The regulations required midshipmen to "promptly and faithfully . . . execute all the orders for the public service, of their commanding officers." They enjoined ships' commanders to see that schoolmasters performed their duties and "diligently and faithfully" instructed their charges "in those sciences appertaining to their department." They required midshipmen to keep journals and, considering the obligation that they had to the country, "to employ a due portion of their time in the study of naval tactics, and in acquiring a thorough and extensive knowledge of all the various duties to be performed on board a ship of war."[32]

In keeping with the latter regulation, Macdonough maintained a journal of the *Constellation* cruise. Generally uneventful, the "Journal Kept on Board the U.S. Frigate of 44 Guns, *Constellation*" allows one to note the daily life on board such a vessel. There are such mundane subjects as "Fresh Breezes and pleasant weather," "a heavy sea from the north and East," "People employed about necessary jobs," "Shortened and made sail occasionally," "Employed Rattling down the Rigging, Blacking the Bends, etc. etc," "Carried away the Main Top Gallant yard, Sent up another, bent the sail and set it," and the notations of the deaths of members of the crew: "Departed this life Jacob Noble, Mariner, . . . George Judge, a seaman, . . . Samuel Monroe, Drummer, . . . Robert Carr, Seaman." One entry must have delighted the pious Macdonough: "Sunday, March 28, 1802—At 11 Mustered all hands and our Worthy Chaplain read Prayers."[33]

On Thursday, 29 April, he sighted Gibraltar for the first time. (Twenty-three years later this would be the last mainland he would ever see.) The *Constellation* sailed on to Málaga, Spain, where it joined the U.S. frigate *Essex* and the *Philadelphia*, commanded respectively by Capts. William Bainbridge and Samuel Barron. Bainbridge subsequently commanded the *Philadelphia* when Macdonough was aboard. Although the young midshipman may never have been formally introduced, he certainly knew Bainbridge by sight before the cruise was over.

For Macdonough the biggest memories of this cruise were the new ports and shorelines he saw. After the visits at Málaga and Gibraltar, the *Constellation* stopped in Syracuse, Naples, Leghorn, Toulon, and the Gulf of Tunis, where several officers went ashore to see the ruins of Carthage.

He saw for the first time the might of the Royal Navy. One can only imagine his awe as he sailed close to his first third-rate ship, the seventy-four-gun HMS *Caesar,* as it rode at anchor in Gibraltar. On board the fifty-gun *Isis* was Prince William Henry, the duke of Clarence (the future King William IV), who received a twenty-one-gun salute from *Constellation.*

From Captain Murray, Macdonough received lessons in how to develop and mature as a junior officer. Murray expected his junior officers to educate themselves, to make the most of the situation with which they found themselves so that they would be cognizant of the duties required "whenever you should be honored with a higher station." The captain enjoined his officers "to preserve harmony and concord among yourselves and enforce your orders, so as to have them promptly obeyed, not with the lash of severity but by a mild and systemic deportment, so as to render this service popular among the sailors." Although Murray's deafness may have contributed to the aloofness he demonstrated in command, his tradition of humane treatment of his tars left a lasting impression on Midshipman Macdonough.[34]

But the most common activity of the *Constellation* was succinctly described in Macdonough's journal as "filled away and stood for Tripoli," for most of the time was spent in a largely vain blockade of that North African port, often in concert with the *Thetis,* a Swedish warship. Part of a small squadron commanded by Rear Admiral Soderstrom, the Swedes were the only nation seriously cooperating with the United States in its efforts to suppress the Barbary pirates. The biggest action came on 22 July when the *Constellation* and *Thetis* fought eight Tripolitan gunboats and forced them to run onto the shore. Because they took refuge beneath the guns of the coastal fortifications, Murray could not destroy the vessels or capture their crews. Macdonough kept close track of the ammunition expenditure, noting the firing of sixty shot, twenty-two grape, and twenty-one canister rounds.[35]

The incident merely reinforced Murray's prejudice against prosecuting the Tripolitan conflict. On 14 August he wrote that unless "the European nations, cooperate more generally with us, & abolish the narrow minded Policy" of paying tribute to the Barbary states, "it will be more prudent for us, also, to submit to the Indignity, at the expence of our Pride." One brief engagement a few days later reinforced this attitude, and he noted the difficulty of enforcing the blockade "after the Blustering Season sets in" and the improper equipment available since the frigates could not sail close enough to shore to intercept the small Tripolitan galleys. The Americans needed what they did not have, schooners and gunboats.[36] Murray went far beyond his duties and tried to make policy rather than carry it out.

At least Murray was on his proper station. That is more than could be said for the commodore of the U.S. Mediterranean Squadron, Richard V. Morris. To subdue the Barbary States, the Jeffersonians sent what was probably the largest contingent of American vessels ever to sail in concert. Accompanied by his wife, child, and nanny, Morris preferred to sail between the Costa del Sol, the Côte d'Azur, Sardinia, and Naples rather than patrol the Barbary Coast. The government became increasingly disturbed at his inaction and ordered Morris and Murray and their ships home. On 10 March 1804 Smith determined that "a close and vigorous blockade of the port of Tripoli hath not been made" and directed a court of inquiry with Capt. Samuel Barron as head of the court. The court eventually decided that there were no facts disclosed "by the evidence, sufficiently clear and explicit, whereon to ground any censure of the conduct of captain Morris." Nevertheless, the court concluded that while Morris might have acquitted himself as the captain of a single ship, his "indolence, and want of capacity" made it necessary to recommend him incompetent to command a squadron.[37] Meanwhile, President Jefferson and Secretary Smith wanted results. To that end they sent Capt. Edward Preble with the *Constitution* to replace Morris.

For Thomas Macdonough the cruise on the *Constellation* expanded his geographic horizons and his knowledge of the sea. It also taught him a lesson in command: unassertive naval leadership was not expected during times of national emergency. The policies of Morris and Murray may have been prudent, but they were not successful. And there was another lesson: being assigned to Alexander Murray's command was not a billet likely to assist with one's early advancement. Murray did not enjoy the confidence of the secretary of the navy.[38] Macdonough needed to serve a commander and commodore who were more likely to have influence when promotion loomed. At this point in his career, there was little to distinguish him from the rest of the navy's 150 midshipmen. All the experience in the world was not going to elevate him into the ranks of commissioned officers if the secretary of the navy did not have confidence in the judgment of his superiors.

With the *Constellation* laid up for repairs, the midshipman, now nearly twenty years old, awaited a new assignment. Fortune now smiled on Thomas Macdonough. Secretary Smith selected him to serve under Preble's most aggressive subordinate, William Bainbridge of the *Philadelphia*. He was now the fourth most senior of eleven midshipmen on board. Besides the two frigates, *Constitution* and *Philadelphia*, Preble received the brigs *Syren* (Charles Stewart) and *Argus* (Isaac Hull) and three schooners— *Enterprise* (Stephen Decatur Jr.), *Nautilus* (Richard Somers), and *Vixen* (John Smith). (All but Somers would be important figures in Macdonough's career.) In the customary language of the day, Secretary Smith noted the president had the utmost confidence in Preble's "skill, judgment and bravery" and therefore entrusted this command to him with the expectation that he would make most "most strenuous exertions" in behalf of the national strategy.[39] Specific instructions informed Preble to maintain "an effectual blockade of Tripoli," to capture "vessels, Goods & Effects belonging to the Bey of Tripoli or his subjects," to "aid, succor, relieve and free any American public or private vessel attacked by the Enemy or in their possession," and to "keep a vigilant Eye over the movements of all the other Barbary powers." This mission was given to the commodore "in full confidence that you will maintain the dignity of your station and that the flag of your country will not be dishonored in your hands."[40] Jefferson and Smith would not be disappointed.

Bainbridge received similar orders and immediately set about to execute them. On 26 August 1803, the *Philadelphia* captured the Moroccan twenty-two-gun ship *Mirboka*, which had recently seized the American merchant brig *Celia*. Bainbridge released the captain and crew of the *Celia* and sent the *Mirboka* to Gibraltar as a prize. In what was by far the most responsible position he had held to date, Midshipman Macdonough went on board the Moroccan cruiser as the second officer of the prize crew. Later he found himself in charge of the ship as it moored in Gibraltar Harbor awaiting disposition as a prize. It proved to be an exceptionally fortunate assignment for him, although at the time he may have considered it unlucky since he was away from Bainbridge and the action off the Tripolitan coast.[41]

While he collected his squadron in Gibraltar, Preble ordered the *Philadelphia* and the fourteen-gun *Vixen* to cruise off Tripoli. It would be well, cautioned Preble, "to send the *Vixen* well in shore to look into the Bays, and snug places, along the coast." Alerted to the possibility that two Tripolitan warships were roaming the Mediterranean, Bainbridge sent the *Vixen* to cruise the narrow passage between Tunis and Sicily. This deprived Bainbridge of a shallow-draft vessel to sail in close to the coast. Captain Murray's warning about the treacherous waters off Tripoli did not deter Bainbridge. When he sighted a Tripolitan xebec he immediately gave chase. The xebec's captain skillfully lured the *Philadelphia* onto an uncharted sandbank known only to those familiar with the local waters.

Bainbridge's frigate ran aground and it, along with its crew, had to submit to capture. The whole diplomatic situation, which Preble had been sent to turn around, now became a most embarrassing one for the United States. From Macdonough's perspective the *Mirboka* incident "providentially saved" him from "prison and the apprehension of death which surrounded those of my shipmates in the power of a merciless foe."[42]

Relations with Algiers, Tunis, and Morocco that had been turning in American favor were now jeopardized. The Pasha of Tripoli had Preble's second largest vessel and 307 prisoners plus confidential dispatches that Bainbridge had not destroyed. Macdonough learned a lesson in naval prudence. As Preble wrote in confidence to his brother, if Bainbridge had kept the *Vixen* with him "it is probable he would have saved his ship." Moreover, he expressed surprise that the *Philadelphia* "was not rendered useless before her Colours were struck."[43]

Publicly, Preble was cautiously optimistic. He ordered Macdonough from his prize duty to become the senior midshipman on board Decatur's *Enterprise*. Preble sailed for Tripoli in expectation of undertaking an extended blockade. Macdonough described Preble as "a daring and vigilant officer." Preble confirmed this observation when from Syracuse he wrote Secretary Smith that he would "hazard much to destroy" *Philadelphia*. It was such hazarding that provided Thomas Macdonough a chance to distinguish himself.[44] In fact, Preble had a determined group of young officers and midshipmen ready to risk their lives in an effort to redeem the situation. Many fine young men would die before the conflict ended in 1805.

The first element in Preble's plan emerged after Decatur captured a sixty-four-ton Tripolitan ketch named *Mastico*. Decatur immediately brought to Preble's attention that the *Mastico* could sail into Tripoli without being thought of as an enemy ship. Once in the harbor, the Americans might be able to board the *Philadelphia* and burn it before being attacked by the Tripolitans. Preble approved the rash scheme. Decatur renamed his prize *Intrepid* and chose sixty-two of his most physically fit sailors and midshipmen to join him along with five midshipmen from the *Constitution*. Later a midshipman and eight men from the *Syren* boarded the *Intrepid*, making its complement eighty-four. Among those aboard was Macdonough, who had intimate knowledge of the American frigate from his service on her.

It was a simple but daring plan. Since the capture of *Mastico* was unknown in Tripoli, *Intrepid* would enter the harbor flying a British flag, come along side the *Philadelphia*, seize it, and set it afire. The *Syren*, dis-

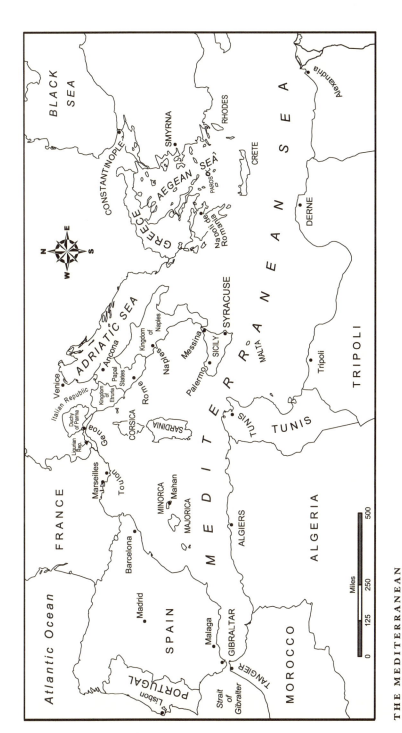

THE MEDITERRANEAN
Courtesy of Karen Mulcahy

guised as a merchant vessel, followed the *Intrepid* in order to supply fire-power and boats should something go wrong. Contrary winds twice kept the two ships from sailing into the harbor. The absence of the American blockading squadron should have raised suspicions, but did it not.

On the evening of 16 February 1804 the *Intrepid* sailed close to the captured vessel and, when challenged, claimed to be a Maltese ship that had lost its anchors and needed to tie alongside in order to avoid drifting aground. The agreeable Tripolitans not only accepted the flimsy excuse but also sent a boat with a line to assist. As the two ships were being tied together the guards noticed *Intrepid*'s anchors and cried "Americanos!" It was too late. The Americans stormed aboard the *Philadelphia* and, without firing a shot, seized the vessel using swords, cutlasses, and daggers. One U.S. sailor received a slight wound; at least twenty Tripolitans died.

With combustibles they had brought with them, Decatur's men quickly went to store rooms, gun room, cockpit, and berth deck. Macdonough and another midshipman took ten men to the berth deck, the lowest and most dangerous position on board. Decatur shouted, "Fire!" and the men started flames that quickly spread throughout the vessel. The Americans rushed back to the *Intrepid* and barely escaped being trapped in the rapidly expanding conflagration. Macdonough was one of the last to leave the frigate. By now the harbor's fortifications had begun firing at the fleeing *Intrepid*, but it escaped with only a single cannon shot through its topgallant sail. Forty miles away on board the *Constitution*, Commodore Preble could see the night sky lit by the flames and the explosions on the *Philadelphia*. His satisfaction only increased when he learned that success had come with no loss of American life. Decatur reported that he hoped the "coolness and intrepidity" displayed by his officers and men "will ever characterise the American Tars." With an outlook toward his enlisted men seldom found in contemporary correspondence, Decatur listed not only his officers but also his "tars" in his after-action report to Preble. British admiral Horatio Nelson pronounced it "the most bold and daring act of the age."[45]

This incident constitutes the turning point in Macdonough's career. He was mentioned in official correspondence and in documents sent to Congress. He had demonstrated his audacity and bravery in front of the navy's rising star, Stephen Decatur Jr. More than that, Macdonough had learned that an important part of a successful military operation is careful planning, including an attention to contingencies that saves lives and contributes significantly to an enterprise's success. This lesson stood him in good stead at Plattsburgh ten years later.

Despite the burning of the *Philadelphia*, the blockade of Tripoli accomplished little to move the bey to negotiate either about the prisoners or the neutral shipping rights of the American merchant marine. Preble decided to attack Tripoli Harbor directly. Nineteen Tripolitan gunboats presented Preble his greatest problem. Shallow-drafted, mobile, armed with one or two cannon, capable of being either sailed or rowed, they provided a defensive flexibility unavailable to Preble's squadron near the rocky shore at the entrance to the harbor. He needed to reduce the number Tripolitan gunboats and decided that U.S. Navy gunboats were the best tools for achieving that objective.

Preble secured permission from King Ferdinand IV of the Kingdom of the Two Sicilies to buy the six gunboats and two bomb vessels and to allow twelve of that government's bombardiers, gunners, and sailors to serve on each of the bomb vessels. He assigned a force of 1,060 men from the frigate *Constitution*, brigs *Argus*, *Syren*, and *Scourge*, schooners *Nautilus*, *Vixen*, and the *Enterprise*, to the bomb vessels and gunboats. Preble divided the gunboats into two divisions commanded by newly promoted Capt. Stephen Decatur and Master Commandant Richard Somers. Macdonough served with Decatur on Gunboat No. 4.

The gunboat-versus-gunboat battle of 3 August started off with an exchange of musketry and grapeshot which drove the Tripolitans to cover. There followed a dramatic boarding operation with hand-to-hand fighting. Gunboat No. 4 captured two enemy gunboats. When Stephen Decatur learned that his brother, Lt. James Decatur, had been mortally wounded while leading an attack on another gunboat, he requested volunteers to go after his brother's killers. Tired and exhausted as his men were, eleven, including Macdonough, volunteered to follow their commander. They killed the enemy gunboat's captain and secured the offending boat's surrender. This engagement resulted in twenty-one Tripolitans being killed or wounded and three taken prisoner. Alonzo Chapelle would immortalize this attack in a painting, giving Macdonough a prominent place. Throughout this effort Macdonough displayed extraordinary courage and daring. Captain Decatur noted that "nothing could surpass the zeal, courage and readiness" demonstrated by the young midshipman. He received a special honor when Decatur had him present the flags of the captured gunboats to Preble. The midshipman was one of those mentioned in Preble's report to the secretary of the navy. He seemed the epitome of the old hymn line, "When duty calls, or danger, be never wanting there."[46] And he learned from Decatur's conduct that the successful commander leads by example.

Now known as Decatur's "favorite midshipman," Macdonough received a growing list of responsibilities. When the notice of Decatur's promotion to post captain came from Washington, he was too high ranked to command a vessel the size of the *Enterprise*. Preble ordered Master Commandant Thomas Robinson Jr. to that vessel. At the same time, 6 September 1804, Preble appointed Macdonough a lieutenant on the *Enterprise*. It was indeed a rapid promotion for a young man who had arrived on board the vessel as midshipman just months earlier. Such a "gunboat promotion" gave him the rank without the pay of the new office until his confirmation by the Senate. Nonetheless, Macdonough now placed on his left shoulder the epaulette of a commissioned officer.[47]

Just as these changes occurred, there was a modification in command of the Mediterranean Squadron. Upon learning of the loss of the *Philadelphia* (the most disastrous loss to the United States since the Revolution), President Jefferson and Secretary Smith decided to replace Preble, on whose watch the incident happened, even though it was not his fault. Before they knew of the burning of that frigate, they sent Capt. James Barron and the U.S. frigate *President* to replace Preble. A letter of appreciation from most of the squadron's officers, including Macdonough, only partially assuaged Preble's disappointment.[48]

Commodore Barron sent the *Enterprise*, which had been almost constantly at sea since coming to the Mediterranean in 1800, northward into the Adriatic for repairs. It went from Malta to Trieste and then to Venice, where Macdonough spent one of the more delightful winters of his life. His grandson described the interlude in romantic terms: "Venice, moonlight, a pair of dark eyes, a young lieutenant, and a gondolier conveniently deaf, dumb and blind is not an impossible combination nor one forbidden by naval regulations, and perhaps rumor did couple his name with some daughter of Italy." The report of these activities reached a young daughter of Delaware to whom the handsome lieutenant was reportedly engaged. Although the temptations of the Italian lady did not result in marriage for Macdonough, the rumor allegedly sent the Delaware lady to the altar with another man. It is probably at this time that he had a portrait painted which shows the lieutenant a steely eyed, square-jawed, and serious young officer.[49]

Preble informed Barron of the need for more gunboats. Barron designated Macdonough to supervise the construction of three of them at the Adriatic port of Ancona, about halfway down the Italian peninsula, an assignment that took him from the charming lady of Venice. The construction of the gunboats took a few months, and, escorted by *Enterprise,* he sailed with them in June 1805 to Syracuse, where he learned that peace had been negotiated with Tripoli.[50] This interlude gave him an opportunity to expand his professional horizons by allowing him the chance to supervise ship construction. It would be an experience of significance when he received the Lake Champlain assignment seven years later.

Before his return to the United States in 1806, Macdonough served under David Porter on the *Enterprise* and became first lieutenant on the brig *Syren,* Capt. John Smith commanding. "Having not much to do," he recalled, we "visited many of the interesting ports and places along the shores of this sea. From Naples I went to Rome by land, visited Pompeii, Herculaneum, Mount Aetna, Malta and the towns of the Barbary Powers."

One day, as the *Syren* lay moored in Gibraltar Harbor, Macdonough witnessed the impressment of a sailor from an adjoining American merchantman. The young lieutenant took a boat alongside the British one and demanded the release of the sailor. When his request was refused, Macdonough "took hold of the man and took him in my boat and brought him on board the *Syren.*" Upon determining his United States citizenship, Macdonough kept the sailor in American employment.[51] Even in the midst of the Royal Navy's vast armada and despite the demands of a British officer that he return the man in question to British custody, Macdonough steadfastly enforced the American sailor's rights. Such conduct endeared him to American seamen.

Since his arrival in the Mediterranean, first on the *Constellation* in 1802 and later on the *Philadelphia, Enterprise,* and *Syren,* Thomas Macdonough had witnessed the successes and failures of his seniors and contemporaries. Three years' service against the Barbary powers had cost him many friends and acquaintances—James Decatur, Richard Somers, James R. Caldwell, and John S. Dorsey among them. But the experience matured many junior officers, who profited greatly from the lessons of operational planning, logistics, strategy, and tactics that would be put to use on salty and freshwater seas in the near future. Such men as William Henry Allen, Isaac Hull, James Lawrence, Oliver Hazard Perry, David Porter, John Trippe, and Lewis Warrington would continue to distinguish themselves in the future. The experience was one of lasting importance to Macdonough. Years later he recalled that the Mediterranean service "was the school where our navy received its first lessons, and its influence has to this day and will continue as long as the navy exists."[52]

Opportunity

One does not become famous as a warrior unless one has the chance to prove one's mettle in battle. The interlude of seven years of peace that followed Thomas Macdonough's three years of combat in the Mediterranean provided him with new professional, as well as social, development opportunities. By the start of 1812, however, there was a serious question as to whether he would even stay in the navy, much less become a naval hero.

Part of his apprehension revolved around the naval strategy proposed by the Jefferson administration. Jefferson's Republican Party was the usual American amalgamation of factions with different agendas. One of these agendas was governmental economy. Another faction wanted to eliminate the navy, or at least restrict it to a purely defensive mission of protecting the national shoreline. A third group wanted a navy that sailed blue waters to protect the merchant marine. A fourth desired a navy that contained large ships-of-the-line that posed a threat to the major navies of the world. In the middle of all this was a large antiregular military group that saw both the army and navy as threats to democracy and desired to rely on the more "republican" and virtuous militia as the principal arm of defense.[53] Most Jeffersonians agreed on the need for fiscal restraint and felt that an offensively capable military would become involved in overseas conflicts. Thus both military services underwent a severe cut in personnel and funds in the first years of Jefferson's administration.

Moreover, the experience in the Mediterranean convinced many that gunboats were a necessary addition to the naval force. The loss of the *Philadelphia* and the inability of Morris, Preble, and Barron to enforce a strict blockade of Tripoli were seen as a consequence of the lack of such vessels in the American inventory. Not only were such vessels purchased and built in the Mediterranean, but ten were built in the United States and nine sailed across the Atlantic (with the loss of one) too late to impact on the war's outcome. Still, as part of a coordinated harbor fortification policy, gunboats appealed to the defensive-minded president and secretary of the navy as a prudent, peaceful, and politically acceptable solution to the national defense posture. Moreover, like port fortifications, they required limited regular forces in peacetime and could be augmented by militia during wartime. From a Jeffersonian point of view, the success of the policy appeared in the British refusal to attack Boston, Newport, New York, Philadelphia, or Charleston and in the triumphant defense of Baltimore during the War of 1812. On the other hand, the Royal Navy's ability to blockade the American coast and to maintain a squadron in the Chesapeake demonstrated to its critics the failure of the gunboat defense policy.[54]

How did all of this affect Thomas Macdonough? After his return to the United States, he briefly visited his family in Delaware and then found himself detached to Middletown, Connecticut, under the command of Capt. Isaac Hull. Middletown was a moderately important port on the Connecticut River, where the river's ten-foot depth allowed waterborne commerce with the West Indies and the North American coast. Little did Macdonough know at the time that this community would become his home port for the rest of his life.

The Middletown of the early nineteenth century was in the midst of a great transition. A generation earlier it had made the gradual transition from a sleepy New England farming community to a bustling port. Along the river were a growing number of merchants' houses, wharves, warehouses, and shops where blacksmiths, blockmakers, rope makers, shipwrights, and sailmakers plied their crafts. Economic diversity brought a wave of new people to the community who also divided the social and political solidarity of the town. One historian wrote that the "old landed families that had always led the town affairs . . . were being pushed aside by newcomers whose wealth was based in trade. . . . By the first decade of the nineteenth century, Middlesex County was in the grips of a full-blown ecological disaster caused by overpopulation and intensive commercialized agriculture."[55] The town was also experiencing economic, religious, and political rivalries, and these too contributed to the community's stagnation.

One of those new families was that of Nathaniel Shaler. His father was a sea captain who married a local woman and died at sea. Nathaniel's widowed mother ran an inn, strongly recommended by John Adams, on Middletown's main street. The Shalers were Anglicans in a town where all the old families were members of the Rev. Enoch Huntington's First Congregational Church. Nathaniel was briefly a captain of a militia company in 1776 but refused to serve when called upon to help George Washington defend Long Island. (The irony is that Thomas Macdonough's father fought at Long Island.) Shaler became a Loyalist refugee in 1777 and spent the war years on St. Christopher in the West Indies. He briefly returned to Middletown in 1783 before moving to New York City. Shaler and his second wife, Lucretia Ann Denning, daughter of a New York Patriot, returned in 1790 to Middletown, where they resided with his aged mother. Using whatever profits he made in the West Indies and New York, Shaler soon became one of the town's most prominent businessmen.

He was involved in fishing, farming, milling, and storekeeping. Most important was his investment in a local stone quarry at Chatham in partnership with Joel Hall. The quarry was said to produce an annual return of 90 percent on the investment.

Nathaniel and Lucretia Ann Shaler's third child was Lucy Ann, born in 1790 in New York. She was sixteen years old when the handsome young lieutenant came to Middletown on his new assignment. In all probability they met at Christ Episcopal Church, where her father was a prominent layman. Despite her father's Toryism, Thomas Macdonough had to be intrigued not only by the young lady but also by the sophistication of the Shaler family. As a boy Nathaniel Shaler was known for his proficiency in music, playing the flute, harpsichord, spinet, and other instruments. As a father he frequently kept his children at church after the services and entertained them by playing the organ. Shaler was fond of books and delighted in reading Shakespeare to his family around the fireplace. To young Lucy Ann, the lieutenant's tales of the Caribbean and Mediterranean must have seemed romantic. In addition, both shared similar religious inclinations. But any chance of an early marriage was put off by two impediments—her age and his poverty.[56]

In Middletown Macdonough also struck up friendships with prominent local individuals, including William Vandeursen. As he sought to recruit sailors in New York at what was known as a "rendezvous," he wrote his friend "Van" a humorous note that he would have made his letter longer except "the sailors are making such a noise together with the drum and fife and fiddle they confuse me or would the devil himself, who has a larger rendezvous open than I have."[57] Another close friend was Henry "Hank" DeKoven, local merchant and childhood friend of the young Miss Shaler. Macdonough would have many reasons to return to Middletown.

After spending three months supervising the building of the gunboats in Middletown, he went to Washington, D.C., where he joined the *Wasp*, Master Commandant John Smith commanding. Smith had been so pleased with Macdonough's performance as first lieutenant of the *Syren* that he requested the lieutenant's services again. Smith took an increasingly important role in mentoring Macdonough's development as an officer. Only slightly older than Macdonough, Smith was a good man for his first lieutenant to emulate. After several years in the merchant service, Smith entered the navy with a direct lieutenant's commission, never having served as a midshipman. He assembled a solid record during the Tripolitan War and advanced rapidly in the expanding navy of Jefferson's second administration. He made the rank of captain at the age of thirty without having distinguished himself in combat. As historian Christopher McKee noted, "The earlier years [of the U.S. Navy] had been less structured; opportunity for rapid advancement was more open for persons with unusual abilities and the good fortune to be in the right place at the right time." Smith was known for his strong sense of duty, for setting an elegant mess, for gentlemanly conduct, and for professionalism.[58]

Officially promoted to lieutenant effective 6 February 1807, the cruise on the *Wasp* has to have been one of the most challenging times of Macdonough's young naval career. The first lieutenant was critically important to the success of any vessel. Unlike his first lieutenancies in the Mediterranean, he found the crew of the *Wasp* was entirely new. Many had never been to sea. He was responsible for managing the daily details of ship routine. The *Naval Regulations* of 1802 required the first lieutenant "to make out a general alphabetical book of the ship's company, and proper watch, quarter and station bills, in case of fire, manning of ship, loosing and furling of sails, reefing of topsails at sea, working of ship, mooring and un-mooring, &c." Soon Macdonough learned that "&c" covered a multitude of duties. He saw that the commissioned, warrant, and petty officers' tasks were performed, that the watch, station, gun, and berthing assignments were made, that the crew practiced gunnery, boarding, and small arms, and that the vessel itself and the sailors' uniforms and equipment were clean and ready for the captain's inspection. He recommended men to the captain for promotion, demotion, or punishment. Since the *Wasp*'s crew included three other lieutenants and eight midshipmen, Macdonough would not normally stand watch but would allow the watch officer to continue to operate the vessel. At the same time, he had to be ready to assume command of the vessel should illness or death demand it.[59]

The *Wasp* sailed to England and France with dispatches. While in Britain, Captain Smith reported that visiting the Royal Navy dockyards enhanced his officers' professional development. Here too Macdonough probably found opportunities to add to his growing library of professional literature. The *Wasp* would be one of the last American vessels to visit England prior to the outbreak of animosities between the two countries following the *Chesapeake-Leopard* incident of 1807. Prior to that time the two navies cruised the same seas—Mediterranean and Caribbean—and visited many of the same ports, including Gibraltar, Port Mahon, Syracuse, and Malta. Historian McKee queried, "Is it to be doubted that in these almost daily contacts, the careful observation, the admiring emulation—and in the avid study of the older navy's professional literature—one touches the fundamental means by which British naval culture became American naval culture?" In his estimation, the obvious answer to this question is a resounding no; there can be no doubt that the Royal Navy provided the example of excellence for officers of the young Republic's ships.[60]

Upon returning home, the *Wasp*'s crew faced a new, different, and difficult assignment. As part of its response to the British Orders in Council and the French Berlin and Milan Decrees, the Jefferson administration secured passage of the Embargo Act, which prohibited trade with any nation. For fifteen months from December 1807 until March 1809, the navy was the principal instrument attempting to enforce this highly unpopular law. The *Wasp* spent most of this period cruising along the coast from Boston to Charleston. This was a most unpleasant task and took the navy into the role of police officer in an operation neither conducive to navy professionalism nor to furthering the navy's popular image among the general populace. In a few years Macdonough would face the same onerous task on Lake Champlain.

One can only imagine Macdonough's great pleasure when Congress repealed the embargo and he received orders to join Captain Smith aboard the recently refurbished frigate *Essex*. His assignment with the vessel was brief, only eight months, from February to September 1809. These three consecutive sea tours with Smith were unusual and reflect that officer's deep appreciation of Macdonough's professionalism, experience, and conduct. There had to be a most cordial relationship and respect between the two and their personalities had to be closely allied. For most of the previous five years the two had served with one another. And apparently the enlisted men were impressed with Macdonough and expressed their "heartfelt sorrow" at his "intention of leaving the Ship." They noted his "officer-like Conduct and Philanthropy" during his brief stay. They ended with a maritime farewell that evoked the religiosity Macdonough left among all that knew him: it was the "Hearty prayer" of his subordinates that "He who holds the Destiny of Mankind [might] guide you Safe through life and Pilot you at last to the harbour of Rest."[61]

But Macdonough had another association he wished to further, and he desired not to sail with the *Essex*. He secured what may be considered a less-career-enhancing assignment as commander of the gunboats in Connecticut and Long Island Sound headquartered in Middletown. Why did he desire such a billet? For one thing it allowed him to rekindle his romance with Lucy Ann Shaler. For her, the impediment of age no long interfered; she was now nineteen. For him, the impediment of poverty (at least when compared to her father) still existed, and prospects had not improved with the post-embargo navy, which had increasingly fewer assignments. Over a fifth of the navy's officers went on furlough, at half pay. He stayed in Middletown seven months before requesting furlough in order to make a merchant voyage to the East Indies. (One may assume that his maritime skills and his prospective father-in-law's influence secured for him this opportunity to enhance his material wealth.) He sailed from New York in June 1810 for Liverpool and Calcutta, in command of the brig *Gulliver* of Boston. The ship returned to Boston in August 1811, its cargo containing a variety of goods, including silk, twine, lines, cords, rope, cotton canvas and other cotton goods, gunny bags, canvas, 100 tons of Campeachy logwood, 94 barrels of pot and pearl ash, various medicines, and 42 boxes of Brazil sugar, which indicates a stop in that country on the return voyage.

The *Gulliver* voyage marked an increased opportunity for Macdonough. For the first time in his maritime career he was solely responsible for a ship. He took it halfway around the world and back, into new and exotic ports, on new and hazardous seas. Such an occasion prepared him for independent command of a naval vessel. Moreover, he learned how to command without the punishment authority allowed by naval regulations. The willingness of his backers to send him on another cruise indicated they thought him an individual who shouldered the burdens of command and the custody of both ship and cargo with reliability and accountability.

Upon his return he hurried to Middletown, from where he requested permission for a second furlough to captain the *Gulliver* on another trip to India. There followed an exchange of letters between Macdonough and Secretary of the Navy Paul Hamilton that illuminates both men's view of the current situation. Macdonough requested the furlough continuation on grounds that he was "honor bound to fulfill a domestic engagement, returning to the naval service would prevent it and expose me to censure and reproach." Hamilton replied that he could not grant such a request, presumably because the possibility of war with Great Britain loomed large. Macdonough pleaded that he did not want to leave "the navy entirely" but must meet his obligations to the Boston merchants as well as his engagement of "a domestic nature" or he would have to resign. This brought a delayed reply from Hamilton that the "high character" Macdonough "sustained in the service" disposed the secretary "to grant you every reasonable indulgence." He granted the furlough. The same day, 15 October 1811,

Macdonough wrote Hamilton offering his resignation. The two letters crossed in the mail. Hamilton wrote "resignation to be accepted" on Macdonough's letter and then crossed it out. Why? We do not know the reasons behind the secretary's change of heart, but it was fortunate for the naval service that he did. Macdonough went to New York in March 1812, intending to sail for Lisbon as commander of the *Jeannette Snow,* a ship in which he held one-fourth interest. It is this investment that is the likely "domestic engagement" to which Macdonough referred, not his intentions toward Miss Shaler. However, before he could sail, Congress enacted an embargo of ninety days on all American vessels heading for foreign ports.[62]

Economic advancement and domestic felicity were not the only items on Macdonough's agenda. He increasingly became a committed Episcopalian and sought full sacramental entrance into that denomination. He had his baptism reaffirmed at Christ Church, Middletown, and subsequently received confirmation at Christ Church, Hartford, by the bishop of Connecticut. His regular practice of religion was well known in a service in which even high-ranking officers were known to drink to excess, curse with vigor, and carouse when in port. Macdonough was different, and that difference impacted all those that served with him. Profanity never came from his mouth, "By zounds" being his most emphatic expletive. He refused to gamble, to drink immoderately, and to behave in an unofficerlike manner. He set an example that many of his subordinates felt necessary to follow even if they were not so inclined. One midshipman later described him as a "high-minded, honorable and religious officer and truly conscientious in the performance of his duties, and withal openminded man, strictly moral & correct in his deportment."[63]

A contemporary later recalled Macdonough exhibited "Spartan firmness with . . . Christian virtues. His bravery was never for a moment doubted, but he was so reserved, temperate, and circumspect, that the envious, sometimes, strove to bring him to their level, and often set snares for him; but he was never caught."[64]

And that reputation was known in the Navy Department. On the eve of the War of 1812, Macdonough stood twentieth on the list of lieutenants in the navy. Yet Secretary Hamilton offered him a choice assignment which many of his seniors, such as Oliver H. Perry, lusted after: the first lieutenancy of the U.S. frigate *Constellation,* Capt. William Bainbridge commanding.[65] For reasons as yet unexplained, Macdonough resigned the position and sought the command of gunboats off northern New England. Up to this point in his career he had done almost everything to enhance his reputation and seized every opportunity to increase his favor in the eyes of his professional colleagues and the Navy Department. There are several considerations for his request for reassignment.

First, was he reluctant to serve under Bainbridge? This is difficult to answer. He had served under Bainbridge on the *Philadelphia* previously. Was there something in this experience that caused him to seek another assignment? Did the memory of Bainbridge's somewhat reckless captaincy of that vessel that resulted in it running aground and capture affect Macdonough's attitude in serving with this officer? Were there Bainbridge personality traits that Macdonough deplored? Was Bainbridge's reputation as a harsh disciplinarian of enlisted men a factor? We will probably never know the answers to these questions. It is certain that Bainbridge wanted Macdonough. When information reached Bainbridge that Macdonough would rather have a gunboat command at Portland than serve with him, he wrote a most complimentary letter. Its critical first paragraph read,

> I regret exceedingly this change [in your assignment] for several considerations. First, that the country will lose your valuable services on the main. Secondly, that you will, I think, lose an opportunity of acquiring fame and making your fortune, for if *I can only run away* from our coast I feel confident the *Constellation* will do something clever. Thirdly, I shall lose an excellent first lieutenant, one in whom I have the highest confidence. But if *love* and the Gods have decreed it otherwise I must be satisfied, and wherever you go you carry my best wishes for your happiness.[66]

What did Bainbridge mean when he said "and the Gods"? Was this merely casual reference to Fate, or did he know of some deeper meaning that might reflect differences in religious and private morality practices between the two?

Second, did he resign the position because the *Constellation* was being refurbished and would be several months before it would see action? Macdonough's grandson thought this to be the case.[67] The first lieutenant of the *Constellation* would be immediately in charge of all the minutia of seeing to it that this vessel was prepared for service. Macdonough might well have wanted to avoid this irksome duty when he could command small vessels that would immediately be at sea. Or perhaps Macdonough foresaw what actually happened. The *Constellation* would not be ready for sea until early 1813, and by then the British naval blockade kept it bottled up in the Chesapeake for the rest of the war. Eventually Bainbridge sought a new command rather than waste months waiting for the *Constellation* to set sail.

Third, did Macdonough expect that his seniority entitled him to a command of his own rather than being someone's second? Since the *Constellation* was docked at Washington Navy Yard, Macdonough had ample time to see Secretary of the Navy Paul Hamilton. Did he determine just what other assignments might be available and lobby for one of them? Did he know of the possibility of a command on Lake Champlain? Did he assume his seniority would result in promotion to master commandant and therefore make him too high ranking for the *Constellation*'s first lieutenancy? For that matter, did Macdonough foresee significant prize money off the New England coast, especially in the Bay of Fundy? Maybe Bainbridge was wrong; fortune, if not fame, could be made commanding gunboats.

Fourth, did Macdonough want to wait until after his marriage before going to sea, or did he not want to absent himself from his bride for an extended period demanded by a frigate's cruise? This is the least likely explanation, but Bainbridge certainly felt it was a factor in Macdonough's deciding against the *Constellation* assignment. Still, Macdonough went on active service and waited until December 1812 before getting married. Yet the reassignment request seems most unusual since most officers wanted frigate billets on the high seas. Was Lucy Ann Shaler worth such a career sacrifice?—perhaps in the eyes of a man deeply in love.

All too little is known of Lucy Ann, who was known as "Ann" to her family so as not to confuse her with her mother Lucretia Ann, who was called Lucy. It is highly probable that it was to Ann that her cousin Elizabeth Denning wrote the poem "To Miss Shaler," which proclaimed,

> In Festive Hall, or rural bower,
> Her charms can ev'ry scene improve,
> And still enhance the pleasing power,
> Of nature, friendship, grace, and love.

The young couple's long-postponed wedding occurred on 12 December 1812 after Lieutenant Macdonough took leave from his assignment at Lake Champlain to come to Middletown. There at Christ Church the Right Reverend Abraham Jarvis, bishop of Connecticut, married the young couple. (That the Episcopal bishop, the former rector of the parish, would come to marry Ann testifies to her father's importance in the church.) The best man was Henry Louis "Hank" DeKoven, local merchant, childhood friend of Ann's, and close friend of the groom, who soon would take a privateer to sea. Their honeymoon trip was a winter journey to Vergennes, Vermont, spent in rather primitive rented quarters.[68]

Macdonough had been in Portland, Maine (then part of Massachusetts), only a few days when new orders came from Secretary Hamilton directing him to Lake Champlain. He was not to wait for a successor to come to Portland; instead, he was to go directly to the lake where all of the vessels were to be under his "direction & command." He replaced Lt. Sidney Smith, who was seen as lethargic in the performance of his duties on this most critical invasion route between the Hudson and St. Lawrence Valleys.[69]

Macdonough was only twenty-eight years old when he made the four-day overland journey from Portland to Burlington. And yet the young man was reasonably well prepared for the arduous duty he now undertook. From family and church he acquired the sense of high moral conduct and integrity that characterized his entire career. From the day he boarded the *Ganges* at New Castle until he left the *Gulliver* in Boston, he increased his knowledge of seamanship and sailed all the world's major oceans except the Pacific. From the time he boarded *La Fortune* off the coast of Cuba until he fought in gunboats in the Tripoli Harbor, he demonstrated the courage and combat leadership that distinguishes a successful combat commander. From his duty in the Mediterranean, he learned the consequences of being overcautious and over aggressive in tactical deployment. From Preble and Decatur he observed the importance of detailed planning before going into an operation. From his supervision of gunboat construction at Ancona, Italy, and at Middletown, Connecticut, he mastered skills of logistics and leadership in port that would be critical to any success on Lake Champlain where the American squadron was in disrepair and insufficient in numbers and size. From his experience with the *Gulliver*, he discovered how to lead men without the compulsion of naval regulations and punishments. From Mullowney, Decatur, and Smith, plus his prospective father-in-law, Macdonough gained an understanding of all the courtesies of the service and of gentlemanly traits that distinguish the exemplary officer. All of these experiences prepared him for the responsibilities he now faced on Lake Champlain. He was what some call a "tarpaulin captain," one who earned his position by exhibiting the character traits, professional expertise, tactical experience, and career development that qualified him for his new command.

We must keep in mind, however, that the competency demonstrated in the junior ranks does not necessarily transfer into success at more senior levels of command. Secretary Hamilton took an extraordinary degree of risk and placed an enormous responsibility in the hands of Lieutenant Macdonough when he wrote orders transferring him to Lake Champlain. Only time would tell how well placed this decision would be.

Chapter Three

Lake Champlain, 1812–1813

The threatening cloud was gathering fast
O'er Plattsburgh's heights, and Champlain's wave,
While firm as oak amid the blast,
Or rock when the ocean's billows rave—
Undaunted stood our heroes brave,
Resolved, with Freedom, all, at stake,
To conquer there, or find a grave
Within the bosom of the Lake.

   Anonymous, "The Battle of Lake Champlain"

ONE HISTORIAN called Lake Champlain "a silver dagger from Canada to the heartland of the [British] American colonies that forged the destiny of France and England in America, and of the United States." It contains 435 square miles and is 107 miles long and 14 miles wide at greatest width. It connects at Ticonderoga to Lake George, and the northward flowing Richelieu River drains it. Located between the Green Mountains of Vermont and the Adirondacks of New York, in the early nineteenth century the lake had only a few small settlements on each side—Whitehall and Plattsburgh, New York, and Burlington, Vermont, were the only communities of any size, and they were quite small. The natural outlet of commerce was down the 75-mile-long Richelieu River, which joins the St. Lawrence River at Sorel. Because one had to cross the international boundary with Lower Canada—the "lines," as the border was called—all commercial traffic was subject to the normal restraints of international trade. But at the time Thomas Macdonough first arrived, the locals paid little attention to the niceties of tariffs and wartime non-intercourse constraints.[1]

The great "Mahican Channel" between the northeastern United States and Lower Canada dominated by the Richelieu River, Lakes Champlain and George, and the Hudson River had long been an avenue of military advance and retreat during the struggles between New France and British North America and between the United States and British Canada. Numerous fortifications rose, fell, and decayed along the route as international

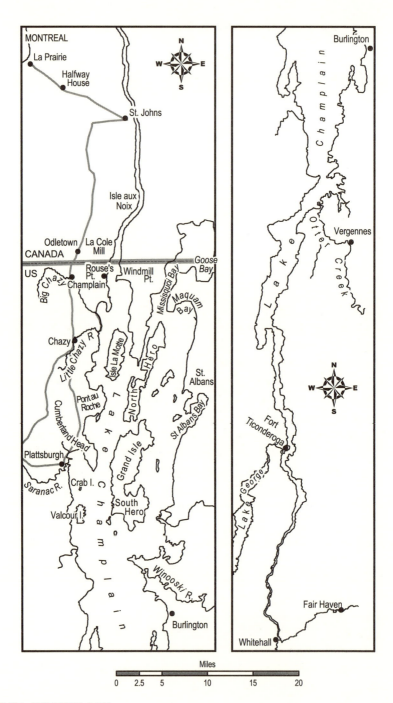

LAKE CHAMPLAIN
Courtesy of Karen Mulcahy

tensions increased and declined. Today some of them, such as Fort Ticonderoga and West Point, are well known; others, such as Fort William Henry, have been immortalized in literature such as James Fenimore Cooper's *Last of the Mohicans.*

Because of Gen. Isaac Brock's 1812 offensives on Lakes Huron, Erie, and Ontario, American strategic and operational interest shifted from this traditional invasion route to the Great Lakes and their environs. This shift meant that for two years the American army and navy's role on Lake Champlain was more defensive than offensive. Gov. Gen. Sir George Prevost's position in Lower Canada was largely defensive. Stretched thinly from Lake Superior to the Gulf of St. Lawrence, he wisely husbanded his limited forces on the St. Lawrence River frontier and on the Lake Ontario littoral. At the war's beginning all this was not apparent. Most assumed that American major general Henry Dearborn would use the Lake Champlain corridor for an advance on Montreal. That officer's lethargy combined with a genuine reluctance from the New England governors to support any war effort contributed to the shifting emphasis toward the Great Lakes frontier.

Prevost concentrated his defensive efforts on building the fortifications and reinforcing the garrison at Île aux Noix a few miles from the head of the Richelieu. There he also brought the gunboats that constituted the basis for a fleet. He had one unusual problem: every time his regulars came close to the lines, they deserted south in large numbers.[2]

The United States gathered its forces at Plattsburgh, where a logistical base and fortifications were constructed. Initial command of the forces there rested on Maj. Gen. Benjamin Mooers of the New York militia, a fifty-four-year-old veteran of the Revolution. Mooers was not expected to wage an offensive campaign. His major accomplishment was placing the first American forces on the Lake Champlain frontier and securing Vermont militiamen for the more militarily vulnerable New York side of the lake. He remained the regional militia commander throughout the war. His superior (despite being junior in rank) was Brig. Gen. Joseph Bloomfield of the regular army, another Revolutionary veteran and the current governor of New Jersey, who did not arrive at Plattsburgh until 2 September 1812. (President Madison gave general officer commissions to two state governors and two territorial governors. Of these only William Henry Harrison of Indiana Territory proved worthy of the trust imposed upon him.)

John G. Freligh of Plattsburgh expressed typical Federalist skepticism concerning the situation: "Democracy [by which he means the Republican Party] will not or cannot see what is for the best good of the country; for this war, like all the rest of their measures, has been commenced in folly, directed in weakness, and will end in ruin." General Mooers proved more optimistic. He felt the steamboat that regularly plied the waters of the northern portion of the lake between Plattsburgh and Burlington "might be of great service to us in case of actual hostilities." Probably he saw its importance more in terms of a logistical support vessel than a military one. Peter Sailly, a French immigrant who settled in the Plattsburgh area in 1785, forwarded rumors that the schooner *Royal Edward* at Île aux Noix was being fitted out for use on Lake Champlain even though it was only a hulk that never sailed again. General Mooers urged Lt. Sidney Smith to put the two gunboats that were laid up near Vergennes to be made ready and brought to Plattsburgh. This Smith did "at his own risque" without orders from Washington. Even Mooers noted local "apprehensions" that British naval and ground forces might stage a raid on Plattsburgh and seize the fleet and destroy the depot located there.[3]

General Bloomfield's illness forced Dearborn to assume operational command. Although he thought a winter campaign might succeed in gaining ground to the St. Lawrence, his irresolution and some of the militia's reluctance to cross the international boundary forced him to withdraw to winter quarters. Only Col. Zebulon Pike proved aggressive during this operation by taking a reconnaissance in force on 20 November toward the British outpost at Lacolle, which his troops took during a confused night attack. Always ready to blame someone else for his failures, Dearborn argued that the one reason for this fiasco was the non-appearance of the naval squadron in support of his movement.[4]

The young commodore had his own problems. A seeming absence of interest in Washington regarding the lake war brought great confusion on Lake Champlain. Two gunboats built in 1809 had been derelicts at Basin Harbor, Vermont, before Lieutenant Smith rescued them and brought them to Plattsburgh. Without authorization from the Navy Department but with General Mooers's advice, he began repairing one of them. Mooers also felt the navy ignored the need to expand the squadron on the lake and wrote Dearborn to that effect. Midn. Horace B. Sawyer accepted a warrant and reported himself to Smith in the summer of 1812. He remained without orders for six months, and the purser refused to pay him until they were received. Meanwhile, the army began constructing 160 bateaux at Whitehall as amphibious assault vessels that would transport forces and supplies down the Richelieu. The War Department purchased 6 sloops, of which 3—the sixty-five-foot *President,* the sixty-four-foot *Bulldog* (renamed *Eagle*), and the sixty-one-foot *Hunter* (renamed *Growler*)—would become navy property shortly after Macdonough's arrival. To counter these vessels the British brought three small gunboats from the St. Lawrence River to Île aux Noix. Even before Macdonough arrived the two small squadrons maneuvered, but never skirmished at the northern end of the lake.[5]

In addition to their tactical duties, Smith's naval forces and army contractors provided ships for the transportation of troops to the northward during the fall campaign. For instance, during September 1812, Capt. John Scott's and Ens. Lucoes Goes's units sailed on navy vessels from Whitehall to Plattsburgh, where they participated in Dearborn's abortive campaign toward the Canadian lines. John Freligh summarized the fall campaign in a letter to his brother: "The Army has again returned . . . without effecting anything. They were absent precisely one week, during which time they were exposed to many inconveniences and privations to no purpose."[6]

Taking Command

Although he was allowed to remain on the scene as Macdonough's second in command, Smith's removal as the senior officer on Lake Champlain must be viewed as a departmental lack of confidence in his capacities. Smith undoubtedly resented being replaced by someone only slightly above him on the seniority list of lieutenants. A native of Plattsburgh, Smith possessed knowledge of the lake and its environs that would assist Macdonough, who had never been there before. On the other hand, that a junior lieutenant such as Macdonough would be given naval command of a critical avenue of approach to Canada reflects the lack of interest in such freshwater assignments among his seniors. Little is known of the decision-making process by which Macdonough's name came to the fore, but undoubtedly his reputation and association with such men as William Bainbridge, Stephen Decatur, Isaac Hull, and John Smith were a contributing factor. He had experience as a supervisor of ship construction and as a leader in combat, skills that would be sorely tested in the next three years. The Lake Champlain posting did not conceivably anticipate the type of prize money that the position at Portland promised, but it involved a much more responsible command. It also promised a quick promotion to master commandant.

When he took command on 8 October, Macdonough found himself with three principal responsibilities. First, he had to obtain and retain naval control of Lake Champlain. Second, he had to cooperate with the army in any offensive or defensive actions on the lake littoral and assist in transportation of troops and supplies as necessary. Third, he had to assist in suppressing illicit commerce with Lower Canada.

Macdonough quickly toured his new command, going from Burlington to Plattsburgh to Whitehall. What he found would tax his abilities as a leader. His tasks were multiple. He had to be an administrator—to supervise the construction and maintenance of vessels; to see that guns, stores, and provisions were available for his growing squadron; to request more personnel of the right type to be sent from distant rendezvouses and see to their correct distribution among his ships and their discipline and training in the tasks before them; and to supervise the accounts of the squadron. He had to be a strategist—to acquire intelligence of enemy dispositions, intentions, and policies; to request sufficient supporting vessels to meet expected contingencies; and to coordinate with his army counterparts in the prosecution of the war in his theater. He had to be a tactician—to direct his subordinates in their activities; to dispose his squadron over the length of Lake Champlain to maximize its impact upon situations; to train his sailors and their officers in the proper conduct of operations; and to be ready at a moment's notice to lead his crews in the fight of their lives. He had to be a naval professional—to exhibit those skills of seamanship, gunnery, and fortitude that his officers and men expected from one in command. He had to remain physically fit so that the stress of command did not interfere with his ability to perform his duties. He had to be able, in the words of Carl von Clausewitz, "to summon the titanic strength it takes to clear away the enormous burdens that obstruct activity in war."

Above all, Macdonough's leadership traits had to exhibit strength of character. It was imperative that he possess self-control, steadiness under stress, rationality in an irrational situation, and imagination at times when one is prone to follow only routine or to freeze when faced with burdens of responsibility and the trauma of combat. All this required, again in Clausewitz's words, "the inquiring rather than the creative mind, the comprehensive rather than the specialized approach, the calm rather than the excitable head to which in war we would choose to entrust the fate of our brothers and children, and the safety and honor of our country."[7]

Whenever he stood on the quarterdeck, or inspected his crews, or supervised ship construction, naval leadership required that Macdonough exhibit a self-assuredness, presence, and confidence that would inspire his subordinates to do more than they may have felt they reasonably could.

Behind what historian John Keegan called this "mask of command," he had to hide all the insecurities, frustrations, and fears that bothered him. For two years Macdonough did just this, and finally, on 11 September 1814, he would have the opportunity to show the man behind that mask.[8]

Secretary of the Navy Jones gave him an autonomous command rather than one under the supervision of a senior officer such as Capt. Isaac Chauncey, commodore of the Great Lakes. This increased the weight of responsibility on the young commander, but it freed him from much of the outside interference that would burden Oliver Hazard Perry on Lake Erie, where he fell under Chauncey's control. Thus Macdonough reported directly to the secretary rather than through a chain of command. It was a command relationship that enhanced the Lake Champlain commodore's place in the naval hierarchy and allowed him to directly increase his logistical support facilities without going through a more senior officer.

It was Macdonough's administrative skills that received the severest test in the first months of command. By mid-January he had the sloop *President*, sloop *Eagle* (formerly *Bulldog*), and two gunboats under his command. Work was progressing on the *Growler* (formerly the *Hunter*). On all three sloops he hoped to reduce the length of the quarterdeck so that the main deck could be lengthened and two more carronades added to each side for a total of five per side plus one long gun on a circle that was on the forward part of the same deck. In addition there were three unarmed sloops used for transports.

Anticipating renewed British efforts to gain superiority on the lake, Macdonough requested more vessels, guns, supplies, officers, men, and shipbuilders. He knew few senior lieutenants would want to join him and requested instead that "old Midshipmen or Sailing Masters" be sent to officer his vessels. Macdonough never received as many men as he had hoped, so in May 1813, he laid up the gunboats and manned the three sloops which had greater firepower than the three sloops with two guns apiece that the British had at Île aux Noix.[9]

Other trials demanded Macdonough's administrative supervision and patience. He hoped to relieve some of the accounting burden by employing a naval agent and purser as had been authorized by Secretary Hamilton when he sent Macdonough to the lake. When Macdonough appointed a temporary navy agent for Lake Champlain, the navy went for months without formally authorizing the status. Even worse was the situation regarding the purser post supposedly awarded George Beale. The Senate delayed confirming this choice, so Beale departed in the spring, leaving all his duties to Macdonough. Beale finally received Senate approval in July and returned to the post in August. Moreover, the seamen Macdonough received were either incompetent or quickly deserted their post.[10]

Were this not enough, the administrative minutiae required to procure and transport the carronades to Macdonough's headquarters at Shelburne, Vermont, would have tasked the patience of Job. Macdonough requested them in January, and Secretary Jones pushed his naval agents in Philadelphia and New York to forward them to Lake Champlain with dispatch. Even their mode of transport up the Hudson River required correspondence. They were still not mounted by the first of May.[11] All this detail was monotonous, routine, and dull; but it was necessary. The attention that Macdonough paid to it reflects credit upon his administrative skills and his willingness to closely monitor these critical essentials of command.

With the carronades mounted and the ice melted, the small American squadron moved down the lake toward the lines to demonstrate the Republic's control of this waterway. It appeared as though Macdonough's strategic calculations were correct. With so much at stake on Lake Ontario and Lake Erie, the British paid little attention to the Lake Champlain region. They moved from Quebec three forty-five-foot and forty-four-foot gunboats, the *Beresford, Brock,* and *Popham,* to Île aux Noix, but this was hardly sufficient to contest Macdonough's three sloops. Strategically, enough had been done to ensure American dominance of Lake Champlain for 1813.

At the north end of the lake, the biggest threat to the United States was smuggling. Ever since the Embargo Act of 1807, smuggling contraband goods to and from Lower Canada had been a major economic occupation for those living along Lake Champlain's shores. Trading with the enemy was looked upon with great favor by many of the lake's inhabitants, who viewed the smuggler much in the way many today look upon Robin Hood and his antics against the Sheriff of Nottingham. Governor General Prevost reported that two-thirds of the army's beef came from Vermont and New York. In an era before canals and railroads linked the region to the Hudson Valley, the lake's environs were tightly linked to the St. Lawrence Valley. "It is surprising," wrote the Rev. Charles James Stewart, Anglican rector in St. Armand, Lower Canada, "how many cattle for our Army Contractors are driven here from Vermont."[12]

Settlers on both sides of the forty-fifth parallel found that economic necessity and geography compelled them to trade with one another. For instance, Pliny Moore, a merchant of Champlain, New York, located almost at the forty-fifth parallel, had long engaged in commerce with Montreal, where he owned property. His son, Royal Corbin Moore, was apprenticed to a Montreal merchant when the war broke out. The seventeen year old begged his father for advice on what to do. Surviving letters do not fully document just what went on, but Royal stayed in Montreal. He sometimes visited his parents in the United States, and his mother visited him in the Canadian city. Another son rafted logs to Canada in 1812 and served as a U.S. Army barracks master in 1814. We will never know how much trade went on between the Moores of Canada and those in America. Throughout the war, the family home frequently entertained officers from both sides, served as a hospital for both combatants, and silently watched as soldiers marched through and stragglers pilfered homes in the little village.[13] Pliny Moore's situation was not that unusual. For Thomas Macdonough, restraining trade between Americans and Canadians would prove one of his more demanding and delicate tasks.

One of those assisting Macdonough in these efforts was Peter Sailly. He had established himself as a local merchant and a leading member of the Republican Party (in contrast with Pliny Moore's Federalist leanings). Sailly served one term in Congress before President Jefferson appointed him collector of customs for the district of Champlain in 1808. In peacetime, Lake Champlain lumbermen shipped millions of cubic feet of timber, and many backwoodsmen moved cattle and other products overland into the St. Lawrence Valley and imported British goods back. Throughout the War of 1812, Sailly and his Vermont counterpart, Cornelius Van Ness, were among the most effective enforcers of non-exportation in the region, but despite their efforts, their neighbors were deeply involved in the shipping of cattle, army provisions, naval stores, and spars into Lower Canada. Canadian agents openly contracted for supplies along the border area. One moderately literate American officer reported that "the host of smuglars that huver on our lines is beyond description. Since the first of August . . . there has been from the best calculation more than sixty yoak of oxen besides other beef cattle drove to Canada." In November 1812 William Sweetson wrote from the Vermont frontier that his regiment had "taken some goods and some Cattle" but that their duty was "very hard . . . for want of men sufficient to Gard every passage into Canaday."[14]

Without the cooperation of the army and navy, the customs officers could do little to stem the tide of illicit trade. For instance, Sailly wrote Gen. Alexander Macomb late in the war that with army assistance the trade could be curtailed and then he would not "despair of rendering that unlawful traffic both difficult and hurtful to the speculators."[15] However, officers of both the army and navy had other missions besides regulating trade. Besides, beneath all the infighting over trading with the enemy was the political rivalry between Federalists and Republicans. The former often assisted in or turned a blind eye to such commerce, while the latter frequently took great delight in frustrating such endeavors.

Master Commandant Macdonough and his subordinates became reasonably effective in curtailing the waterborne trade. Sails could be spotted miles off and chased down with some degree of efficiency. On the other hand, navigating the narrow and shallow waters of the lake proved somewhat hazardous. For instance, Macdonough ran the *President* aground outside Plattsburgh and a sudden gust of wind upset a gunboat commanded by Midn. Horace Sawyer. Despite these problems, Macdonough's greater task was to maintain naval supremacy on the lake. In this he failed for a short time in the summer of 1813.

The Loss of the *Growler* and *Eagle*

Strategically, Macdonough's situation changed after Capt. Stephen Popham, RN, wrote a memorandum to Robert S. Dundas, Viscount Melville, first lord of the Admiralty, regarding future operations on the American lakes. He first established the necessity of learning where the Americans would focus their effort. Would they concentrate on Lake Ontario or Lake Champlain? Second, he proposed sending ordnance and ship's stores to America along with "a selection of good Officers, Seamen, and Workmen, with a proportion of Marines." He noted particularly the criticality of skilled artisans to build the necessary craft, as "too much dependence should not be placed, on the resources to be derived, from the other side of the Atlantic." Clearly understanding the quantity of officers and sailors necessary to meet the expanding American effort, Popham emphasized the importance of lake service and the need to provide "the most ample means of every description" in order to avoid "the grave responsibility of undertaking a Service with inefficient means."[16] In reality the Royal Navy consistently minimized the effort required to secure control of the lakes. In the long run, a series of intelligence, logistical, and personnel errors led to defeats on Lakes Erie and Champlain and a naval stalemate on Lake Ontario. In both the Royal Navy and the United States Navy, officers and men sought to avoid lake duty as much as possible.

Strategic commentary on the American side varied considerably, but former U.S. senator Jonathan Dayton advised President Madison to concentrate on the Lake Champlain route. While the upper St. Lawrence was dangerous because of "its rapids, its rocks, its shoals," the Richelieu River route "exposed . . . no such risks or dangers. . . . Transportation of baggage, stores, Artillery & provisions & clothing will be managed [there] with great comparative cheapness, ease, expedition & safety." Moreover, Dayton argued, the British emphasis on the defense of Kingston meant that the back door to Montreal was open to an advance via the Lake Champlain–Richelieu River corridor. Former congressman John Nicholas of Geneva, New York, wrote the president a naval truism in the tradition of Alfred T. Mahan: "With command of the lakes it is almost a plain mathematical calculation that equal forces in the hand of the assailant must be victorious" on land.[17]

Nevertheless, during 1813 both sides placed their emphasis on Lake Ontario. Secretary Jones wrote optimistically about American prospects to a friend: "I feel confident of our decisive superiority on all the Lakes which I trust will play itself as decisively as on the Oceans. This will settle the war on that frontier for the naval superiority there effectually includes the military command of both shores."[18]

At the start of the season on Lake Champlain, Thomas Macdonough's squadron, consisting of three sloops—the *President, Eagle,* and *Growler*—plus three gunboats, was the dominant naval element on the lake. The *Eagle* and *Growler* contained eleven guns each and often carried an army compliment as well as their naval crew when on cruises. Commanded respectively by Lt. Samuel Smith and Sailing Master Jarius Loomis, these two vessels received orders from Macdonough to prevent British gunboats from entering the lake, but to stay within the American lines. Still smarting from his replacement by Macdonough, Smith sought to enhance his reputation with the Navy Department and his local friends by disobeying Macdonough's rules of engagement and following a riskier course.

Smith augmented his force by picking up army Capt. Oliver Herrick and forty-one men at Champlain and began his search for the pesky British gunboats. On 3 June he entered the Richelieu River over the protests of his pilot, who thought the stiff south wind combined with the current posed an undue risk for the two vessels. Smith overruled his objections and went after three galleys. Decoyed into going farther downstream than was wise, the Americans suddenly found themselves being attacked from both sides by well-armed British ground troops. For over four hours they fired at one another until the *Growler* and *Eagle* surrendered along with over 113 officers and men.

Pliny Moore wrote Congressman Elisha J. Winter a description of what he called, with a somewhat derisive reference to the *Growler*'s commander having the same name as a famous contemporary English knight, the "Grand battle of Sr Sidney." He noted that "everyone with the smallest descernment [*sic*]" knew that entrance into the river would lead to the loss of the sloops. He also wondered how an engagement of such length and supposed intensity resulted in the American losing one killed and eight seriously wounded with few casualties among the British. Whatever the nature of the battle's ferocity, everyone knew its consequence: with these captured vessels the British now had naval superiority on Lake Champlain. Even though there were threats on the Lake Ontario littoral of greater urgency, the capture of the two sloops created an opportunity the British could not ignore. Maj. Gen. Francis de Rottenburg, commanding at Montreal, immediately urged the sending of an expedition to capitalize on the opportunity to destroy "the whole of their naval force Boats &c on that Lake" and to seize military supplies being assembled along the lake's shore. John Freligh expressed the locals' indictment of their neighbor's conduct when he wrote his brother, "This disaster was solely occasioned by the inconsiderate folly and imprudence of Lieut. Smith." He noted how Macdonough had ordered Smith only "to be on look out and to prevent the enemy's gun-boats from coming into our waters; and had Smith been contented to remain there according to his instructions, the misfortune we now have to deplore would never have taken place." He concluded, "What is worse than all the rest, [is] the command of the Lake, which as respects the safety of the inhabitants is of the utmost importance" was now lost.[19]

Macdonough expressed outrage at his subordinate's misguided and disobedient conduct. Several months of work were lost in one afternoon. Immediately upon hearing of the loss, Secretary Jones wrote Macdonough that he was "upon no account . . . to suffer the enemy to gain the ascendancy on Lake Champlain." He gave the commodore "unlimited authority, to procure the necessary resources of men, materials, and munitions for that purpose." While he was not going to stop the Royal Navy's dominance of the lake in the immediate few weeks, Macdonough began the slow process of building up his squadron. He purchased two merchant sloops (*Commodore Preble* and *Montgomery*) while he continued to build gunboats. But it was going to take weeks to secure the necessary ordnance and manpower to utilize them. On 2 July the *Plattsburgh Republican* reported that "thirty hearty jacktars" were coming from New York City to help man the *President.* This scarcely replaced what had been lost in the Richelieu River a month earlier.

In the meantime, the British sought to assert their new authority. They reinforced Lt. Thomas Pring at Île aux Noix with sailors commanded by Cdr. Thomas Everard of HMS *Wasp* from Quebec and with Lt. Col. John Murray's 945 picked troops for the raid up the lake. Unlike what was to follow a year later, Murray's venture was not an invasion designed to hold American territory as a bargaining chip in negotiations; instead, he was "to create a diversion in favor of the Army in Upper Canada, by alarming the Enemy with his expedition of Attack and thereby checking the movement of reinforcements" to the Great Lakes region. Maj. Gen. Roger Hale Sheaffe ordered Murray to destroy all public stores and buildings, capture shipping vessels he found, and preserve inviolate all private property in the region.[20]

In the meanwhile, Macdonough withdrew to Burlington, and Maj. Gen. Wade Hampton, the newly arrived ground commander in the region, moved over three thousand American troops of the Ninth, Eleventh, Twenty-first, and Twenty-fifth U.S. Infantry into barracks on the east side of the lake. He and Macdonough collaborated with civilian contractors in moving as much as possible of the stores at Champlain, Plattsburgh, Swanton, and elsewhere on the west side into storehouses at Burlington. But they could not move it all, and the remaining stores, storehouses, and barracks were left to the not-too-protective New York militia. From a military point of view the concentration at Burlington was a correct move, as Hampton had no idea how many men were coming on the raid and he had to protect Macdonough's vessels at all costs. For those left on the western shore, however, the situation was grim. When the hamlet of Champlain petitioned for military assistance, General Hampton prudently but haughtily replied, "My duties are purely Military, and extend not to the police of the Country." Leading citizens of Plattsburgh petitioned General Mooers not to defend their city with his militia unless he thought it would be successful because such a defense could only lead to significant destruction of private property. Along the lake's shore citizens went inland with as many household treasures as they could carry in order to avoid loss and confrontation with the British. As one American noted, the British "have the entire command of the Lake and they are sailing at pleasure, whenever they hear of plunder."[21]

Most of that plundering took place on the New York side of the lake. Murray's raid became, for the lake's inhabitants, one of the more memorable events of the war. Commander Everard commanded the *Shannon* (formerly the *Eagle*), and with Lieutenant Pring in the *Broke* (formerly the

Growler) and three galleys and forty-seven bateaux, he sailed into American waters on 29 July. When the flotilla arrived at Plattsburgh on the thirty-first, Mooers had only three hundred militiamen to oppose Murray's troops. The New Yorkers precipitously but prudently withdrew. The British quickly destroyed the arsenal, a blockhouse, the barracks, and several storehouses, all legitimate military targets. But before the troops left the next morning, household furnishings, books, clothing, and groceries were gone from private residences. Although British adjutant general Edward Baynes would subsequently draft general orders commending the "promptness and regularity highly honorable to the Officers directing the Expedition," it is clear that Murray did not restrain his troops during their occupation of the town. The *War,* a newspaper of military and naval affairs published in New York by S. Woodworth and Company, reported that Plattsburgh was a "scene of cruel and wanton waste and plunder," where "tables, bureaus, blocks, desks, cupboards and crockery, were cut and broken into pieces and thrown about the houses—books and writings were torn to pieces and scattered about the streets." Well it was, the reporter concluded, that "our wives, sisters, and daughters . . . trusted not their persons to the mercy of the invaders" and fled the town. Similar criticisms were leveled by local citizens against British troops who destroyed blockhouses and stores at Champlain along with private property. Minor expeditions to Cumberland Head, Point au Roche, and Chazy Landing in New York and to Swanton, Vermont, destroyed government property and resulted in charges of rape and attempted rape against the British.

On 1 August, Commander Everard sailed the *Broke* and one gunboat to the Burlington shore. There he found Macdonough with the *President* and two sloops covered by ten guns on the shore and two scows mounting one gun each. Everard sought to entice the American out into the lake, but despite cannonading the town, Macdonough wisely refused to leave the protection of the shore batteries. The British flotilla sailed as far south as Whitehall, but it found little to attack as the Americans regularly sounded the alarm alerting the militia, which kept an armed force along the lake's shore. Along the way they captured eight American commercial vessels and took half of them back to Canada, destroying the others. Those lost and their cargo tonnage were the *Mars* (thirty-five tons), *Enterprise* (forty-five tons), *Essex* (sixty tons), *Burlington Packet* (twenty-five tons), *Lark* (fifteen tons), *Willing Maid* (twenty tons), *Federal Victory* (twenty tons), *Red-Bird* (ten tons), and a Durham boat with eighty barrels of flour. Among those captured was a civilian named James M. Wood, who was held by the British to exchange for Canadian civilians held by the Americans. By 4 August, Murray, Pring, Everard, and their vessels and booty were back at Île aux Noix. Everard returned to Quebec, and Pring remained in command of His Majesty's naval forces on the Lake Champlain frontier.

The *War*'s reporter in Burlington noted that it was the insufficient number of seamen that prevented the American naval force from meeting the British. In the edition of 17 August, he made one of the first compliments to Thomas Macdonough's Lake Champlain campaign that has been recorded. The American commodore was "a brave and experienced naval officer, in whom we venture to say, the honor of the American flag will ever find an able support; but situated as he was, it would have been the height [*sic*] of rash presumption in him, to have hazarded the dominion of the lake . . . upon a contest with so disproportioned a force." But this correspondent prophesied the Americans would soon secure the "dominion of the lake." This sentiment duplicated the promise Secretary Jones made to President Madison on the fourteenth, but two weeks later he wrote more skeptically about Macdonough's prospects of securing mastery over Lake Champlain.[22]

For whatever reason Everard had been sent to support the Murray Raid, his return to the St. Lawrence River constituted a telling indictment of the importance His Majesty's commanders attached to the Lake Champlain command. That such a junior officer as Pring was left in command of such a critical position constitutes one of the most incomprehensible aspects of the War of 1812 on this lake. Such inattention to leadership on this vital waterway became most costly later on. Moreover, the British failed to exploit their naval superiority. No serious effort was made to build at Île aux Noix a ship that would ensure British naval dominance of the lake. Everard and Pring recommended that a sixteen-gun brig and two gunboats be built immediately, but the brig remained an idea, not a reality, even though sufficient timber for its construction lay at Île aux Noix.[23]

Whether the blame for this neglect falls on Commo. Sir James Lucas Yeo, commander of all Royal Naval operations on the lakes, or on Adm. John B. Warren, commander of Royal Navy forces in North America, is open to question. In the late summer of 1813, Yeo focused his attention on a desperate cat-and-mouse game with Commo. Isaac Chauncey on Lake Ontario. He narrowly escaped strategic defeat at what are known as the "Burlington Races," 26 September, just a few days after his subordinate Cdr. Robert Barclay lost control of Lake Erie, 11 September. Warren, on the other hand, centered his attention on the blockade of the Atlantic Coast of the United States and raids into the Chesapeake Bay. As a consequence, Lake Champlain received little attention even though it would become the locus of a major operation a year later.[24]

Reestablishing American Naval Supremacy

Thomas Macdonough's promotion from lieutenant to master commandant became effective on 24 July. This good news came while he anticipated a British raid, needed to reconstitute his squadron, and sought to regain naval supremacy. In the weeks that followed Lieutenant Smith's loss of the *Eagle* and *Growler*, the Navy Department urgently went to remedy the situation on Lake Champlain.

Secretary Jones not only sent the previously mentioned letter to Macdonough insisting he immediately begin rebuilding his squadron but also sent messages to critical departmental officials to carry out his objectives. He ordered John Bullus, naval agent at New York, to provide Macdonough with everything he needed on Lake Champlain. In particular Jones wanted New York recruiters to forward men to Macdonough's command. Lt. James Renshaw of USS *Alert* in New York sent fifteen men to reinforce Macdonough in June. But Macdonough complained to Capt. Samuel Evans of the New York Navy Yard that the first men sent him were totally useless. In mid-July Renshaw sent fifty more men to Macdonough. Meanwhile, Jones urged that guns from the *Alert* and the *John Adams* be sent from New York to the lake. Evans provided 9-pounders from the yard rather than 12-pounders from the *Alert* because the latter were both lighter and longer than the former. As these men and supplies came up the Hudson and over the mountains to the lake, Macdonough still lacked officers to command his squadron which he expected to be ready to reassert itself by early August.[25] But even by mid-August he did not have commanders or enough men. Fifty men reached him in late August and another two hundred officers and men arrived in early September. After securing a few soldiers from General Hampton's command, he was able to sail from Burlington on 6 September. These manning problems were a common complaint facing the secretary. Oliver H. Perry on Lake Erie and Isaac Chauncey on Lake Ontario bombarded the Navy Department with similar requests for officers and men to fill the personnel needs of the rapidly expanding lake squadrons. Jones stripped the blockaded frigates in eastern ports to fulfill them as best he could. He wrote the president in early September, "I cannot but hope from the measures taken, & the character of McDonough, that it [command of the lake] will be regained" in time for the navy to cooperate with army operations in the region.[26]

While these supporting activities were going on, Macdonough refitted his three sloops, hired two others, and converted the gunboats into row galleys. The squadron contained the *President, Commodore Preble, Montgomery,* and four gunboats. His two hired merchant vessels, named *Frances* and *Wasp,* sailed so poorly that he soon returned them to their owners. Still, he reconstituted his strength enough to reassert control over the lake. His small squadron kept Pring's Royal Navy sloops and gunboats in the Richelieu River for the last weeks of the summer and throughout the fall. One Plattsburgh resident reported that with the navy in control of the lake, "we now feel tolerably secure."[27]

Châteauguay Campaign

Few military operations in the history of the United States have been more poorly planned, ineffectively led, and inexpertly conducted that the army's campaign against Montreal in the fall of 1813. The troubles began when Secretary of War John Armstrong brought General Hampton and Maj. Gen. James Wilkinson from the South to lead operations in the North. Wilkinson was perhaps the most corrupt, inept, and duplicitous general officer in the history of the United States. He spent years in New Orleans, where he was jointly in the pay of America and Spain and connived with both governments to enhance his fortune if not his reputation. His conduct was bitterly resented by many of his subordinates, and the army was torn between Wilkinson and anti-Wilkinson factions. Were this not enough, the appointment of rich South Carolina planter Wade Hampton to colonel and eventually to brigadier general in the expansion of the army following the *Chesapeake* affair resulted in a new faction around the vain and arrogant former congressman. The men detested one another.

Now a major general, Hampton made it clear he would not come northward without a command that reported directly to Washington, not through the commander of the ninth military district—at the time Henry Dearborn. The argument was militarily sound; communications between Lake Champlain and Lake Ontario were so primitive that it was easier to correspond with Washington than with the departmental commander. Moreover, caught between the Kingston and Niagara fronts, Lake Ontario operations were demanding in and of themselves. Since the navy had given Macdonough a command separate from Chauncey's, why should not the army do the same? Hampton understood that if the two armies were joined on a Montreal operation, Dearborn would be his superior. Thus Hampton secured from Secretary Armstrong what he thought was a separate command on Lake Champlain.

Much to Hampton's disgust he learned that Wilkinson had been named to relieve Dearborn. As historian Robert Quimby deftly expressed it, "The succession of Wilkinson to command was most mischievous in its effect." Even so, as long as Hampton's objective was Montreal and Wilkinson's Kingston, this arrangement had some validity. But if both men received orders to take Montreal, the potential for conflict, noncommunication, and noncooperation rose exponentially.

Armstrong knew he faced difficulties with these two men and had Wilkinson visit him in Washington before taking command. The secretary hoped he might clarify the general's objective and arbitrate the differences between the two senior officers. But such would not be his fortune. Again, as Quimby describes it,

> Armstrong had, partly by inadvertence and partly by the sheer ill luck of circumstance, thus placed the two most antipathetic characters among the upper ranks of the army in positions that required their close cooperation for the success of proposed operations. He had, moreover, placed one in command of a military district that covered all troops within its boundaries, while to the other he had given separate command within that very same district. The lack of wisdom in combining the command of an army or armies with that of a definite geographical area was soon to be conclusively demonstrated, although the lesson was not learned. Of the two principals, Wilkinson was certain, as always, to advance his pretensions by asserting his authority even if only to demonstrate that he had it. Hampton was certain to resent the slightest infringement on his independent position by anyone, let alone his bitterest enemy in the army.[28]

In a memorandum of 23 July, Armstrong proposed three objectives for a summer-fall campaign: Niagara, Kingston, or Montreal. He rejected the first, desired the second, but left the third as an alternative. He even suggested a feint toward Kingston and a move down the St. Lawrence, where Wilkinson's eight thousand would unite with Hampton's four thousand to seize Montreal.

Even more ominous than the failure to focus on the bird in the hand at Kingston rather than the one in the bush at Montreal was the command relationship. Armstrong clearly let Wilkinson understand that Hampton was his subordinate. When Wilkinson sought to assert this authority in correspondence with Hampton, the South Carolinian responded bitterly. Armstrong promised Hampton that his orders would come from the War

Department. This, of course, contradicted what he had told Wilkinson. To smooth over the situation, the secretary decided to go to Sackets Harbor and consult with Wilkinson. For the secretary of war to leave his command post for a remote site five hundred miles from the capital while his small staff conducted a war from Louisiana to Maine boggles the imagination of a modern reader.

In the midst of all this animosity, indecision, and delay, General Hampton and Thomas Macdonough sought to conduct operations on and about Lake Champlain. As noted earlier, the young commodore was ready to reassert his command of the lake on 6 September. At that time Hampton began moving his troops from Burlington to Cumberland Head outside Plattsburgh. On the nineteenth, they embarked and began moving down the lake toward the Little Chazy River. There they disembarked and marched across the border. The usually skeptical John Frelign declared himself impressed by the excellent condition of Hampton's troops. He found them well clothed, clean, neat, healthy, and well disciplined. "To draw a contrast between them and those that were stationed here last fall would not be much to the credit of the latter. In short," he observed, "they only want experience to make them everything that a good general would require for the accomplishment of the most hardy enterprize." He complimented General Hampton's "exertions as a disciplinarian. How he will appear in the field remains yet to be determined." Frelign certainly knew what he was talking about, as time would tell.[29]

Macdonough's squadron escorted the army toward the head of the Richelieu River, but, after the loss of the *Growler* and *Eagle* earlier in the year, the commodore refrained from entering the river itself. Hampton's troops entered the Lower Canada hamlet of Odelltown, and he stopped to reconsider his proposed march down the Richelieu toward Montreal. He found a number of impediments to his progress. First, the wells had dried up and there was little water for his troops. Second, the roads were mere cart paths and allegedly inadequate for logistical support of his four-thousand-man force. (One must note that a year later Prevost would march a larger force down these same roads.) Third, he would have to use his mostly raw troops to take the fort at Île aux Noix before advancing down the river toward the St. Lawrence and a position east of Montreal. Such a location would place the object of his and Wilkinson's attack between their two armies thereby threatening defeat in detail from the British if they used their interior lines to attack one American army and then the other. Moreover, in such a position, he invited a British attack from Quebec against his rear.

For these and other reasons, Hampton decided to stop the advance to the north and instead move west to the Châteauguay River. He planned to use that route to move toward the St. Lawrence and unite with Wilkinson somewhere west of Montreal where the combined American force could assault the unfortified city.

As a map problem, Hampton's solution looked the best. On the ground, however, he would find the situation not nearly as logical as it appeared on the map. First and foremost was the logistical situation, which was far more difficult than moving down the Richelieu route. Second, if the two American armies were not coordinated, the Châteauguay operation would draw to Hampton's force British troops not being used to counter Wilkinson's movement down the St. Lawrence. The British could use their interior lines of communication and concentrate against Wilkinson and then turn to attack Hampton. From an operation point of view, noncoordination between the two armies placed both in danger of defeat in detail. Third, there was no way Macdonough could support the Châteauguay operation. On the other hand, if Hampton cleared the upper Richelieu's banks of the enemy, he could utilize Macdonough's vessels for firepower and logistical support. Finally, if they took Île aux Noix, Hampton's troops could interdict the supplies coming from New York and Vermont to the St. Lawrence Valley. This would severely impair the British war effort. In the long run, such a limited Richelieu operation threatened not only the British forces currently in the Canadas but also any future operations that might come in the next campaign season. Moreover, a Richelieu campaign would maintain Hampton's independence of command and still assist Wilkinson by threatening Prevost's St. Lawrence lifeline.

The Châteauguay decision proved fatal to Hampton. There was no coordination with Wilkinson. In fact, Hampton began his march on 21 October before the senior officer had even decided to make Montreal his objective. The route went over cart tracks through dense woods, felled trees and destroyed bridges obstructing and delaying the advance. Hampton lacked adequate intelligence concerning the size and disposition of the force in front of him and knew nothing about the commander he faced—Lt. Col. Charles-Michel d'Irumberry de Salaberry. A battle-hardened veteran of West Indian and European campaigns, he was a favorite of General de Rottenburg, who brought Salaberry to his home province of Lower Canada in 1810. There the Canadian raised a regiment of Voltigeurs, light infantry skilled in combat in the wooded environment.

Salaberry's principal subordinate was Lt. Col. George Macdonell, who brought his six hundred Glengarry Light Infantry (a regular unit recruited for Canadian service only) over 210 miles on a three-day boat trip down the St. Lawrence and forced march to join Salaberry on the Châteauguay River. Both he and Salaberry constructed log fortifications and abatis at defensive positions along the trail down which Hampton advanced.

Hampton sent one brigade against the fortifications on the trail and another in a flanking maneuver on the opposite bank. Both failed to meet their objectives and Hampton withdrew. Now Secretary Armstrong's worst fears came to pass. His two columns received defeats in separate engagements—Hampton at Châteauguay on 26 October and Wilkinson at Crysler's Farm on 11 November.

On Lake Champlain, Benjamin Mooers of Plattsburgh wrote General Hampton that he considered the military situation on the lake particularly dangerous. With Hampton and his army off to the west, the lake region became vulnerable to attack from Canada. While he was certainly overly sanguine regarding British capabilities, Mooers's intelligence indicated that "the Enemy's Flotilla is about Equal to ours and better manned, that [if] the fleets come in contact and the Enemy get the ascendancy our situation without a body of Troops being Thrown into this place be critical [to] the great depot & public stores" in Plattsburgh. Macdonough sought to remedy this situation by expanding his flotilla. In early October he launched two gunboats built at Plattsburgh.[30]

Meanwhile Col. Isaac Clark of the Eleventh U.S. Infantry raided into Lower Canada from Burlington, attacking St. Armand (now Philipsburg, Quebec) on 12 and 27 October and taking over ninety prisoners from the local militia as well as horses and cattle, most of which had been "smuggled in from the States." While one Canadian observer reported the raiders came "from the [Missisquoi] Bay," there is no evidence that Macdonough's vessels provided their transportation. Clark's aggressive enforcement of the trade restraints with Canada provoked aggressive opposition among Federalist politicians in his home state of Vermont. The British also used the fall season for raids. On 4 December six row galleys took advantage of the calm to row to Cumberland Head outside Plattsburgh Bay, where a detachment burned a barn and escaped faster than Macdonough's men could row after them. Pring wrote his superiors that he destroyed a military storehouse and provisions, bateaux, and ammunition. Americans reported a barn containing whiskey was all that was lost.[31]

Finally the raids died down as the lake began to freeze over. Before Christmas the Lake Champlain flotilla left Plattsburgh for a winter at

Otter Creek on the Vermont side of the lake. From there Macdonough could provide protection from any British raiding party to his squadron and at Vergennes were lumber and iron to construct new vessels for the next campaign season. Macdonough knew his ship and personnel strength would not likely be enough for 1814. Intelligence reports indicated that the British brought from the St. Lawrence to Île aux Noix from nine to a dozen galleys each mounting a 24-pound long gun on the bow and a 32-pound carronade on the stern and carrying a crew of fifty men.[32]

For Thomas Macdonough, the first year on Lake Champlain proved a quick course in naval leadership and joint operations. Of his first principal responsibility, he obtained and retained naval control of Lake Champlain for all but a few weeks of the year. Murray's raid was an unfortunate event that hindered military operations for a few days, but the British never achieved naval dominance for a long period and did not capitalize on the opportunity the loss of the *Eagle* and *Growler* presented them. On the other hand, Macdonough's dominance was not total and continuous. Throughout the year the British conducted limited operations out of Île aux Noix into the northern part of the lake when wind and the absence of the American flotilla allowed them. In other words, their fleet-in-being constituted a continuous threat to American forces.

Cooperation with the army, Macdonough's second major responsibility, proved fruitful. His control of the lake for most of the year allowed General Hampton to move a five-thousand-man army into place at Burlington and to cross the lake for operations against both the Richelieu Valley and the Châteauguay operation. Had Hampton desired to push southward toward Île aux Noix Macdonough was ready to support such an operation. Certainly the young commodore recognized how important Hampton's force at Burlington was in saving his crippled squadron during Murray's raid.

Macdonough's final major responsibility, suppression of illicit trade with Lower Canada, proved elusive. Most American traffic with British quartermasters went by land, but certainly some traveled by water. A flotilla as small as his, plus the threat posed by British vessels if he dispersed his squadron, kept him from exercising a tight naval blockade of the Lake Champlain coast. This aspect of his command continued to vex him throughout the time he spent on the lake.

Macdonough's administrative skills grew as his responsibilities increased. He demonstrated an ability to effectively request necessary workmen, sailors, and stores to maintain his growing flotilla. The failure of the

Table 3-1. U.S. Naval Strength, December 1813

Ship Type	Name	Armament
Sloop	*President*	6 18-pounder columbiads, 4 12-pounder long guns
Sloop	*Commodore Preble*	7 12-pounder long guns, 2 18-pounder columbiads
Sloop	*Montgomery*	7 9-pounder long guns, 1 18-pounder columbiads
Sloop	*Wasp*	3 12-pounder long guns
4 galleys		1 18-pounder long gun

Source: TM to Jones, 28 December 1813, Dudley and Crawford, *Naval War of 1812* 2:606.

Navy Department to secure confirmation of George Beale's appointment as purser proved frustrating and added to his administrative burdens. Continuously receiving raw recruits and newly promoted officers and petty officers, Macdonough trained his men in their new tasks and built that confidence in their abilities that is a hallmark of effective leadership. The most trying circumstances came after the loss of the *Eagle* and *Growler*. Short on officers and men, without a secure line of communication, he proved resilient and patient as the secretary of the navy and naval officials provided him with sufficient support to overcome the British advantage.

During this first year there was no severe trial of Macdonough's combat leadership skills. He regarded the protection of military stores at Plattsburgh to be particularly important, and he desired not to hazard this important duty in the narrow, shallow, reef-filled waters north of Plattsburgh. His most galling defeat was the consequence of a subordinate's disobedience of explicit orders. The lake commodore could not forgive Lieutenant Smith for entering the Richelieu River and losing the two sloops. Perhaps the most demanding test came when Cdr. Thomas Everard stood off Burlington and tried to tempt Macdonough to leave the protection of General Hampton's guns and troops and engage in a ship-to-ship battle. Macdonough's prudence contrasted sharply with the impetuosity exhibited that summer by Capt. James Lawrence of the USS *Chesapeake,* who engaged in an unnecessary losing battle with HMS *Shannon* off Cape May. His conduct impressed local citizens such as John Freligh, who wrote his brother that "Capt. McDonough who commands at this station is a man of prudence, and possesses every quality calculated to inspire the most unlimited confidence. To his exertions we now look for safety and repose." Late in the year Macdonough reputedly issued a challenge to the British commodore to come out and fight, but the invitation was not accepted.[33]

With his squadron safely laid up at Vergennes on Otter Creek, he left Lt. Stephen Cassin in command and went to Middletown to visit Lucy Ann and her family for a few weeks. The following year would bring an even more trying test of his leadership capabilities.

"The Trap," Thomas Macdonough's boyhood home, Newcastle County, Delaware.

Burning of the frigate *Philadelphia* at Tripoli, 1804
Reproduced from the collections of the Library of Congress

USS *Constellation* by Nicolas Camillieri
U.S. Naval Academy Museum

Macdonough's mentors and associates:

Stephen Decatur Jr.
U.S. Naval Institute

Edward Preble
U.S. Naval Academy Museum

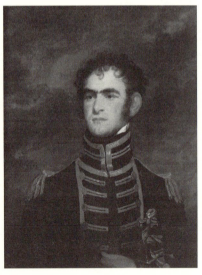
John Rodgers
U.S. Naval Institute

Charles Stewart
U.S. Naval Academy Museum

William Jones, Secretary of the Navy, 1813–14
U.S. Naval Institute

Macdonough House, Middletown, Connecticut, as it appeared in the mid-nineteenth century

Middlesex Historical Society, Middletown, Connecticut

U.S. Navy frigate *Constitution*

U.S. Naval Institute

Thomas Macdonough by Alonzo Chappel
U.S. Naval Academy Museum

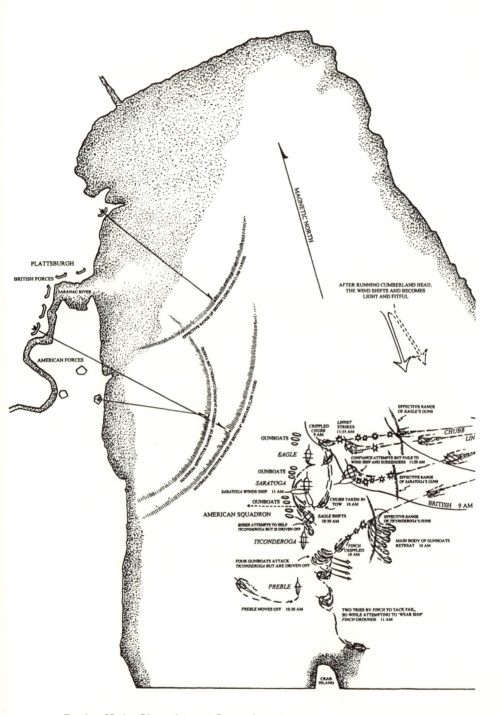

Battle of Lake Champlain, 11 September 1814
Dean Mosher Studio

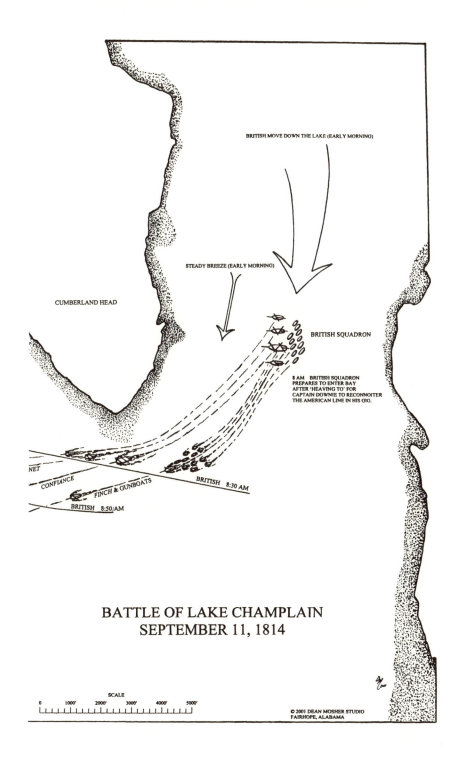

BATTLE OF LAKE CHAMPLAIN
SEPTEMBER 11, 1814

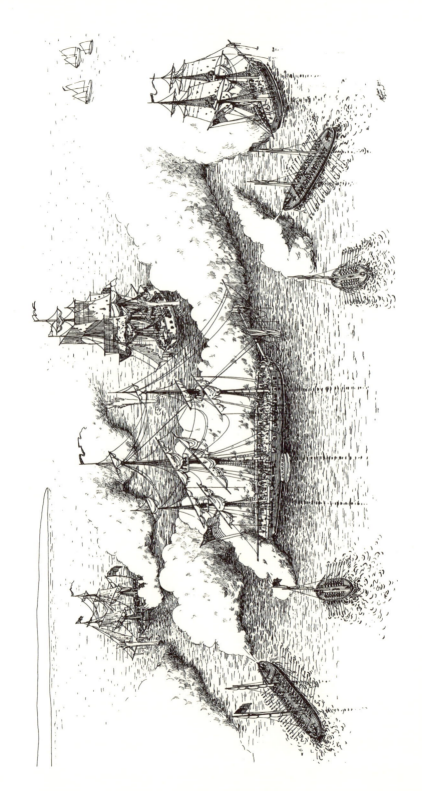

Sketch of the Battle of Lake Champlain
Dean Mosher Studio

Chapter Four

Lake Champlain, 1814

DARK was the hour, when o'er our land
The storm of war portentous hung;
When swept the foe with sword and brand,
And loud the peal of battle rung.
To arms the gallant warrior sprung,
While swelled in air the martial strain,
And wide our eagle banners flung,
From Orleans to thy wave, Champlain!

    Anonymous, "The Battle of Lake Champlain"

THE FAILURE of the American campaign of 1813 terminated any chance for the United States to win the war by conquering Upper Canada. The Allied victory over Napoleon at Leipzig in October 1813 laid the strategic groundwork for the French emperor's abdication the following April, thus freeing British ground and naval forces for redeployment to North America. The British gained the initiative and could now go on the offensive against the pesky Americans, who, they believed, had tried to stab them in the back while they fought the Corsican usurper in Europe. For the United States the offensive campaigns of 1812 and 1813 turned into defensive efforts from New Orleans to Penobscot Bay. As the *War* noted, "The enemy are . . . active and sanguine in their expectations." Gov. Daniel D. Tompkins of New York warned the state legislature, "We ought not to permit the hope" of successful peace negotiations "to lull us into a fatal security; for it may be that we must ultimately depend upon an unanimous, vigorous and successful prosecution of the unavoidable contest, in which we are involved, for the establishment and security of our just rights."[1]

Indeed, His Majesty's government was both expansive and confident in its plans for 1814. The strategic options confronting British planners were many. Perhaps the United States' eventual salvation resulted from the fact that British senior officers and political leaders, rather than focusing on a few possibilities, exercised a variety of operations, few of which would be successful.

Reflecting this divided 1814 strategy was a letter written by Adm. Sir

John Borlase Warren, RN, to the Admiralty in late December 1813. He called for increased numbers of ships and crews to enforce the blockade of the East and Gulf Coasts. Admiral Warren's letter omitted any interest in reinforcing the lakes with his officers and men.[2] In other words, the senior naval officer in North American waters displayed no interest in the lake frontier and hoped to deploy the Royal Navy on the Atlantic and Caribbean littoral rather than in the continental interior's fresh waters. Whatever other strategic circumstances existed, the Royal Navy would concentrate its 1814 efforts on salt water.

For reasons having little to do with the lakes, the Admiralty sought to correct various problems of theater command. Admiral Warren commanded all of North America from the Caribbean to the Gulf of St. Lawrence, and the difficulty of such regional size, combined with the feeling in London that the blockade was not as successful as it should have been, resulted in a series of changes in organization. First, the Jamaican and Leeward Island commands were separated from Warren's control. This allowed the Admiralty to conclude that a full admiral such as Warren was not needed and could be replaced by a vice admiral. Thus Warren came home in the spring of 1814 and the much more aggressive Vice Adm. Sir Alexander Cochrane replaced him.

Admiral Cochrane extended the blockade to include pro-British New England. Warren had allowed illicit trade between New England and Nova Scotia, but the changing situation in Europe supposedly negated the necessity of such commercial intercourse. Similarly, the British decided to conduct small raids at various American out ports. On 24 April Cochrane ordered his principal subordinate, Rear Adm. Sir George Cockburn, RN, to "act with the utmost hostility against the shores of the United States." He urged that American seaport communities "be laid in ashes and the country invaded...[in] retaliation for their savage conduct in Canada." From the Chesapeake Bay to the New England coast, small communities felt the wrath of boat raids. Cochrane also proposed incursions along the South Carolina and Georgia coasts, establishment of a fortified island refuge for fleeing blacks, and arming the Creek Indians.[3] All this was part of a concerted British strategy that sought to end the war by infuriating the Americans so much that they would demand President James Madison sue for peace on British terms. Like so many raiding strategies from time immemorial, it had much the opposite effect and made the American public more resolute.

Perhaps a more important part of the new strategy was the desire to conduct large operational raids against Washington and Baltimore. In August 1814 Maj. Gen. Sir Robert Ross arrived in the Chesapeake with four thousand European theater veterans to join Cockburn's sailors and marines. It was a formidable force, and most Americans recall the disastrous defeat of U.S. forces at Bladensburg, Maryland, on 24 August, the subsequent burning of many public and private buildings in Washington, D.C., and the successful American defense of Baltimore on 12–14 September. Although designed to lure U.S. troops from the lakes region, it had the opposite effect on the British. The principal consequence of the Chesapeake operation was the diversion of Ross's troops and Cochrane's sailors from the lakes to the Chesapeake, keeping them from having an impact upon the more critical British objectives in the northern theater.

Also dominating British decision making was arrogance, a belief in Albion's invincibility. Defeats in single-ship actions on the high seas and the loss of a squadron on Lake Erie did not diminish the typical Royal Navy officer's belief in American inferiority and British dominance of the waves. Such hubris often is an antecedent to military defeat.

British Strategy for the Lakes

Whatever the emphasis on coastal raids, Americans knew that the lakes merited considerable attention. The *War* noted on 29 March 1814 that "great preparations are making on part on the lakes Champlain and Ontario, to obtain naval ascendency [*sic*] in the ensuing campaign." It was in this theater, critical to the United States surviving with all its territory intact, that the Americans concentrated their forces.

The British raiding strategy's failure to draw important American regular forces from the lakes meant that proportionally the United States could concentrate more soldiers and sailors in the critical lakes region. These troops would be far different from the ill-trained, ill-equipped, and ill-led men the British confronted in 1812 and 1813. While 1814 saw a successful British conquest of the Penobscot region of Maine and a favorable defense of outposts at Mackinac Island, Michigan, and Prairie du Chien, Wisconsin, they failed in their effort to dominate the Lake Ontario basin and control the Champlain Valley.

The Duke of Wellington wrote in February that Royal Navy forces must dominate the lakes before ground operations commenced. Even were this accomplished, the Iron Duke cautioned, it was problematic as to whether operations could so injure the Americans as to cause them to sue for peace on terms desired by the British.[4]

These sentiments supported London officials who focused on the lakes, but it did not stop the coastal raiding strategy. In December 1813 and January 1814 the government decided to construct the hulls of two frigates and two brigs at the Chatham shipyards and ship them to Canada. These fir-built ships-in-frame would compensate for the lack of British ship-building facilities in North America. To these frames, local contractors were to add planking and decking. With this process the Admiralty ex-pected the Royal Navy could match the American effort. But London of-ficials failed to comprehend the difficulties of transporting the frames from the St. Lawrence Valley to the lakes. Wood was not nearly as important to ship construction on the lakes as ordnance, gunpowder, shot, anchors, stores, and sails. These items had higher logistical priority in the Canadian governor general's mind than ship frames.[5]

Lord Bathurst, secretary of state for war, and the Admiralty decided on a sweeping change in command arrangements for the coming campaign season. In particular, Governor General Prevost lost his control over naval forces on the lakes. The Royal Navy took charge of all fleets and dockyards on the lakes and placed them under Commodore Yeo. Sir James received a new title, "Commander-in-Chief of His Majesty's Ships and Vessels em-ployed on the Lakes," to replace his previous one, "Senior Officer on the Lakes."[6] This removed him from subordination to Prevost. Given the huge influx of ships and crews to the lakes, the continuance of Yeo, a junior cap-tain, in command of flotillas whose size merited at least a rear admiral of the blue, reflected either great confidence or an overconfidence in his com-mand abilities in a theater demanding greater experience that Yeo had heretofore exhibited. Moreover, a command arrangement involving Yeo as a captain and Prevost as a lieutenant general created a great disparity in rank that could only exacerbate interservice rivalries. The Royal Navy's quest for service autonomy, which violated the military principle of unity of command, bedeviled both sides in this conflict.

This did not mean that the lakes would not be reinforced. But there would never be the emphasis on the interior that was necessary to achieve Whitehall's enlarged strategic objectives. A major reallocation of forces came with this new arrangement. Capt. George Downie, RN, led three other newly promoted captains and nine hundred junior officers and men to the lakes. Their presence was part of an effort to gain dominance on Lake Ontario in preparation for ground offensives against Sackets Harbor and the Niagara frontier. In March 1814, a convoy brought six hundred sailors and dockyard workers to Canada, but Prevost had difficulty finding transportation for them and the ships-in-frame, ordnance, and stores provided for the lakes. Only one of these vessels, the frigate HMS *Psyche*, would be launched on the lakes, and it came down the ways at Kingston a day after the Treaty of Ghent ended the War of 1812.[7]

Throughout the fall of 1813, Prevost emphasized the Lake Ontario region. To him Lake Champlain was not a major campaign theater. When Cdr. Daniel Pring sought to construct a sixteen-gun brig and two gunboats at Île aux Noix, Prevost authorized only two fifty-foot gunboats. Pring kept insisting on a 370-ton brig but was turned down in August 1813. That October, learning that Macdonough was increasing his armaments to five sloops, Pring called for either the brig or two sloops. Finally, in November Prevost directed shipbuilder William Simons to construct the brig for expected completion in May 1814.[8] Still, compared with what was going on at Kingston, the Lake Champlain efforts were minuscule. By the time the ice melted on Lake Ontario in 1814, Yeo had a new flagship, HMS *Prince Regent*, fifty-eight guns, which, combined with the new forty-gun HMS *Princess Charlotte* and his old squadron, gave him naval dominance on that lake for two months.

Any push for increased effort on Lake Champlain would have to come from London, and it did. While Prevost sought mostly to preserve the Canadas from invasion in the first two years of the war, Whitehall clearly had more ambitious objectives for him in 1814. Lord Bathurst wrote Prevost on 3 June 1814 that the end of the war in Europe allowed His Majesty's government to reinforce Canada with over ten thousand soldiers, most of them veterans of the Napoleonic Wars. There was no desire to reincorporate the United States into the British Empire, but there were intentions to readjust the boundaries between Canada and the young Republic along lines more favorable to the British than those concluded in the Peace of Paris of 1783. The governor general was "to commence offensive operations on the Enemy's Frontier before the close of this Campaign." Prevost was to secure the destruction of the Lake Ontario and Lake Champlain fleets, capture and destroy Sackets Harbor, secure the Niagara frontier, and reconquer Detroit and Michigan Territory. Were this not enough, he was to take an advanced position on Lake Champlain that would significantly improve Lower Canada's security. Bathurst also counseled, "Always however taking care not to expose His Majesty's forces to being cut off by too extended a line of advance."[9] This last line merely reinforced the caution that always characterized Prevost's conduct of military affairs.

Trying to improve his deflated reputation following the disaster of the

Montreal expedition of 1813, Maj. Gen. James Wilkinson moved his head-quarters to Plattsburgh and sought to advance on Île aux Noix in the late winter. With the snow still on the ground, he advanced with 4,000 troops across the lines at Odelltown. Shortly north of this point Maj. Richard B. Handcock of the Thirteenth Regiment of Foot occupied the small stone Lacolle Mill (in modern Cantic, Quebec) with 180 soldiers. Handcock's troops were about to run out of ammunition on 30 March when Wilkinson, believing he faced 2,500 men, ordered a withdrawal without assaulting the improvised fort. Thus ended the final disgrace of a most shameful military career. Secretary of War John Armstrong relieved Wilkinson of command and sent Maj. Gen. George Izard to replace him.[10]

Constructing the Lake Champlain Squadrons

Because of the ice in the lake, Macdonough's flotilla played no role in Wilkinson's Lacolle fiasco. President Madison wrote Gov. Daniel Tompkins of New York that both Sackets Harbor and Lake Champlain had "an essential and constant claim to attention."[11] As was usual, it was the administrative and logistical aspects of Macdonough's command that demanded his constant attention. For both his winter quarters and his shipyard he chose the hamlet of Vergennes, located seven miles up the winding Otter Creek from the lake. The local falls provided waterpower; iron ore in nearby Monkton supported a series of blast and air furnaces, forges, and rolling mills. The town had good road connections to Boston and was convenient for waterborne supplies being shipped up the Hudson and, after portage between that river and the upper lake, down that waterway to this easily defended location. For a while Secretary of the Navy Jones preferred building gunboats to square-rigged sailing vessels. Learning of the British intent to build a brig, however, Macdonough sought permission to build one himself. Jones quickly consented and directed the employment of Adam and Noah Brown of New York to build this vessel, eventually known as the *Saratoga*. "I urge the propriety of building a ship without delay," the secretary told the commodore.

The Brown brothers were shipbuilders of note. In 1806 they secured a contract to construct four gunboats for the navy and they later built the U.S. sloop of war *Peacock* in 1813 and the famous privateer *Prince de Neufchatel*. The latter had an illustrious career in European waters that took $1 million in ships and cargo before being captured by four British frigates in December 1814. The former became famous for her victory over HM brig *Epervier* off Cape Canaveral on 29 April 1814. It eventually took fifteen prizes; no U.S. Navy vessel took more. Noah Brown achieved a fine reputation with the department after building of Oliver Hazard Perry's fleet at Erie, Pennsylvania, the previous campaign season.[12] Certainly this firm was the correct one to employ in constructing satisfactory ships in a short time.

The Browns contracted to build the *Saratoga* in sixty days, but they managed to complete it in forty, a remarkable feat. They had several advantages. In New York were many out-of-work ships shipwrights, carpenters, sailmakers, and other workers. For them such work in the wilderness offered an opportunity to make money when the wartime blockade and subsequent downturn in ship construction and repair denied them the employment to which their skills entitled them. Noah Brown possessed the intimate knowledge of construction of lake ships from his work on the Lake Erie squadron. The *Saratoga* was similar in construction to the two brigs that Brown built for Perry, except it had much less rake at the bow. Brown had extraordinary organizational skills. He brought several dozen workmen with their tools from New York, constructed barracks for them, contracted with the Monkton Iron Works for the necessary iron to fasten the timbers together, and began assembling the wood necessary for construction. Construction speed was far more important than long-term durability for this vessel, so unseasoned lumber and a variety of woods, not just choice oak, would be used for the *Saratoga*.[13]

Macdonough secured permission to construct the vessels across the creek from the Monkton Iron Company. While the construction was an economic boon to the company and village, it also posed a threat to the town if the British ever took the place and saw it as a government manufactory that should be destroyed.[14] The shipwrights laid the keel on 7 March from lumber that had been a live tree just five days earlier. In this humble shipyard they laid out the keel of several pieces fixed together with overlapping joins called scarphs. At the stern they erected a sternpost of a several pieces of timber. At the bow was a stempost, also made of several pieces scarphed together. After Brown lined and plumed them, the workmen shored the keel, sternpost, and stem with timbers to rigidly hold them in position. The keel, sternpost, and stempost constituted the fundamental elements around which Brown then added the frames or ship's ribs. The shipwrights used axes, augers, draw knives, chisels, gouges, hammers, mauls, saws, and, above all, adzes—the most characteristic tool of the trade—to form the frames. The key to making frames involved a careful selection of naturally curved trees and the sawyers cut the timber along the curve to maximize the strength of each frame. Workmen also established a system of scaffolding that allowed them to work as the ship rose up from the keel. To some of the scaffolding poles were added pulleys and tackle that assisted in raising the heavy frames into position. Once the frames were installed, the shipwrights added a series of longitudinal members, the most important of which was the keelson, which ran fore and aft along the centerline directly above the keel.

Once all the frames were in place, the workmen added horizontal planking. Both internally and externally the rows (called strakes) of planks held the frames together. External planking kept the water out and provided longitudinal strength to the structure. Internal planking kept ballast and debris from falling between the frames and provided additional structural strength. In a similar manner, the carpenters covered the main and berthing decks with strakes of wood and then scraped them smooth so that the sailors could walk on them in bare feet. They secured the exterior planks and main decking to the frames by boring a hole through the plank and frame and by inserting wooden pegs known as trenails. With exposure to moisture, the trenails expanded to make a tight fit. On the exterior planking and decking, caulkers used their mallets and caulking irons to drive oakum—tarred hemp—into the seams. Then the caulkers coated the seams with hot pitch to seal them watertight.

The *Saratoga* was called a "single-decker" because its armament was carried only on the main deck. Along the centerline of the main deck were several gratings which gave access to the berthing deck below and provided ventilation to the vessel. Aft of the mainmast the workmen installed the capstan, the cylindrical revolving mechanism by which the deck hands laboriously wound the cables that weighed the anchor. This was but one of the several critical fittings added once they completed the structure of the vessel. Others were the rudder, tiller, and wheel of the steering mechanism, and the pumps necessary to eliminate water in the hold. Below the quarterdeck at the stern was the cabin for the captain consisting of a day cabin where he ate and conducted business, and a small sleeping compartment.

Below the main deck on the lower or berthing deck the shipwrights constructed the accommodations for the ship's company and remaining officers. At the stern was the gunroom, which served as both cabin space and the officers' wardroom. (Since all the artillery was on the main deck, the "gunroom" had no guns.) Here they constructed cabins for the ship's first lieutenant, the lieutenant of marines, the sailing master, and the surgeon. There may have been additional cabins for the purser and others. The other officers slept on cots suspended from the deck head and stored their belongings in chests that also served as the wardroom's desks and seats. In the middle of the room was a large table that served as both the master's chart table and the mess table. The remainder of the ship's company lived and ate forward of the bulkhead that divided the gunroom from crew's quarters. The crew would sleep in hammocks suspended from the beams. The warrant officers had canvas screens that divided their living area from the others. Here also was the galley for cooking.

In the shallow hold of this lake vessel the shipwrights built storage rooms for the sails, the supplies for the boatswain and carpenter, plus cordage, slops (crew clothing), and spirits. Forward of this was the cable room for the anchor hawsers. The aft portion of the hold contained the magazine, with powder, shot, and cartridges. The *Saratoga* did not need extensive capacity for water and food because it would never be far from port. Ashore, the carpenters worked on the sweeps, boats, and gun carriages. Others began working on the gunboats necessary to compliment *Saratoga*'s firepower.

A mere forty days after Brown's men laid its keel, on 11 April, the ship slid down the ways into the basin on Otter Creek near the foot of the falls. It was 143 feet long, had a beam of 36 feet, 6 inches, and a depth of 12 feet, 6 inches. Noah Brown's work was not entirely done, as it still needed masts and spars, but from here on Macdonough and the naval officers and men of the squadron played an increasingly important role in the ship's completion.

Throughout the entire construction process Macdonough's role as the chief logistician of the squadron became more significant as guns, anchors, cordage, and other equipment came up the Hudson, across the mountains, and down the lake to Vergennes. The correspondence between Macdonough and Secretary Jones and John Bullus, the navy's agent in New York City, grew in stridency and urgency. Theirs was no small task.

The hawsers for the anchors were up to a foot in diameter and hundreds of yards long. The total rigging on a ship of this sort required miles of rope, most of it between three and five inches thick. The *Saratoga* carried eight 24-pounder long guns, six 42-pounder carronades, and twelve 32-pounder carronades. The former weighed 1,120 pounds each, the second some 2,249 pounds each, and the latter 1,904 pounds apiece. The water transportation portion of the ordnance was relatively easy, but teams of men and animals hauled all this from the Hudson to the Champlain Valley using pulleys, leverage, and brute strength of man and animal. Some of *Saratoga*'s guns came from Baltimore, others from ships unable to escape the blockade of

New York. They had not arrived when the brig and gunboats were launched but did so by early May. Some anchors weighed over a ton; they too had to be hauled from the Hudson to the lake. Fortunately, much of the shot needed for the guns could be manufactured at local ironworks such as the Vergennes Iron Manufacturing Company, which contracted for one thousand 32-pound shot. But some shot came by a long and arduous route to Vergennes. In April 1814, Asa Sheldon of Charlestown, Massachusetts, contracted to bring 6,700 pounds of grapeshot to Macdonough. With four yoke of oxen and a horse, he walked 175 miles up the Merrimack River, then across New Hampshire and Vermont to Vergennes, where he sold not only the shot but also the oxen, horse, and harness.[15]

Miscellaneous supplies included slop clothing and shoes for the crews, iron work for the gun carriages, cannon locks, muskets, pistols, battle lanterns, and so forth, all of which had to be brought up the Hudson and along the same route to Vergennes. It is this meticulous attention to logistical detail that distinguishes the skilled manager of military affairs. As we shall see, the British were not nearly so attentive to such things and in the end it meant that they were not as well prepared for combat as Macdonough's flotilla would be.[16]

In the meantime, Macdonough increased his squadron's size by means of a unique innovation. At Vergennes, the newly formed Lake Champlain Steamboat Company began constructing a steamboat in February 1814. On a trip to Washington, D.C., Lt. Stephen Cassin, Macdonough's second in command, reported to the secretary of the navy that a 120-foot hull was being built. Secretary Jones immediately authorized the steamboat's purchase for the navy's use. Initially, Macdonough thought the *Saratoga* was sufficient and did not interfere with the steamboat's construction. Meanwhile, the owners of the hull recognized the risk they were taking in trying to start a commercial venture of this sort in the midst of a war. They also saw considerable profit in a sale to the navy; when the war was over, they anticipated repurchasing the vessel at a significant discount from the navy's initial purchase price. Using the good offices of New York's Governor Daniel Tompkins, they pressured Jones to buy the vessel. Macdonough and Brown inspected it in April and recommended that the hull be used for a sailing vessel, not a steamboat. The rationale for this was that the mechanical equipment was not available on the lake and that it would take longer than desired to acquire it. In fact, Brown could build a new vessel faster than the two months necessary to bring the equipment to Vergennes from Albany. Moreover, should it need any replacement parts, they were not available on the lake and an equipment failure could make it useless. Nonetheless, the hull was useful and it could be adapted to navy use as a sailing vessel. Brown took over the supervision of construction from shipwright John Lacy and had the vessel ready for service by 15 May. Named the *Ticonderoga* and rigged as a schooner, Macdonough put Lieutenant Cassin in command of it.[17]

Soon the sounds of axe and adze, of hammer and saw, of mallet and chisel died down. Their task completed Noah Brown and his men left the lake and returned to New York. The *War* proudly reported that "on 2d March the timber of the ship *Saratoga* was standing in the forest. Its keel was laid on the 6th of the same month and she was launched on the 11th of April! ... The country is much indebted to Mess. Brown, master builders, for their exertions in completing these vessels [*Saratoga, Ticonderoga,* and six gunboats], in season to secure us the mastery of the lake."[18]

Still Macdonough could not sail onto the lake, even though the British were now at sea. No more persistent problem plagued the young commodore more than the shortage of sailors and officers. He wrote Secretary Jones on 30 April, "The *Saratoga* is rigged, her sails are made. . . . Her Gun carriages at the Ports, ready for the Guns, part of which have arrived, which we are mounting—the other expected daily." He anticipated the powder in a few days. He also reported the new gunboats were finished. All was ready "to receive her officers & men."

The dearth of officers and crew allowed the British to take command of the lake for a few days in May. In early April, Commander Pring had his guard boat making sorties up the lake as far as Rouses Point. With the ice breaking up north of the lines, the British began making efforts to sail farther up the lake. General Mooers warned, "Our situation in this frontier is daily becoming more alarming." Not only was the lower end of the lake threatened, but the militia general cautioned, "Even White Hall may be visited by the Enemy if their Flotilla are as formidable as he [our informant] presented—provided our fleet is not in readiness to meet them; by accounts we little expect they will be."[19]

On 8 May the British squadron departed Île aux Noix. Word quickly reached General Izard that the *Linnet, Chub, Finch,* and seven gunboats were on their way up the lake. Peter Sailly reported to Macdonough that the British were taking every vessel they could and their design was to load them with stone at the mouth of Otter Creek and seal the American squadron off from the lake itself. Taking every boat they could find ("even to a canoe" wrote the *Plattsburgh Republican*), the British beat against a south wind and arrived off Split Rock Point about three miles north of the mouth of Otter Creek on the evening of 13 May. The same newspaper lamented that Macdonough was "poorly prepared" to defend his position. Why "the tardy preparations to maintain the superior power we had on Lake Champlain last year?" it asked. "The neglect lies somewhere—a neglect, through which, consequences of the most serious nature may ensue."

The newspaper even proposed tactical dispositions for the Americans. It suggested that if the army had cooperated with Macdonough and established a battery of artillery near the lines the two services could have "infallibly, blocked up the British floating force within their own waters, and prevented the injury that the neglect of that precaution will probably produce."[20]

Tactical defensive issues bothered the young commodore throughout the spring. For defensive purposes the narrow creek provided ample warning of any approaching enemy force. Before the lake ice melted the army built and the two services situated an artillery battery at what would be called Fort Cassin at the creek's mouth. Vergennes was about as secure a location for protecting and enlarging his squadron as Macdonough could find. As the war assumed a more defensive character and memory of the depredations in Plattsburgh during Murray's raid shocked Vermonters, Gov. Martin Chittenden of that state became more bellicose, despite his Federalist and antiwar views. In mid-April he ordered five hundred militiamen to Burlington and a thousand to Vergennes to protect the federal depots and naval squadron stationed there. As Pring's force sailed up the lake, the *Burlington Northern Sentinel* shouted "ALARM" from a headline and suggested the British intended to "make a visit to Vergennes." If they did so, the newspaper suggested that Macdonough would come out to meet them, and it doubted "not but that the result will be favourable to our navy." Obviously they knew little of Macdonough's manpower problems.[21]

The slow progress brought about by the headwinds and the signaling system used by the Americans prevented Pring and his men from surprising the defenders at Fort Cassin. Warned by General Macomb, Col. Aquila Davis sent 50 artillerymen and 140 infantrymen to reinforce Otter Creek's mouth and Fort Cassin. To Macdonough Macomb sent a message promising "to afford you every aid in my power to protect your naval Depot from interferences of the Enemy." Pring found a battery of four boats and artillery ashore commanded by Lieutenant Cassin and army light artillery captain Arthur Thornton. In addition, there were numerous militiamen. There ensued an artillery duel of about three-quarters of an hour which killed 1 British seaman and injured very few on either side. Reconnoitering the American position from his gig, Pring decided to call off the attack he hoped to make with 130 Royal Marines and 60 seamen. As Pring noted in a letter to a friend, "Every Tree on the Lake shore seems to have a Jonathan [American] stationed behind it." Unable to inflict significant damage on the Americans, Pring withdrew down the lake. Before he left, however, militia units mobilized on both sides of the lake to repel expected attacks. It was increasingly clear that for the British to raid as they had before, it would have to be done with substantial numbers of men, because the Americans increasingly demonstrated an ability to communicate alarms the length of the lake and to mobilize militiamen with considerable effectiveness. Writing years later, army captain George H. Richards said, "Macomb afforded Commodore McDonough [*sic*] every assistance in his power. . . . Thus by his *coup d'oeil*, vigilance, and foresight, Macomb anticipated the designs of the enemy, and effectually frustrated a well-concerned plan to destroy our incipient Navy on Lake Champlain." While this may overstate the degree of Macomb's cooperation with the navy, it does indicate the degree of interservice collaboration emerging on this lake. The two commanders knew the success of their objectives as well as their survival required them to work as a team. Certainly the *Plattsburgh Republican*'s boast that the British raid captured "no vessel of any consequence" and the enemy's expedition "met with nothing but defeat and disgrace" seemed an appropriate summary.[22]

This was not the only instance of army-navy cooperation. In March Macdonough authorized a suit of sails from his stocks be turned over the army for use on a transport vessel being used by that service. In July General Izard agreed to supply Macdonough with a gunpowder surplus he had at Whitehall. But the greatest degree of coordination between service came, albeit reluctantly, in the area of personnel.[23]

Personnel Problems

Manpower needs were the bane of the lake commanders. For several reasons sailors refused assignments to the region. They feared lake fever, a deadly form of typhus. There were greater profit opportunities for them on the privateers sailing out of various ports. There was a demand for sailors on the gunboat flotillas designed to protect the coastline being attacked by the British. Despite an increase in the pay and bounty for lake seamen, recruitment went slowly. Secretary Jones feared that continued stripping of the Atlantic ships of their crews exposed coastal harbors to British depredations. He already had a fourth of the navy's personnel employed defending

Table 4-1. United States Naval Strength, May 1814

Vessel Type	Name / Commander	Armament
Brig	*Saratoga* / Thomas Macdonough	8 24-pounder long guns, 6 42-pounder carronades, 12 32-pounder carronades
Schooner	*Ticonderoga* / Stephen Cassin	8 12-pounder long guns, 4 18-pounder long guns, 5 32-pounder carronades
Sloop	*Commodore Preble*	7 12-pounder long guns, 2 18-pounder columbiads 10 gunboats 1 18-pounder long gun each

Note: Macdonough returned the *Frances* and *Wasp,* used in 1813, to their owners because of their poor sailing qualities.

the lake frontiers, thereby leaving the more settled regions of the country vulnerable to enemy raids.[24]

By mid-March Macdonough had 329 officers and men for a squadron that needed at least 300 more to meet its growing requirements. Moreover, there was a quality problem: "Our men are not the best," he told the secretary of the navy. One reason for this could have been that Commodore Chauncey was recruiting simultaneously for Lake Ontario's expanding squadron. He offered a thirty-dollar bounty plus a salary bonus for service on his lake. Sailing Master E. A. F. Vallette informed Macdonough that if similar terms were not offered for Lake Champlain, Chauncey would acquire all the good men. Attempts to secure men from Boston met with hostile opposition from Capt. William Bainbridge and U.S. Navy Agent Amos Binney, who refused to advance any funds to the officers Macdonough sent to recruit there.[25]

By 5 May, Sailing Master Vallette could raise only 60 men in New York. In desperation Macdonough sought 250 men from General Izard at Plattsburgh. With increasing demands to man both Macdonough's and Chauncey's growing squadrons, the lake commodores turned to the army for personnel. Macdonough wrote Brig. Gen. Alexander Macomb in May that he had "a deficiency of men" and begged the army commander in Burlington for a temporary loan of 250 soldiers. Were he to do so, Macdonough expected to "enter the lake immediately." Izard received a copy of the letter and directed Macomb to comply with the request. Otherwise, Izard told the secretary of the war, the enemy would continue to sulk around the lower lake and intercept troops and stores going from one side to the other. "Paralyzed as I am by this unexpected delay in the advance of our fleet," he wrote, "I can only make Preparations to guard the Position I occupy" in Plattsburgh. Subsequently Izard became upset at Macdonough's requisitions for men. He told Secretary Armstrong that the taking of soldiers to man the squadron was "in every respect a very unpleasant one" which mortified their commanders and was unjust to the men who had enlisted for ground duty.[26]

Macdonough became frantic to fill his officer complement. He was woefully short in numbers and in men with experience. Some wanted to leave. Midn. Joseph R. Jarvis wrote Secretary Jones, pleading for a saltwater assignment by arguing that sailing on Lake Champlain made it "impossible" for him to "obtain the nautical information necessary" for a naval career. By 6 May Macdonough had received only one sailing master and three midshipmen. He was desperate for lieutenants; he had only Cassin and Acting Lt. Charles Budd with him at Vergennes. The former had command of the *Ticonderoga*, the latter one of the sloops. The *Saratoga* had no lieutenant. His other two lieutenants, Joseph Smith and John Stansbury, were on recruiting duty. Perhaps becoming more understanding of Macdonough's manpower predicament, General Macomb became more cooperative and sent enough men to Vergennes to man his vessels. Still short of experienced sailors and officers, the commodore promised General Macomb to enter the lake "when my men come on."[27]

Efforts were being made to bring men to Lake Champlain. In May several wagons filled with sailors proceeded through Middlebury, Vermont, "from the eastward" to Vergennes. In Newport, Rhode Island, Sailing Master Henry Few "was very active in enlisting men" for Macdonough's ever-expanding flotilla. In August he sent with Masters Mate Peter Vanderver twenty-one seamen from that port in addition to twenty-seven Few had shipped earlier.

This shipment raised another issue regarding recruitment. It contained "four Collard men which were Recomd. As Smart Seamen." Few could send "Fifty Collard men" more if Macdonough wanted them. On 22 June Macdonough wrote his recruiting officers not to send more black tars, a request Few and New York recruiter C. B. Thompson found an imposition in their efforts.[28] We do not know whether the prohibition on recruiting

African Americans reflected a personal prejudice or whether Macdonough thought a high proportion of blacks would impair recruiting efforts among whites. Or did it mean that the blacks were not seafaring men and of little use as crewmen? It is clear that Few only wanted to forward African Americans who were skilled seamen.

At the same time, General Izard and Secretary Armstrong grew increasingly reluctant to deplete their ranks with drafts from the army. The secretary of war admonished Izard in late May that such calls were "becoming frequent & producing a very considerable diversion from our field forces." He wanted the general to make sure that Macdonough understood that such personnel loans were "temporary & will be withdrawn whenever wanted for military purposes." Finally he urged Izard to be explicit with "Captain Macdonough, otherwise he will expect from you this campaign as much if not more aid than he had the last one from General Hampton."[29]

Soon Macdonough reported success. His squadron entered the lake on 26 May, the Royal Navy forces withdrew to the Richelieu River, and free communication existed between all points on Lake Champlain. By 17 June his force stood off Point au Fer with the *Saratoga, Ticonderoga, Preble,* and ten gunboats. His report to Secretary Jones sounded optimistic: "I find the *Saratoga* a fine Ship, she sails & works well. . . . The Gallies [gunboats] are also remarkably fine vessels. I have not yet my complement of men, but as fast as they come on I shall relieve the soldiers whom I have on board." The United States, the *Burlington Northern Sentinel* trumpeted, was in "complete command of the Lake." Yet the manpower problem remained unresolved. The army still resented the levies placed upon it by the navy, the navy never fulfilled its recruiting objectives, and the size of the Lake Champlain squadron kept growing, thereby increasing the need for more sailors.

When Vermonter Samuel Elam Albro wrote a friend from Plattsburgh that "something of an interesting nature, will I presume, shortly transpire," he did not know how prophetic he was about to be. For a while, at least, the Americans commanded the lake and the British remained inside their own national boundaries.[30]

The Summer Shipbuilding Race

Secretary Jones exhibited an excessive optimism as *Saratoga* neared completion. He wrote the president that "on Lake Champlain our supremacy will be placed beyond doubt" once it was launched. "Indeed," he added, "there is good reason to believe the enemy will not venture on the Lake."

The Browns' speedy shipbuilding efforts received particular notice: "I know of nothing to equal the exertion and dispatch in this case."[31]

But even as American naval superiority on the lake seem assured, intelligence information arrived confirming new construction was underway at Île aux Noix. Macdonough reported that four frames of vessels had arrived at Montreal from England. His sources said two of these were to go to Lake Ontario, the others to Lake Champlain. When completed, the Americans would lose control of the latter unless more was done to rectify the situation. News from overseas confirmed the need for the United States to construct more vessels on Lake Champlain. While in Europe as part of a peace talks delegation, former Secretary of the Treasury Albert Gallatin and James A. Bayard discovered just how angry the British were. They reported to Washington that not only would His Majesty's government never abandon impressment, but it sought American renunciation of fishing rights off Newfoundland, acceptance of Canadian boundary modifications, recognition of British control of Great Lakes navigation, and restoration of Louisiana to Spain.[32]

Word of these excessive demands reached the Champlain Valley in mid-August when the Burlington newspaper published a report of a London pamphlet indicating boundary changes—including British access to the Mississippi, creation of a British-guaranteed Indian buffer territory in the upper Great Lakes, and cession of all or part of the Louisiana Purchase—as well as exclusion of the Americans from the fisheries off the maritime provinces and trade with the British East and West Indies and no concessions regarding neutral rights or impressment. To support these designs the British were about to send the largest transatlantic expeditionary force since the American Revolution. As Henry Adams would later describe it, "Great Britain had never sent to American so formidable an armament. Neither Wolfe nor Amherst, neither Burgoyne nor Cornwallis, had led so large or so fine an army as was under the command of Sir George Prevost."[33]

For the United States, the military situation became dire. For many antiwar advocates the prospect of becoming British subjects and the loss of territory for the United States made them more willing to defend American soil from invasion. Indignation over British demands roused such newspapers as the Federalist-leaning *United States Gazette* in Philadelphia to cry, "England now turns upon us in the fullness of her wrath and power. No alternative is left us but to resist with energy or submit with disgrace. As the latter is not possible to Americans, we must prepare our minds for an extremely long, arduous, and sanguinary war." A

Plattsburgh correspondent wrote the editor of the *Albany Argus* that there was "no doubt the enemy are making the most vigorous exertions to fit out a force sufficient to command this lake."[34] For Thomas Macdonough, the strategic significance of the Lake Champlain theater was about to change dramatically.

The important information Commander Pring learned in his sortie up the lake was intelligence on Macdonough's fleet: fairly accurate information regarding the size and armament of *Saratoga* and *Ticonderoga* as well as the number of gunboats, now ten. Obviously he needed more firepower if he was to contend with Macdonough for superiority on the lake. While he was gone on the expedition to Otter Creek, the British government contracted with shipwright William Simmons to build a thirty-seven-gun ship (eventually HMS *Confiance*) at Île aux Noix. When British authorities solicited Simmons's opinion regarding the two ships-in-frame now at Montreal, Simmons reported that their twelve- to fourteen-foot draft made them unsuitable for lake service. His proposal to construct a twenty-six-gun vessel failed to receive approval. Undoubtedly a major reason for this decision was the lack of facilities and skilled personnel to construct two major vessels simultaneously. However, the Royal Navy immediately moved two fifty-five-foot gunboats (*Murray* and *Drummond*) up the Richelieu to Île aux Noix.[35]

Construction of the *Confiance* consumed most of the available skilled labor at Île aux Noix. (Its name was an archaic form of the word "confidence"; it was also the name of the ship on which Commodore Yeo had made his reputation.) Over 147 feet in length and 37 feet in beam, it would be the largest warship launched on the lake. It would take Simmons over three months to build the vessel. His lack of facilities and workmen, plus a somewhat lackadaisical attitude, allowed the Americans to nearly match his effort in a much shorter period of time. The laying of its keel raised the stakes on Lake Champlain and pointed, if the Americans could read their intelligence tea leaves, to the possibility of that body of water being used as an invasion route into the United States.

The *Confiance*'s existence also raised the expected rank of the lake's commodore. A flagship and a flotilla of this size required the services of a post captain. Capt. Peter Fisher replaced Pring in command of the squadron on 24 June, but Pring stayed on as second in command. Whether Pring resented the intrusion of this new senior officer is unknown. Certainly, maintaining at this station an officer familiar with the hydrography and anemology of Lake Champlain was a wise move. At the same time, the change in command brought with it unfamiliarity with the local geography and uncertainty regarding strategy and tactics at the highest leadership level. It demanded that new relationships and acquaintanceships be formed between army and navy commanders. The necessary mutual trust and confidence between service commanders requires time to develop; Fisher's tenure was too short one for such intra- and interservice collaboration to develop. Exacerbating the instability in Royal Navy leadership was a growing infusion of new and unfamiliar personnel at lower levels. In contrast, Macdonough's long service on the lake gave him an understanding of local wind tendencies, navigation hazards, and personalities that would hold him in good stead.

If Simmons proceeded with deliberate speed, Macdonough faced an extraordinary task. First he had to determine what was being built in Canada, when it could be launched, and what the British intention was. This information had to be forwarded to Washington with a sense of urgency that would cause an administration facing a host of military emergencies to expend scarce financial resources in a theater that had, to this point, been a rather quiet one. If the administration accepted his information and his conclusions drawn from it, Macdonough needed to oversee the construction of a vessel large enough to provide near equality, if not superiority, to the flotilla being assembled at Île aux Noix. Simultaneously, he and naval authorities had to ensure the necessary cordage, anchors, ordnance, sails, officers, and men would be forwarded to the lake in time to meet the British challenge. No previous assignment had required the administrative and logistical skills this thirty-year-old now confronted. All his ingenuity and experience now focused on the challenge imposed by HMS *Confiance*.

In early June Macdonough received information from four British deserters that the keel of the *Confiance* had been laid and that several gunboats were being towed up the Richelieu toward Île aux Noix. He immediately informed Secretary Jones of this, and of the British intention to secure command of the lake. They were engaged in a shipbuilding race; they intended to risk nothing, but instead "endeavour to out build us, and there is no knowing where this building may stop." He urged an augmentation of his flotilla and suggested that "Messrs. Brown of New York" be employed in the construction of sixteen- to eighteen-gun schooners. Navy Agent Bullus in New York informed Macdonough that he had heard nothing regarding the building of a new vessel but that as soon as he did he would immediately inform Macdonough of the department's decision and "use every exertion in my power to effect what you may require."[36]

While Washington considered his proposal, Macdonough reconnoitered Île aux Noix and found the British position "so strong as to make an attack on him where he now lies, a very imprudent measure. There is no getting round him, or between him, and the Isle Aux Noix." Consequently, Macdonough stationed his squadron at the northern end of the lake, thereby keeping the lake free for military movement and commerce by bottling the British in the river. He recognized, however, that this was a temporary situation. Unless he and General Izard could combine their forces and take the British position, the massing of British troops and the growth of the Royal Navy squadron would undo their current dominance of the lake and its littoral. His reliable information included some understanding of the problems with the ships-in-frame. The four ships had arrived in Montreal, but there was considerable uncertainty as to what should be done with them. Macdonough feared they would be forwarded as a further addition to his opponent's force. Again he proposed new construction, this time of a brig or schooner carrying eighteen long 18-pounders. It was now mid-June and still no decision from the Navy Department. Macdonough seemed to ignore information that construction of the *Confiance* went slowly. Five weeks after Macdonough expressed his fears of naval inferiority, a War Department informant wrote Secretary Armstrong, "The Enemy's New Ship is not very forward." In fact, he thought that instead of a ship, the new British vessel was a floating battery scheduled to mount thirty to fifty heavy guns. This latter misinformation had little impact on the Washington decision-making process, which had already endorsed the construction of a new brig for Macdonough's squadron.[37]

By Independence Day 1814 the administration had made a series of decisions regarding the war and its conduct. In the midst of the financial crisis facing the nation, Secretary Jones wondered where the money would come from to expand the navy. Besides Lake Champlain, he had to worry about British incursions into the Chesapeake, along the coast of Maine, and on Lake Ontario. There did not seem to be enough men, money, artificers, and materiel to meet all the pressing needs. Moreover, he hoped Izard could establish a fortress and artillery that would close the narrows at either Rouses Point, Point au Fer, or Cumberland Head so that no enemy squadron could pass into the upper lake. Were this done, and with naval force cooperation, the Americans would have "effectually secured" command of the lake without any new ships. Jones felt that the British possessed "means and facility of increasing his naval armament, greatly exceed those which we possess, either in equipment, transportation or manning." As late as 2 July, Jones would not authorize any more vessels for Macdonough's squadron. He failed to recognize that his plan for combined army-navy defenses against Royal Navy movement on the lake was unrealistic. Over the objections of his navy secretary, President Madison ordered the construction of a new brig for Lake Champlain. Even though he did not know where the funds for the enterprise were to come from, the president knew that if the British gained control of the lake, the whole northern frontier line might collapse. For not only was Lake Champlain in danger, but the line of communications through Albany to Lake Ontario was vulnerable to a British advance. Too much was at stake not to build a new brig. On 5 July, Jones ordered Messrs. Brown of New York to begin the "irksome contest of shipbuilding" by constructing an eighteen-gun brig on Lake Champlain. The Federalist-leaning *Vermont Mirror* of Middlebury doubted construction could be completed before the British attacked. The paper feared the British would make a "serious effort" soon, and while it hoped that endeavor might "prove a fruitless one," it was "not without doubts and fears."[38]

Instead of Noah Brown, his younger brother Adam assembled two hundred workmen in New York and made the journey up the Hudson, over the seventy-five miles from Albany to Whitehall and then down the lake. Adam Brown went ahead to see Macdonough at the foot of the lake, where they conferred on 18 July. Despite the delays, he beat Jones's letter informing Macdonough of the president's decision to build the brig. An overjoyed commodore and the master shipbuilder decided to utilize the Vergennes shipyard, where cut timber and iron were available. Five days later workmen scarfed together the 106-foot-long keel from maple and oak timbers. Thus began the frantic effort to build a ship faster than the one begun by the British nearly two months earlier. Brown's workmen were both numerous and skilled. The days were long; in the remote village of less than four hundred souls there was virtually nothing to divert their attention from the work at hand. The valley echoed with the sound of axe and adze cutting into wood; men yelled at one another and cursed as they laboriously raised the ribs; chips piled up all over the shipyard; smoke bellowed from the chimney's of the Monkton Iron Works as men formed the iron necessary to hold portions of the ship's interior together and made cannon balls. Adam Brown used numerous shortcuts to speed up construction. As his brother had done to build the *Saratoga*, he used unseasoned lumber. Even the choice of wood was below normal standards. Instead of exclusively relying on oak for the frames, he took whatever were at hand—ash, spruce, white pine, elm, and chestnut. Soon they began planking and caulking the outer and inner hulls and the berth and main decks. On 11 August, just nineteen days after laying the keel, the brig slid down the ways and into the creek. There it stuck in the mud; but shortly thereafter it was afloat in Otter Creek, a wooden monument to the industry of Adam Brown and his workmen. It was not, of course, ready to sail. First the workmen had to step its masts and then the boatswain and his men had to rig it. There were countless other final tasks that kept the carpenters and riggers busy for days thereafter, even as the brig was being readied for combat.[39]

As Brown and his workmen put the finishing touches on her, Macdonough continued the administrative and logistical tasks necessary to make the new vessel a fighting ship. He lacked five things: officers, sailors, sails, stores, and ordnance. The perpetual problem of finding men for the new ship began at recruiting stations established in Boston, Newport, and New York. The response was not encouraging.

Moreover, Macdonough needed a commander for the brig. Initially he sent Lt. Francis Mitchell to attend to its equipment, but he had little faith in Mitchell's abilities or those of any of the inexperienced lieutenants he had in his command. He asked for Master Commandant John O. Creighton. He received newly promoted Master Commandant Robert Henley. The Henley-Macdonough relationship would not be cordial. Robert Henley had once been senior to Macdonough in the navy. He resented what had happened over the past several years as he lost seniority. Between 1798 and 1815 he lost fifteen positions on the seniority list while Macdonough gained thirteen. In 1805, Henley stood thirty places above his new commodore on the lieutenant's list. In the ensuing seven years, Henley did not go to sea. Even his younger brother John passed him on the list as Secretary Jones undertook what historian Christopher McKee calls "a brutal . . . enforcement of the primacy of merit over seniority." Macdonough became a master commandant in July 1813; Henley rose to that rank a year later. The tensions undoubtedly increased when Henley found that Lieutenant Cassin, commander of the *Ticonderoga,* was a Macdonough favorite. Cassin's father, Capt. John Cassin, wrote disparaging reports on Henley's performance at the Norfolk Navy Yard. Captain Cassin's remark that he "would prefer a more active officer" undoubtedly lowered Henley's reputation in Washington. Henley believed he had an "*insidious foe*" inside the Navy Department who had colored the secretary's evaluation of his capacities. But positive evaluations by Oliver H. Perry and David Porter convinced Jones to promote him and to give him command of Macdonough's new brig.[40]

From the beginning Henley strained his relations with Macdonough. He started the contretemps off by writing the secretary directly, not Macdonough, that he had arrived on the lake. They even quarreled over the new ship's name. Henley recommended *Surprise;* Macdonough sought to name it *Eagle.* Over the course of the next few months Henley wrote Jones several times without going through his commanding officer. Such a lack of deference to rank only increased the commodore's displeasure. Macdonough's resentment at Henley's conduct would eventually result in an embittered evaluation of his abilities and character: "I look upon him to be very deficient in seamanship, and in the equipment of a vessel of war he is a stranger; his disposition I take to be malicious."[41]

Regarding ordnance, Macdonough originally desired a ship that carried a full battery of long 18-pounders. But the secretary recommended a mixture of 18-pounder long guns and 32-pounder carronades. Jones advised, "In close action the Carronades are more efficient." Macdonough readily accepted this suggestion. Naval Agent Bullus began to forward the ordnance and ships stores to Lake Champlain shortly after receiving Jones's directive.[42]

Throughout the summer supplies arrived from Albany, Schenectady, and Troy, New York. Bullus kept his promise and forwarded equipment as fast as he could. Hawsers, rigging, cordage, sails, spars, and a spyglass were among the many items he sent from New York. Undoubtedly the gift of six Bibles from the American Bible Society in Philadelphia "for the benefit of your fleet" pleased Macdonough greatly. And he also gained pleasure from some twenty-five hundred gallons of spirits, seventy barrels of pork, vinegar, molasses, flour, and orders of beef and butter that contractor M. D. Woolsey supplied. But Woolsey also made it clear that the government's credit was at an end.[43]

Patrolling along the International Boundary

In the midst of the activity in Vergennes, Macdonough kept a close watch of the British in the Richelieu and of the smuggling activities between Vermont and Lower Canada. Concerning the latter, Macdonough expressed exasperation. "The supplying of the enemy by many citizens of Vermont is in daily practice," he noted. "Fat cattle are continually going from that state to the enemy, some of which have been driven from forty or fifty miles within the state and in a public manner. I am informed upwards of 100 went in three or four days since. Surely there must be a great indifference on the part of the Governor or some other authority of that

state in permitting this to be done." General Izard expressed similar sentiments when he told Secretary Armstrong that on the high roads of
Vermont one found "droves of Cattle" and they were "pouring into Canada
like Heards of Buffaloes." Customs official Peter Sailly described how cattle were driven across the Black River Country in Franklin County, New
York, and found their way to Canada either through the Châteauguay
Woods or across the St. Regis Indian Reservation. He found that the "utmost watchfulness on the part of the [customs] officers could not even
check the outward current. The officers were avoided by those engaged in
the illicit traffic, or were opposed and frequently overpowered by superior
numbers." Even when contraband property was seized, it was in danger of
being retaken by smugglers and sent to Canada. In one instance, a seized
drove of cattle were intercepted by a band of St. Regis Indians, ferried
across the St. Lawrence River to Upper Canada, and delivered to the commandant of the nearest British outpost.[44]

Nevertheless, Macdonough had a few significant successes intercepting
this waterborne commerce with the British. Onetime Sailing Master
E. A. F. Vallette intercepted a shipment of spars between eighty to ninety
feet long. When he learned that "a large Raft of Plank, Timber & Tar" was
being run into Canada via "a narrow and unfrequented passage," Macdonough again sent Vallette to intercept the cargo. Not only was Vallette
successful, but he towed to the squadron approximately thirteen thousand
feet of ship's planking, oak timber, and tar.[45] The importance of this inter-
ception cannot be overestimated. Presumably they sailed the raft to Otter
Creek for use by Brown's workmen.

To assist in the antismuggling effort, Midn. Joel Abbot volunteered to
undertake a most hazardous mission. When Macdonough asked if he was
willing to die for the United States, the young man replied, "Certainly, sir,
that is what I came into the service for." The midshipman took a launch
into the Richelieu River and hid it from British sentries and picket boats.
Then, posing as a British midshipman, Abbot boldly bluffed his way into
the enclosure where the workmen stored the *Confiance*'s yards. He then rejoined his men at the launch. During the night they rowed with muffled
oars to the storage area and cut the yards to pieces. Finally the exhausted
men rowed back up river, sneaked past the picket boats, and after three
days behind enemy lines rejoined the *Saratoga*. Abbot was so weak from
fatigue that he had to be hoisted into the flagship. According to Abbot
family lore, Macdonough later told his midshipman that "if it had not been
for you we should have been sadly beaten" because the *Confiance* would

have been launched before the *Eagle*. It speaks well of his leadership abilities that Macdonough inspired such daring and loyalty among his subordinates.[46]

Sometimes these antismuggling patrols resulted in tragic mistakes. On 16 August members of a guard boat feigned to be British sailors at a Vermont tavern. The owner mistakenly believed Acting Lt. John T. Drury was from the Royal Navy and started to attack the officer. While his wife diverted his gun from killing the officer, the navy enlisted men with him killed the tavern keeper. This "tragical scene," as Macdonough called it, conveyed to all the tension that faced officers, their men, and civilians living along the international boundary. Vermont authorities charged Drury with murder and Macdonough released him from his command and sent him away from the clutches of the local officials.[47]

Despite such an unfortunate incident, the efforts of Vallette and Abbot and their men delayed the completion of the *Confiance*, thereby giving Adam Brown and the workmen at Vergennes a few more days to complete their increasingly more critical task. Brown needed every day such interceptions allowed him. And Macdonough needed every day that delay would permit. He faced the same routine and problems he had in the outfitting of the *Saratoga* and *Ticonderoga*. The logistical support required to furnish the new brig took all the coordination that he, Secretary Jones, Bullus in New York, and dozens of artisans, sailors, teamsters, and laborers could muster to manufacture and to transport the materials necessary to equip the vessel. New York sail lofts measured, cut, and sewed the canvas necessary for the vessel's propulsion. From the navy yard Bullus found anchors, cordage, slops, and the ordnance necessary to equip her.

On 27 August Macdonough reported to Secretary Jones that the new brig, named *Eagle*, had arrived at his station at the lake's foot. He estimated U.S. Navy firepower was now two guns short of the strength of his opponent. More critically, he noted that the *Confiance* had been launched five days earlier and was being hurried into readiness. He saw the more "active part of the campaign" being "to the westward" on Lake Ontario, and therefore the exact date when the new Royal Navy vessel would contest naval superiority on Lake Champlain was in doubt. Such misinformation regarding British operational intentions in the Lake Champlain region was at the core of strategic decisions being formulated in Washington.[48]

By this time Macdonough had done all he could to prepare for any eventuality. His secured permission to build both new vessels and gunboats to increase his squadron's size to one similar to that of his opponent; he supervised the forwarding of necessary stores and ordnance; he acquired sufficient men, many of whom were soldiers sent by the army, to man his ships and gunboats; his subordinates' skill and bravery delayed the building of a new enemy vessel until the *Eagle* came to his assistance; and he maintained naval dominance of the lake for most of the season. Above all, he had time to train the crews of the *Saratoga* and *Ticonderoga* in seamanship and gunnery. Even the *Eagle*'s crew trained together for over two weeks before entering combat. The officers and men knew one another; they knew their battle stations, their weapons, and their ships. Yet he was about to face an enemy slightly superior in combat power that was supported by a vastly superior ground force. The next fortnight would be decisive in the career of Thomas Macdonough. Up to this time he had demonstrated the managerial and logistical skills necessary for any successful combat leader. Now he would face the test of combat leadership.

The Battle of Plattsburgh Bay

> Forth from the squadron bursts at once
> The martial clangour's loud response.
> The bugle shrill, the drum, the fife,
> All summon to th' approaching strife.
> "Prepare," the brave commander cries,
> "Prepare," the echoing shout replies.
> The decks are cleared, the guns prepared,
> The matches flame, the blades are bared.
> Yet ere awakes the battle peal,
> The brave Macdonough bids them kneel,
> And crave His aid, whose sovereign power
> Alone preserves in danger's hour.
>
> Anonymous, "The Battle of Lake Champlain"

FROM THE AMERICAN standpoint the situation was most dire. The *Albany Argus* loudly proclaimed the time for partisanship had gone and "Providence calls Americans harmoniously to unite their spirits in one national soul." Why, it asked, is the need for unity now at hand? "Because the temple of freedom has been polluted and the name of liberty profaned by our enemy—our territory has been seized and declared a part of the British province, and the inhabitants strangled with the oath of allegiance to a foreign prince, who has stolen, enslaved, and in many cases hanged our unoffending brethren." The same paper reprinted the *Burlington Northern Sentinel*'s plea to Vermonters to "repair to the scene of action;—meet your brethren of New-York, in arms; and convince the enemy that the soil of Freemen is sacred."[1]

Command Reassignments

While these calls were going out to the American countryside, a surprising development took place in Lower Canada. On 1 September Capt. George Downie arrived at Île aux Noix with an order from Commodore Yeo placing him in command of the British naval squadron on Lake Champlain. Although Downie was more experienced than Captain Fisher, a change in command on the eve of a major offensive violated all norms of military command. Naturally, Fisher protested his dismissal vociferously. He noted also that "the manner too in which I am removed without the least previous communication [from Yeo regarding inadequate performance] can only carry with it the impression to the Army now assembled on this frontier, and with whom we were expected to co-operate, that I must be either unfit or unworthy in your estimation to retain it."[2]

Yeo's rationale for appointing Downie has never been fully explained. Certainly he may have been disappointed in the slowness of the *Confiance*'s construction and may have blamed Fisher for the incomplete vessel, particularly since the Americans had finished theirs in a much shorter time. Perhaps he felt that such an important invasion effort deserved a more senior naval commander. But if this was the case, why did he not send Downie earlier? Last-minute changes in command are prone to bring confusion. Certainly there was confusion enough at Île aux Noix with the thousands of soldiers moving forward to invade the United States, with all of the new personnel arriving to man the vessel, and with the *Confiance* in a still unfinished state. Whatever the reasons for the change, Downie faced the challenge of preparing the vessel for combat on its first cruise, of coordinating his movements with the ground commander (in this case Governor General Prevost), and of gaining information regarding winds and hydrography of a narrow lake. He knew little about his opponent, except that the Royal Navy had a slight advantage in firepower. He hardly had time to meet his subordinates when he had to move up the river and into the lake.

Downie's arrival came just after the launching of the *Confiance*. The ship came into the river on 25 August and was still incomplete when he arrived a week later. It needed a crew. By 7 September the new captain had scraped together enough men from the vessels in the St. Lawrence to man the ship, but many of these men were not seamen experienced with gunnery. For most of their time aboard the *Confiance* the sailors manned the sweeps and towed the vessel through the river's current and into the lake against a south wind. Thus Downie had little time to train his crew in the operation of the guns as he moved the vessel into combat. For the flagship of a squadron to be manned by men who did not even know the name of their gun captains, much less how to operate the guns, was an invitation to disaster. The *Confiance* lacked that unit cohesion so important to an effective fighting force. To engage a flotilla in which the commodore and the crews of most of the vessels had several months of cohesive experience was to court fate.

There was hubris from Sir George to Sir James, from Downie to the lowest ordinary seaman who assumed the Royal Navy could not lose. After all, they had defeated the best navies Europe could throw against them. What did this young Republic think it was doing trying to fight the world's greatest sea power? Lost from memory were the lessons of the frigate battles of 1812, the defeat on Lake Erie, and the failure of Yeo to destroy the Americans' Lake Ontario squadron. With caution disregarded, prudence overlooked, and discretion forgotten, confident as to the eventual outcome, Prevost and Downie moved their respective commands into the Adirondacks and onto Lake Champlain.

The British Invasion

"We shall probably have upon our frontiers and coast, in three months, a greater force than at any period of the revolutionary war; and a crisis is at hand, which will put in requisition the best exertions of our country—a crisis, in which indifference and inactivity will be, virtually if not legally, treason to the commonwealth."[3] So proclaimed the *Albany Argus* in early July as the intent of the British government became more and more obvious to the Americans. Where should the attack along the frontier be made?

For Prevost the choice was clear. His twelve-thousand-man force assembled in Lower Canada could not be sent to Kingston for a possible attack on the key American base at Sackets Harbor because of a logistical insufficiency in the Lake Ontario basin that could not be remedied for so large an army. Lake Champlain was the logical route. The combination of supplies forwarded to Quebec plus the provisions being smuggled from Vermont, New Hampshire, and New York made this region the preferred one in which to conduct operations. Not only were there sufficient supplies for his army in this area, but His Majesty's government desired that at least a portion of that lake's coast be occupied for possible inclusion in the British Empire in any subsequent peace treaty. Strategically such an annexation would close what historian Robert Quimby called the "Champlain sallyport into Lower Canada."[4] While the British Army focused its strength against the Lake Champlain corridor, the Royal Navy concentrated on securing control of Lake Ontario. What was obvious to Prevost was not so apparent to Secretary of War Armstrong, Secretary of the Navy Jones, and the Washington leadership, who remained fascinated by the Lake Ontario theater in the same manner as the Royal Navy.

When Armstrong requested General Izard construct a battery at Rouses Point to deny the Royal Navy entrance into the lake, the field commander noted that he lacked heavy artillery for such a position. Moreover, Rouses Point left the Americans in a dangerously exposed position close to Canada. Instead, Izard employed Maj. Joseph G. Totten, his chief engineer, in erecting three small forts on the narrow elevated peninsula between the Saranac River and Plattsburgh Bay and in building a small artillery outpost at Cumberland Head. The forts gave Izard an easily defensible position from which he might frustrate any British advance along the lake's western shore. With Macdonough defending the bay itself and his army on the shore, Izard felt reasonably sure of a successful defense of the northern end of Lake Champlain. Moreover, by drawing his opponent more than twenty miles over primitive roads into a forested wilderness, he placed the British at a logistical disadvantage when they arrived at Plattsburgh.

In mid-June, Izard sent Brig. Gen. Thomas Smith's brigade to the village of Champlain near the Canadian border. There both sides conducted a war of raids, counter raids, and ambushes for the next several months. Macdonough's flotilla corked the British squadron in the Richelieu River and thereby denied British troops any deep raids behind Smith's screening forces. Throughout the summer there ensued a degree of army-navy cooperation that facilitated the effective defense of the Lake Champlain frontier. It boded well for a continued cooperation as the British advanced later in the season.

Across the international border Prevost assembled a division of three brigades under the command of Maj. Gens. Thomas Brisbane, Manley Power, and Frederick Robinson, veterans of the Peninsular War against Napoleon's occupying forces in Spain. With both his officers and men, Prevost got off on the wrong foot when he issued an order for dress regulations that conformed to spit-and-polish garrison duty but seemed inappropriate to men who had been so long in the field. The governor general noted that "the dress of several of the officers of corps and departments, lately added to this army from that of Field Marshal the Duke of Wellington," lacked uniformity and consisted too often of "a fanciful vanity inconsistent with the rules of the service." Prevost then directed that brigade commanders "uphold His Majesty's commands" regarding dress and appearance and "only admit of such deviations from them as may be justified by particular causes of service and climate," and even then uniformity was to be retained. Were this not enough, the senior Peninsula War veterans were annoyed at finding themselves under not only Prevost but also men like General de Rottenburg and the newly promoted Maj. Gen.

Edward Baynes. The former they considered an aging officer out of touch with new military realities and the latter a Prevost aide and lackey with little combat experience. Nonetheless, Prevost left a brigade of nearly four thousand men in reserve at Montreal and marched over ten thousand men southward with de Rottenburg, ostensibly the division commander. Still, not even Prevost's most ardent critics doubted the result of the forthcoming invasion.[5]

Prevost recognized it was unlikely that appropriate naval cooperation with his campaign could be acquired before mid-September, and that without such aid "nothing could be undertaken affording a reasonable hope of substantial Advantage." Because Vermont provided so many essential supplies for his military forces, he determined to attack toward Plattsburgh on the New York side of the lake.[6] It is interesting to note that in early August he did not expect the Lake Champlain squadron to be ready until 15 September. Yet when his ground forces advanced far more rapidly to Plattsburgh than predicted, he would become impatient when the Royal Navy was unable to support him nearly a week earlier than previously anticipated.

Had Secretary Armstrong left well enough alone, the outcome of the ensuing invasion would have been more in doubt. Instead, his micromanagement of field operations placed the Americans in serious jeopardy. He, like Prevost, seemed more concerned with inattention to departmental rules than in large strategic concerns. By mid-June, General Smith reported to General Izard that "the enemy are preparing to attack me" and that the British had no expectations of an American attack in the Richelieu River valley.[7]

Despite ever-stronger warnings to the contrary, Armstrong persisted in believing that the main attack was to be on Sackets Harbor. Throughout July and August Caleb Nichols, his perceptive informant on the Lake Champlain frontier, wrote him: "The Enemy has never had so great a force on or near this frontier as we have had"; "The British . . . no doubt intend by Superior Numbers to force their way to Plattsburgh to capture the U.S. Army" there; "All the inhabitants [are] moving off. I am packing up my most valuable things." Izard initially thought he should reinforce Lake Ontario and menace Kingston, but he soon recognized the real threat was to Plattsburgh and sought to change minds in Washington. It was to no avail. On 12 August Armstrong reiterated his directive for Izard to move westward, and two weeks later the defense of Lake Champlain's western shore lay almost bare. "I will make the movement you direct," Izard wrote, "but I shall do it with the apprehension of risking the force under my command, and with the certainty that every thing in this vicinity but the lately erected works at Plattsburg and Cumberland Head will, in less that three days after my departure, be in the possession of the enemy."[8]

All he left behind were fifteen hundred fit regulars commanded by Brig. Gen. Alexander Macomb and some seven hundred New York militiamen headed by Brig. Gen. Benjamin Mooers. While Izard overestimated the ability of the Cumberland Head battery to withstand the British assault, he placed a firm reliance on Macomb's ability to utilize the defensive works at Plattsburgh erected under the supervision of Major Totten. Izard and Totten designated a narrow neck of land in south Plattsburgh as a suitable site for a defensive position. Here the tenth graduate of West Point could use the steep banks of the Saranac River as one side of a defensive network that included Plattsburgh Bay on two sides and required forts to be built on a narrow isthmus. On this isthmus Totten supervised the construction of three redoubts—Fort Moreau in the center, Fort Brown next to the river, and Fort Scott on the lakeside. With their interlocking fields of fire, these three posts could support one another.[9]

While some estimates of Prevost's strength are as high as fourteen thousand, the reality is probably about half that figure. With some four thousand left in Montreal, some two to three thousand in reserve at Odelltown or left along the route to guard various important posts, and others involved in providing logistical support over very difficult roads, the number actually arriving at Plattsburgh was probably closer to seven thousand. This still gives a margin of four to one in regulars against regulars, but American militiamen had given good account of themselves when behind fortifications since the battle of Bunker Hill in 1775. When joined with regulars they demonstrated this ability again in the War of 1812 at Sackets Harbor, Fort Erie, Fort Stephenson, Fort Meigs, Baltimore, and New Orleans. Totten's fortifications enhanced the American situation at Plattsburgh. No post built by West Point–trained engineers fell to the British at any time during this conflict.

But the Americans put up little resistance to the British advance from Odelltown to Plattsburgh. In fact, the British never broke out of a column formation during the six days they took to arrive at their objective. The left column marching down what today is U.S. Route 9 (North Margaret Street) north of Plattsburgh stormed over the bridge across Dead Creek and found itself confronting some of Macdonough's gunboats as they moved close to the shore. These vessels beat a retreat when the British brought up artillery of their own and inflicted a few casualties on the American sailors. Nonetheless, this incident is important. To Prevost the fire from the gunboats constituted a threat to any army formation close to the lake. He did not want any attack to be subjected to enfilading naval gunfire when trying to take Macomb's position on the south side of the Saranac.[10] The two lower bridges (at present-day Bridge and South Catherine Streets) across the river had their planking removed and incorporated into breastworks on the south shore. The high, steep banks of the river made it impossible to attack across the stream. The only avenue of approach was against Totten's three forts.

Macomb's troops may have not resisted well during the British advance, but they retired in good order and inflicted a few casualties on their opponents. On 6 September Prevost found himself in Plattsburgh a full nine days before he had anticipated the *Confiance* would be ready to support him. He was facing a determined foe, the bridges were impassable, his heavy artillery was held up by muddy roads and those he had were inferior in caliber to those of his opponent, it was raining much of the time, men were deserting to the Americans, winter was fast approaching, and the navy was not there to support him militarily or logistically. On top of all this, Macdonough's gunboats could redeploy and fire upon his troops attacking the American forts. Moreover, much to his surprise, hundreds of men from supposedly antiwar and war-weary Vermont were being ferried from Burlington to the New York shore to reinforce Macomb. One conservative estimate gives Macomb about twenty-five hundred militiamen plus his regulars. On 9 September the *Burlington Sentinel* apologized for its single-sheet issue on the grounds that all the men had gone to war. Another two thousand New York militiamen were on the march from the south. Meanwhile, General Mooers's militiamen guarded upriver fords and harassed the British from the rear.[11] Prevost's numerical advantage was considerably less than either his American opponents proclaimed or his British and Canadian critics acknowledged.

Were this not discouraging enough, Macomb saw to it that Prevost received erroneous intelligence regarding a supposed invasion of Canada that threatened Montreal led by Gov. Martin Chittenden of Vermont. Other misleading rumors said that far more militiamen than there were in reality were about to fall on Prevost's rear. Another erroneous report had Izard on the march from Sackets Harbor toward Lake Champlain. Prevost gave little credence to these reports, but the governor general knew that if he did not drive Macomb from his peninsular bastion soon, he might find himself in the same situation that confronted Gen. John Burgoyne in 1777—outnumbered and outgunned, deep in enemy territory, unable to go forward, and with his line of supply interdicted to the north.

Prevost needed naval control of the lake and he needed it soon. He urged Downie to move expeditiously to Plattsburgh Bay and engage Macdonough. On 7 September he sent the naval officer a report of the American strength that underestimated the number of gunboats and number of men on the American vessels. "If you feel that the Vessels under your Command are equal to a contest with those I have described," Prevost wrote, "you will find the present moment offers many advantages which may not again occur." At the same time, Prevost pressed Downie to bring forward some mortars with their stores that were at Île aux Noix "provided you can do so without delaying the sailing of your Squadron."[12]

The next day Downie replied that his ship was not ready and that he could not "hazard the Squadron before an Enemy who will be superior in Force." On the ninth Prevost wrote that his army was coiled to strike pending naval cooperation with the army. He noted that the *Eagle* was using prisoners as crewmen as there were no more sailors available for that vessel. He cautioned that "evils" would arise to both services if delay continued. To this missive Downie replied that he was proceeding south and hoped to be at Plattsburgh Bay the next morning. Because of a wind out of the south, Downie could not arrive on the tenth, and Prevost's disappointed army waited in vain at attack positions for hours. The governor general's last letter impugned Downie's motives when it expressed the hope that the navy's delay was the result of "nothing but the state of the wind."[13] One cannot read this correspondence without reaching the conclusion that both men were preparing a paper trail to cover themselves in case of an inquiry into their conduct following the forthcoming encounter.

Maj. F. Lech Coore, Prevost's aide-de-camp, who delivered this final message to Downie, recalled that he did not convey, nor was he directed to convey, to the senior naval officer on the lake an obligation to attack Macdonough when he was at anchor. According to Coore, Downie understood his squadron to be inferior in firepower to the Americans, yet he "expressed himself full of confidence in a successful issue of the Battle."[14] But how Downie was supposed to draw Macdonough into open waters was not explained and what impact the land attack would contribute to the outcome of the naval engagement remains perplexing.

Among the British there was a hubris that would have fatal consequence. Despite the apprehensions voiced in his letters to Prevost, Downie boasted in the mess hall at Odelltown that with the *Confiance* alone "he could lick the whole American squadron!"[15]

Tactical Comparisons

"Battles are won by the quartermasters," Field Marshal Erwin Rommel is reputed to have said. That is, the outcome of combat is often determined by the logistical support a commander receives before a battle is ever fought—as the situation on Lake Champlain verified. The slowness by which the British finished the *Confiance* allowed Macdonough to acquire near parity with the Royal Navy's squadron. The ability of the United States to construct and man the *Eagle* before the decisive engagement must be seen as a major logistical triumph.

Thus the first key to the outcome of the naval engagement at Plattsburgh was the relative equality of the two squadrons. Standard historical accounts say the British had ninety guns with a weight of metal of 1,864 pounds, of which 1,128 was in long guns, and 736 in short-range carronades. These studies give Macdonough eighty-six guns with a total weight of metal of 2,033 pounds, of which 759 were in long guns and 1,274 were in carronades. There is some dispute regarding exactly how much this difference really was. Part of this arises out of the controversy over how many gunboats the Royal Navy deployed. Macdonough wrote that there were thirteen, Prevost said twelve, Lts. James Robertson and Christopher James Bell, RN, testified there were eleven, and historical accounts list between ten and twelve. Lieutenant Bell's testimony is very explicit and eleven appears to be the most probable number. The British may have had twelve but left one small gunboat behind due to manning problems. Only one gunboat disappeared from the British gunboat list—the *Simcoe*—but Bell testified that it was not closely engaged. There is no evidence other than Macdonough's letter that any gunboats sank.[16]

Macdonough, who captured the vessel, said the *Confiance* had two 18-pounder long guns not reported by the British. But he exaggerated the *Confiance*'s firepower. These two guns were on its berth deck, on which there were no ports through which to fire them. Macdonough added three gunboats with three guns that are unreported in Royal Navy sources. The American's report concluded the *Chubb* had only one 6-pounder long gun instead of three but had ten 18-pounder carronades rather than eight. This significantly reduced that vessel's long-range firepower and may partly explain why it engaged the Americans at such close range. Macdonough's report gave the British ninety-five guns to his eighty-six rather than the traditional difference of ninety to eighty-six. The significant firepower difference between the two squadrons was the twenty-seven long 24-pounders on the *Confiance* to which the Americans could counter with only eight similar weapons on their flagship.[17]

Both sides had troubles securing enough personnel for their latest ships. Prevost correctly reported to Downie regarding American manpower problems. Macdonough sent forty men from his own crew to supply Lieutenant Henley's deficiencies. Still there were not enough, so he sent Lt. Joseph Smith to General Macomb to request men for the *Eagle*. Macomb told the *Eagle's* first lieutenant that he needed every man he had to fight off Prevost. He could spare none. But he gave Smith an order allowing him to take men who were under guard for various crimes; "some were chained by pairs, one with a ball & chain & some was shackeled." Smith removed the irons from forty-six men and brought them to the ship, where he had them washed, barbered, fed, and dressed in the last of the available slops. After a night's rest in hammocks made from sails, Smith "put them to the Guns & kept them at it constantly till the fight & they behaved well for greenhorns."[18]

But Downie's problems in this regard were far more severe. Nothing indicates the Royal Navy's lack of interest in lake service more than the way it manned Downie's flagship. For an action which the army in general and the Duke of Wellington in particular considered of paramount importance if the British were to be successful in achieving their national strategic objectives, the navy did not send its best enlisted men. Lt. James Robertson, the senior surviving officer of the *Confiance*, reported that the ship's complement contained men from eight warships and several transports in the St. Lawrence River. This included fifty-eight from HMS *Leopard* "sent to the Lakes against their inclination." The forty-eight from HMS *Ceylon*, *Ajax*, and *Warspite* were "chiefly men who were in disgrace," some of whom deserted prior to the battle. Although Robertson acknowledged there were several that had volunteered and were excellent seamen, most were not. As a contemporary historian wrote, the "men of the *Confiance* . . . were all strangers to each other and to their officers; and Captain Downie was acquainted with no officer on board his ship but his first lieutenant, and the latter with none of the other officers."[19]

There can be little doubt that a contributing factor to the *Confiance's* combat performance was a consequence of the fact that this was a vessel whose officers and crew lacked unit cohesion. The poor preparation of Downie's command for battle can in part be attributed to the Royal Navy,

Table 5-1. United States Naval Strength, September 1814

Vessel Type	Name / Commander	Armament
Brig	*Saratoga* / Thomas Macdonough	8 24-pounder long guns, 6 42-pounder carronades, 12 32-pounder carronades
Brig	*Eagle* / Robert Henley	12 32-pounder carronades, 8 18-pounder long guns
Schooner	*Ticonderoga* / Stephen Cassin	8 12-pounder long guns, 4 18-pounder long guns, 5 32-pounder carronades
Sloop	*Commodore Preble* / Charles Budd	7 12-pounder long guns
6 gunboats	*Allen, Burrows, Borer, Nettle, Viper, Centipede*	1 24-pounder long gun, 1 18-pounder columbiads
4 gunboats	*Ludlow, Wilmer, Alwyn, Ballard*	1 12-pounder long gun

Source: Letter from the Secretary of the Navy, 15; Wood, *Select British Documents* 3:373.
Notes: Cdr. Daniel Pring, RN, reported that the *Ticonderoga* had four 18-pounder and ten 12-pounder long guns and three 32-pounder carronades and that the *Preble's* long guns were 9-pounders.

which paid little attention to this aspect of their Lake Champlain squadron. Just as the fine combat performance of Daniel Pring's *Linnet* can be explained in part by the crew's long service together, so also can the opposite characteristic of the squadron's flagship be ascribed to a ship's company without the training, association, and teamwork distinctive of effective fighting units. The same lack of unit cohesion characterized the crews of the various gunboats. Pring cautioned Downie that the American vessels would be well manned and efficient. The new British commodore reportedly wanted to fight Macdonough before he took shelter up the lake. Downie saw an opportunity to gain complete dominance of Lake Champlain and desired to take it and not allow Macdonough to keep a fleet-in-being that could be supplemented and regain American naval control.[20]

Normally an apologist for the Royal Navy, British historian William James, who undoubtedly knew many associated with the Plattsburgh battle, wrote in 1837 a damning critique of the situation: "On the 10th, just as the last draught of this motley crew...was ascending the side of the *Confiance,* while the loud clank of the builder's hammer was still sounding

Table 5-2. British Naval Strength, September 1814

Vessel Type	Name / Commander	Armament
Ship	*Confiance* / George Downie	27 24-pounder long guns (1 on pivot), 6 24-pounder carronades,[1] 4 32-pounder carronades,[1] 2 18-pounder long guns
Brig	*Linnet* / Daniel Pring	16 12-pounder long guns
Sloop	*Chubb (Growler)* / James McGhie	3 6-pounder long guns, 8 18-pounder carronades
Sloop	*Finch (Eagle)* / William Hicks	6 18-pounder carronades, 4 6-pounder columbiads, 1 18-pounder columbiad
1 gunboat[2]	*Wellington*	1 18-pounder long gun, 1 18-pounder carronade
3 gunboats[2]	*Yeo, Prevost, Blucher*	1 24-pounder long gun, 1 32-pounder carronade
1 gunboat	*Wellington*	1 18-pounder long gun, 1 18-pounder carronade
3 gunboats[2]	*Murray, Drummond, Beckwith*	1 18-pounder long gun
4 gunboats[2]	*Brock, Simcoe, Popham, Beresford*	1 32-pounder carronade

Source: Prevost to Bathurst, 11 September 1814, and Plattsburgh Court Martial, 18–21 August 1815, Wood, *Select British Documents* 3:351, 429–36, 476; Letter from the Secretary of the Navy, 15–16.

[1]"No Men quarter'd at the 4-32 pʳ or 2 of the 24 pʳ Carronades," wrote Lt. James Robertson, RN, for the Plattsburgh court-martial in 1815.

[2]Most of the gunboats were "luggers"—small coasting vessels carrying one or more lugsails, which are four-sided sails, bent to a yard that hangs obliquely on a mast and is hoisted and lowered with the sail. All could be maneuvered with long oars called sweeps.

in all parts of the ship, while the guns were being breeched and pointed through the ports, and while the powder, for the want of a place fitted for its reception, was lying in a boat alongside, an officer from Sir George Prevost came to solicit the instant co-operation of the British squadron."[21]

This was a ship ill prepared for the task it was about to face. The army cannot be blamed for the hasty, last-minute assembly of "this motley crew." The army cannot be blamed for the absence of the correct gunlocks to fire the ship's guns effectively. Nor can it be blamed for the failure of HMS *Junon*'s commander to loan Downie the desired gunlocks or for the slow construction of the flotilla's flagship. It was Commodore Yeo and the Royal Navy that placed the emphasis of shipbuilding on Lake Ontario, thereby neglecting Lake Champlain until it was too late to supply the latter with sufficient shipwrights and crews.[22] Prevost's insistence that the squadron be brought into battle before it was fully ready undoubtedly contributed to the eventual outcome in Plattsburgh Bay, although his impatience and growing anxiety over his situation are understandable.

Downie's plight was a disaster about to happen. British commentator James wrote in 1817:

> Captain Downie's situation was one of peculiar delicacy. While he was fully aware of the unprepared state of his own ship, he knew that a powerful British Army was anxiously waiting to co-operate; and that the season for active warfare was rapidly closing. The slightest backwardness on his part might injure the reputation of himself and those placed under his command; and,—had he not the most positive assurance, that the enemy's works should be stormed by the troops, at the very moment he was seen advancing to attack their fleet?[23]

But the Royal Navy had overcome worse odds before; its officers and men often "muddled through" battles in which it appeared the outcome would be adverse. Units that were not cohesive have been victorious. From the British standpoint, the critical question of this battle revolves around the degree of cooperation each service expected from the other.

Prevost never indicated that his attack on Macomb's fortifications would assist Downie's attack by gunfire from the shore. Obviously, Prevost expected Downie's squadron to keep Macdonough's gunboats from providing supporting fires in the American defense of south Plattsburgh. On the other hand, the navy expected the successful storming of Macomb's position might force Macdonough to sail into the lake where the Royal Navy's advantage would be most telling in comparison with an attack on a squadron at anchor. The implication is the two services would conduct a simultaneous effort, but there was no assurance of mutual assistance between the army and navy. Although the naval officers after the battle conveyed the impression that they anticipated Prevost's assault would assist their efforts, nothing in Prevost's correspondence indicates this. The navy counted on the army to capture the American artillery and turn these guns on Macdonough's squadron. But at their maximum range none of Macomb's guns would have reached the American flotilla. Even if they could, in the midst of battle, it is doubtful if they would have forced Macdonough into a more disadvantageous situation by trying to break into the lake's open waters from his position at anchor. Nothing so indicates British hubris regarding the expectations of a ground victory than the statement by British naval historian William James that Wellington's men "all panted to rush forward; but, in truth, a third part of the troops would have done all that was required."[24] The navy seemingly anticipated that the Americans would not spike any guns before surrendering and that their gun carriages would be in such condition that the artillery could be moved into position to support Downie.

From Prevost's reports, Downie knew the American fleet lay outside the effective range of Macomb's guns before he rounded Cumberland Head and he could not have expected significant gunfire support against Macdonough from captured American field pieces. Downie also knew that if he did not attack when Macdonough was at anchor, the Americans might escape up the lake and constitute a threat to his squadron in the future. Victory by Prevost and not by Downie meant that any ground force at Plattsburgh faced isolation in the midst of unfriendly enemy country. Macdonough's squadron had to be defeated, and the likelihood of a better opportunity to accomplish this was remote.

However, the surviving naval officers reported Downie anticipated mutual support of the navy by ground forces. Captain Pring later testified that "Captain Downie had somewhat *more* than a common prospect of success, and that he had every expectation of such assistance [from the army], as would effectually provide against one of those accidents which often defeat the best concerted plans of the most able Commanders." Pring continued, "That it was the duty for Captain Downie to Co-operate with the Land forces cannot admit of a doubt, that he went into Action with the full expectation of receiving a simultaneous assistance from the Army, is equally clear." Sailing Master Robert A. Brydon of the *Confiance* also testified that as the ship rounded Cumberland Head, Downie said, "There are the Enemy's Ships, our Army are to storm the Enemy's works at the moment we engage, and mind don't let us be behind."[25] A close reading of this sentence does not indicate the army was to provide any direct support to the navy.

Brydon's testimony also includes a passage almost never discussed in the descriptions of this engagement. When asked what sail he might have set had the army controlled the shore batteries in Plattsburgh, he replied that *Confiance* could have "set sufficient Sail to have run her under the Batteries."[26] Did this question and the answer imply that Downie contemplated crossing the American line and occupying a position between Plattsburgh and the American squadron? If so, that scenario implied a successful army attack not simultaneous with the navy's but prior to it, something Prevost never promised. The whole question of what support, if any, Prevost verbally promised Downie is unverifiable, since Downie died in battle and Prevost died before he could present his arguments.

One can verify that the British placed their nation's strategic objective in the hands of a recently assigned junior post captain who had never sailed on this lake's waters with a "motley crew" in a ship on its first voyage. To expect success in such a situation was an extraordinary gamble.

The Americans gambled also. Unlike Downie and Pring, Thomas Macdonough had little naval combat experience. His midshipman's service in the Barbary Wars involved combat in gunboats and on a night cutting-out expedition against the *Philadelphia*. He had never seen a fleet action, never fought a ship-to-ship battle, never witnessed shot and splinters tearing flesh, canvas, and wood, and he had never stood on a quarterdeck with men dying around him and others crying out from their wounds. He had never tried to issue orders when the clouds of smoke obscured one's understanding of the situation and the noise of artillery drowned out rational thought. Yet he clearly understood his mission: ensure that their mutual foe would not surround General Macomb by land and water and maintain American naval superiority on Lake Champlain. He decided to fight a battle at anchor, something about which he knew only from the history books and naval literature, not from any experience. The two recent examples of such combat had been won by the attacker, not the defender— Adm. Horatio Lord Nelson's victories over the French at the Nile and over the Danes at Copenhagen. President Madison and Secretary Jones placed an enormous responsibility on the shoulders of a thirty-year-old master commandant without much seasoning in the art of combat leadership.

We have one record of Macdonough's command style on the eve of the battle. John H. Dulles of Philadelphia, a young Yale student, received an invitation to visit the squadron on Sunday, 4 September 1814, just a week before the British and Americans met in mortal struggle. The commodore's gig met him at the Plattsburgh landing and took him and a chaplain to the *Saratoga*. At noon, with the officers seated on the quarterdeck, the chaplain standing on the capstan, and the crew assembled from midships to the bow, the parson performed divine services. When Dulles remarked to Macdonough at the attentiveness of the crew to the devotions, the commodore remarked wryly, "The men do behave well, but there are other considerations controlling their conduct."

At dinner afterward, Dulles observed how Macdonough "conversed with the singular simplicity and with the dignity of a Christian gentleman on whose shoulders rested the weightiest responsibility that bore on any man at that period in our history." He discussed religious topics and regarded the Epistle of St. James peculiarly adapted to naval life, with its references to "He that wavereth is like a wave of the sea driven with the wind" and "Behold the ships, though so great, are turned about with a very small helm." Obviously he had a command of religious literature. Macdonough appeared younger than his age, was "of a light and agile frame, easy and graceful in his manners, with an expressive countenance, remarkably placid."

Particularly impressing Dulles was the unbounded confidence his officers had in their commander. When Dulles asked one midshipman ,"What do you think about the coming battle?" The young man replied, "We know the British force to be superior to ours, but we will do our duty." The calm, resolute composure of that response typified the attitudes that Dulles encountered throughout the squadron's officers. It demonstrated a trust in the commodore's leadership abilities that Dulles found "great leaders only can secure." One other incident expressed the impact of Macdonough's personal conduct and expectations of his officers. After the commodore left the dinner table and the conversation became more informal, one officer uttered an oath to which another responded, "Sir, I am astonished at your using such a language. You know you would not do it if the Commodore was present." The rebuke was, the visitor felt, approved by the rest of the officers present.[27] Obviously Macdonough brought a sense of duty and of decorum to those serving under him.

Macdonough's officers were a mixed bag. His second in command was Master Commandant Robert Henley, whose checkered career has already been discussed. As Henley's first lieutenant on the *Eagle* Macdonough assigned Lt. Joseph Smith, who had been with Macdonough since his arrival at Lake Champlain in 1812. Lieutenant Cassin received command of the *Ticonderoga*. A junior lieutenant who had already proved his combat mettle at the battle at the mouth of Otter Creek earlier that year, Cassin would not disappoint his commander at Plattsburgh Bay. Commanding the sloop *Commodore Preble* was Lieutenant Budd, who had served with Macdonough before. Subsequently Macdonough gave Budd a very critical personnel report describing him as "a very intemperate man whose habits of intemperance are, I believe so firmly rooted as to be nearly immovable." Budd spent over eight years as a midshipman and had been passed over for a lieutenancy several times before his promotion on the eve of the battle. There was little in his record to indicate he deserved a combat command, but Macdonough had no choice in the matter. The *Saratoga's* critical first lieutenancy fell to Raymond H. T. Perry, younger brother of Commo. Oliver Hazard Perry. Unfortunately for Macdonough, Perry fell ill and could not be present at the battle, even though he received commendation from his commodore for the "care and attention [he gave] in disciplining the ship's crew" while serving on board. That meant that Peter Gamble, a lieutenant with less than a year's service in that rank, became the *Saratoga's* second in command.[28] Scattered among the officers were men who had already distinguished themselves, including Sailing Master Vallette, Midshipman Abbot, and a young midshipman who would eventually rise to the rank of rear admiral, Hiram Paulding. With the exception of Henley and Budd, all served well on 11 September 1814. But compared to their opponents' experience, the American officers lacked seasoning. If the United States had an advantage in the forthcoming battle it was in the experience and cohesiveness of its crews.

Preparation for Battle

On Monday morning, 5 September, Macdonough called his officers to a conference on the *Saratoga*. They received instructions on how their various vessels were to be placed in the battle line. That afternoon the squadron weighed anchor and warped into the line with anchors out and spring lines bent. The *Eagle,* the northernmost of the major American vessels, anchored about two miles north northeast of Crab Island. Macdonough directed the five northernmost gunboats to concentrate their fire on the *Confiance* to ensure its capture or destruction. From the fifth through the tenth, the crews of the various ships prepared their respective vessels for combat.[29]

Of course Macdonough did not know he was going to have a week to prepare, but the time provided gave him the opportunity to take every precaution he could imagine. While the *Confiance* was assembling its crew and making the first efforts to form its ever-changing manpower into cohesive units, the Americans carefully laid their ships in line and set out anchors so that they might alter their respective ships' position during the battle as the situation warranted. Macdonough placed his main anchor directly off his bow with kedge anchors broad off the bow carrying hawsers to the quarters. The design was such that by winding in one or the other of the hawsers, the stern of the ship could be swung one way or the other, while the cable of the main anchor would keep its bow in place. Each vessel provided springs, hawsers attached to the bow anchor cable and extended to the stern. This allowed the vessel to be canted to port or starboard as desired. Stern anchors also provided some stability to each vessel's position. Moreover, the various cables allowed for winding the ship if required, thereby allowing a fresh battery to be brought into action. At the hospital on Crab Island Macdonough mounted a 6-pounder long gun that could be manned by mobile invalids at that installation.

Macdonough knew he had several advantages in the forthcoming engagement. He could adapt his formation to the circumstances of the anchorage and to wind conditions, allowing him to turn his guns in any direction. His crews had no obligation to work the sails, so they could fully man each of the guns. His assailant had to man both sails and guns and had to anchor while under fire, making it more difficult for Downie, who had to consider both wind direction and enemy fire, to place his vessels exactly where he desired them. The American commodore located his heaviest vessels to the north, to windward, which gave them the weather gauge and the better ability to maneuver should circumstances require.

Macdonough placed the *Eagle* to the north, followed by the *Saratoga, Ticonderoga,* and *Preble* in that order. Macdonough calculated his position so that it would force his opponents to anchor within the range of his carronades, since there was not enough sea room to round the head and anchor at long-gun range only. Between and inshore of these four vessels were the ten American gunboats whose principal tasks were to keep the British from crossing the T by maneuvering between the larger ships. They also were to counter an attack from their opponent's gunboats. He directed each ship's boats be lowered to the unengaged larboard side of the respective vessels. The American commander expected his gunboats to attack the British when they approached and could not fire back and then to dart out from behind the larger vessels as the situation and opportunities beckoned.

After anchoring just north of Cumberland Head, Downie reconnoitered the American position from his gig and returned to the flagship and gave orders to his captains. While behind this peninsula, he scaled his guns to alert the army of his pending attack. There was no response from the shore. While one presumes Prevost heard the signal, no record of this appears in the surviving army accounts. Downie directed gunboats to attack either of the two southernmost American ships and the *Finch* to assist the gunboats in taking either the *Ticonderoga* or *Preble*. His orders directed the gunboats to sustain three volleys from the *Ticonderoga* and then board her. Concurrently, Downie intended to sail up the American line, fire a starboard broadside at the *Eagle*, put the flagship aport, and anchor the *Confiance* athwart the bow of the *Saratoga*. He would then engage the American flagship with his larboard guns. The *Linnet* and *Chubb* were to engage the *Eagle* at the head of the American line. At 0740 the British squadron made sail in order of battle.

While Downie sailed toward the Americans, Macdonough offered the following from the Book of Common Prayer before his assembled officers:

> O Most powerful and glorious Lord God, the Lord of hosts, that rulest and commandest all things; thou sittest in thy throne judging right: And therefore we make our address to thy Divine Majesty, in this our necessity, that thou wouldest take the cause into thine own hand, and judge between us and our enemies. Stir up thy strength, O Lord, and come and help us; for thou givest not always the battle to the strong, but canst save by many or by few. O let not thy poor servants begging mercy, and imploring thy help, and that thou wouldest be a defence unto us against the face of the enemy: Make it appear that thou art our Saviour, through Jesus Christ our Lord. Amen.[30]

Officers and their men then went to their battle stations. Macdonough ordered his signal midshipman to raise flags containing an inspirational communication to his tars: "Impressed seamen call on every man to do his duty." Aping Lord Nelson's famous signal at Trafalgar, "England expects that every man will do his duty," Macdonough's message appealed to the typical sailor's hatred of the British impressment system, which had been a *casus belli* for this war. Such a communiqué also increased the commodore's reputation as a friend of seamen.[31] We also know that the crewmen were fond of cock fighting and that they brought a prized bird on board and kept him in a cage on the deck. That animal would become famous during the subsequent combat.

The Battle Begins

As the Royal Navy squadron moved in, Macdonough faced the lingering doubts that confront all commanders as they enter their first serious combat. Have I done all I could to prepare my vessels, officers, and crews for the forthcoming battle? Will they and I be able to withstand the carnage we are about to endure? Is there anything more I can do before we go into action? In the awesome silence and seemingly endless wait as the British squadron approached there was the opportunity for the Christian to med-itate on the temporality of this life. A sternly religious man like Macdonough surely prayed, "Good Lord deliver us through this time of trial." Undoubtedly his thoughts also turned to his beloved Ann, now in the eighth month of her second pregnancy: "Will I ever see her again?"

After rounding Cumberland Head, Downie found the wind had shifted from north northeast to west northwest. Now, instead of having the de-sired crosswind, he faced a headwind. The wind direction forced him to enter the bay close-hauled, the worst point of sailing, and once under the lee of Cumberland Head he found the breeze light and fitful. The shallow-draft Royal Navy vessels found it increasingly difficult to attack in the de-sired formation. The *Linnet* had no sea room to turn the line to the north. In particularly bad sailing position was the *Finch*, which failed to haul as close to Cumberland Head as its fellow vessels; it slipped farther and far-ther southward, less toward its target vessel and more toward the shallow waters off Crab Island. The wind also forced the *Confiance* to sail directly toward the American flagship since it could no longer sail upwind toward *Eagle*. As a consequence, *Eagle* escaped a broadside from Downie's flag-ship. With its topsails, topgallant sails set, and jib and spanker out, *Con-fiance* went into action.

Henley was the first to lose his nerve. He began the firing with a broad-side of the *Eagle*'s long 18-pounders that fell well short of their mark. While the British close-hauled on a starboard tack and sailed directly toward the Americans, Macdonough waited patiently for *Confiance* to come into range. The young commodore personally sighted one of his long 24-pounders and, finally, ordered it to be fired. The shot entered the *Confiance*'s hawse-hole and ranged the whole of the deck, killing and maiming several British sea-men. He then ordered the signal for "close action" to be raised. His gunboats advanced forward of the line and unleashed what Pring called "a heavy and galling fire" at the *Confiance*, which it could not return because it had no guns firing directly forward. As their foe advanced, these gunboats with-drew behind the four larger U.S. vessels.[32]

The first shots from the gunboats and *Saratoga* had an immediate effect upon Downie's flagship. Before it reached its destination it lost its sheet anchor and bower anchor, and when it dropped its best bower, the spring was shot away. The loss of these anchors and of the spring line to the best bower anchor's hawser contributed significantly to the battle's eventual outcome. Rather than at the bow of the *Saratoga*, *Confiance* found herself at the beam with little ability to fire at the *Eagle*.

While the *Linnet* took its station abeam the *Eagle*, the *Chubb* boldly passed astern the *Linnet* and sailed directly into the *Eagle's* range. Before it could seriously contribute to the action, two broadsides from the *Eagle* left the *Chubb* with its sails shot away and much of its standing rigging cut. Soon its foresail unrove and fell into the water over its lee bow. The ship's captain was slightly wounded and went below deck, and two marines were killed; seven soldiers, two marines, and at least one seaman serving in its crew went below, where they hoped to find security from musket fire of the *Saratoga's* marines.[33] Deck command devolved on Midn. John Bodell, who had only half a dozen men working with him. Each time he ordered the sweeps out to bring it into position, the oars were shot away. The *Chubb* drifted between the two flagships a helpless wreck, and finally Bodell received the captain's permission to lower its colors. Soon thereafter one of the American gunboats towed it out of the action.[34] The British had lost one of their four largest vessels before the *Confiance* had fired its first broadside. Still, this was not a disastrous loss; Downie carried on without it and brought the *Confiance* into position athwart the *Saratoga*.

The drifting *Chubb's* passage between the two flagships delayed Downie's first barrage for several minutes. At approximately 0930 the Royal Navy flagship commenced its first broadside. Scarlet tongues of fire leaped from the cannons' mouths and smoke covered the scene as thirty 24-pound iron spheres burst forward from double-shotted long guns. They hit the *Saratoga* with tremendous force. It shuddered from bow to stern; the impact threw over half the crew to the deck. Most were not seriously hurt, and, though stunned, they passed the wounded below, dragged the dead to the larboard side of the main deck, and returned to their guns. The blast deprived Macdonough of the services of his first lieutenant, Peter Gamble, who lay dead beside the bow gun he had been sighting. Remembering that Gamble was a replacement for the ill Raymond Perry, Macdonough's executive officer was now his original third lieutenant. This placed the American command situation on the thin reed of Macdonough's survival; for it was doubtful if anyone else could adequately replace his experience, coolness, and reputation with the *Saratoga's* crew.

At the same time, American gunnery exacted its toll on the *Confiance*. As the Royal Navy's commander stood behind one of his guns, a shot hit the artillery piece, threw it off the carriage, and killed Downie instantly. Thus, less than fifteen minutes into the battle, the British flotilla had lost its senior officer. But the situation was even worse than that. One of Downie's relatives,[35] Lieutenant Robertson, took command of the

Confiance. Somehow in the confusion of Downie's death and the chaos of battle no one could find the signal book. Robertson could not signal Pring on the *Linnet* that squadron command now devolved on him. Moreover, a message could not be sent to Pring via one of the *Confiance*'s boats because all of them were damaged beyond usefulness. The battle raged on with the British command and control system in total disarray.

Actually the same situation almost happened to the American flotilla. Around the time of Downie's demise, the *Confiance* unleashed a second broadside. A shot hit the spanker boom, sending a portion of that heavy spar against Macdonough and knocking him senseless to the deck. The crew watched in dread until after a few minutes he rose, shook off the cobwebs in his brain, and continued working the guns like a common sailor. Another time a shot took off the head of a gun captain and sent it hurling against Macdonough with such force that it sent him sprawling across the deck between two guns. With his uniform now soaked with blood and brains, he rose and resumed command. One could hear the enemy's shot passing overhead with a sound like the tearing of sails; other shot hit the vessel's sides, sending sharp-pointed splinters through sails, hammocks, and flesh. The whole scene grew indescribably confused and ghastly. Torrents of blood dyed the deck; bodies, bones, and body parts lay strewn everywhere. The screams of the wounded and dying combined with the roar of cannon contributed to the pandemonium and horror. But coolness amid the chaos of combat is a dominant characteristic of great commanders, and Macdonough exhibited that trait throughout the day.

But this battle was not merely a contest between the two flagships. In reality there were two separate engagements. One to the north involved the *Eagle* and *Saratoga* against the *Linnet* and *Confiance,* and the other to the south saw the *Ticonderoga* and *Preble* fight it out with the British gunboats and the *Finch.* Here, at the foot of the American line, the action became heated about 0940. Three of the British gunboats, *Yeo, Prevost,* and *Blucher,* had 24-pounder long guns that clearly outranged the four 18-pounders and eight 12-pounders on *Ticonderoga* and the seven 12-pounders on the *Commodore Preble.* But the Americans had more stable gun platforms and their ships were more sturdily built than those of their opponents. Moreover, Stephen Cassin's five 32-pounder carronades on the *Ticonderoga* constituted a violent threat to any gunboat approaching at close range to his vessel.

The gunboats advanced in a rough line toward the *Ticonderoga* under the command of Lt. Mark Raynham. Upon reaching within approximately

five hundred yards of their target Raynham hoisted the signal for close action and boarding, but instead of setting an example for the rest of the gunboats, he promptly withdrew the *Yeo* from the action, saying that the
touch-hole on his long gun was clogged. A number of the gunboats got
into grapeshot range of Cassin's carronades. Several men were killed and
wounded from these rounds. The *Beresford, Blucher, Murray, Popham,* and
Wellington were close enough for their crews to receive grapeshot wounds.
The *Beckwith, Brock, Drummond, Prevost, Simcoe,* and, of course, *Yeo* did
not actively participate in the close action. Despite Macdonough's report
that his vessels sank three British gunboats, all escaped. In their testimony,
the Royal Navy officers tried to disparage the conduct of the Canadian
militia volunteers on board the gunboats, who only spoke French and, the
British said, ducked when enemy shots were fired at them. For the most
part, these Canadian infantrymen were not on board to man the guns but
to become part of a boarding party. The Quebecois volunteers suffered severely, with nine killed and three wounded in the action. Only on board the
Linnet and *Confiance* were more men killed. Of the American gunboats in
this sector of the fight, only the *Borer,* commanded by Midn. Thomas
Conover, tried to support *Ticonderoga.* As it came around the *Ticonderoga's*
bow, a volley from a British gunboat killed two of the *Borer's* men, wounded
another, and forced it to withdraw before being of significant assistance.[36]

The *Finch* sailed so far to leeward that it focused its attack on the *Preble,*
not *Ticonderoga.* Its commander, Acting Lt. William Hicks, argued that his
orders were only "to lead the Gun Boats in and support them" as they
boarded the *Ticonderoga* and to concentrate on the *Preble.* This meant that
the five combatant gunboats were badly outgunned by the *Ticonderoga* and
driven off under heavy fire from the American schooner. During the gunboat attack, Cassin shifted his cables from time to time to fire some telling
rounds at the *Finch* that cut away its rigging and hulled it several times.
The *Finch's* broadsides against the *Ticonderoga* had little effect.

The *Preble,* on the other hand, failed to exhibit the combativeness Macdonough expected of her. By 0945 it and the *Finch* were within half a gun-
shot of each other. After an exchange of fire for over three-quarters of an
hour, *Preble's* commander, Lieutenant Budd, slipped the vessel's cable and
sailed toward the south Plattsburgh shore. The commodore subsequently
excused Budd's conduct as necessary to avoid capture by the gunboats.

With the *Preble* out of action, Hicks turned his attention to the
Ticonderoga about the same time the American schooner had dispensed
with the gunboats. It was an unequal contest. Soon the British sloop had

its forestay cut away, its main boom nearly cut through, and its mainmast severely hit. Its rudder became unserviceable, and over three feet of water filled its hold. Drifting to the leeward, it approached a reef off Crab Island, and to avoid it, Hicks tried to wear the ship. Before this could be accomplished it struck ground. From this position Hicks fought off *Ticonderoga* on the one hand and the 6-pounder manned by the Crab Island hospital invalids on the other. Desperate to get off the shoal, he ordered his carronades to be thrown overboard trying to lighten the vessel and raise it off the rock on which it was stuck. It was to no avail. With his ship aground and taking water, Hicks kept up a desultory fire until after the gunboats fled and the *Confiance* and *Linnet* struck before doing the same with *Finch*'s colors.[37]

Winding the *Saratoga*

The slackening of the gunboat attack allowed Lieutenant Cassin to observe the action north of him. There he found the *Saratoga* and *Confiance* and the *Eagle* and *Linnet* engaged in a continuing struggle. Cassin ordered his schooner to shift its fire from the gunboats and to concentrate on the *Confiance*. Aboard the other four vessels gun crews heaved and grunted; matches glowed and flintlocks sparked; cannons roared and smoke billowed; the rhythm continued over and over again—swabbing, ramming, heaving in and heaving out, firing. After each firing, the gun captain went through his ritual of commands—"Stop your vents," "Sponge your gun," "Load with cartridge," "Run out your gun," "Prime, . . . point, . . . fire!" But the rate of fire declined as more and more cannons on the engaged sides of the respective vessels became disabled. The battle became so intense and desperate that one Royal Marine who had been at Trafalgar later said that Lord Nelson's great victory was "a mere fleabite in comparison with this."[38]

The effectiveness of the *Confiance*'s fire declined rapidly as the gun crews unfamiliar with the new 24-pounder Congreve long guns failed to notice that each time they fired the recoil caused the quoin or wooden wedge which controlled elevation to slip to the rear and thereby raise the muzzle of the piece. Consequently, each successive round went higher than the previous one. In the heat of battle with smoke obscuring the target, the gun captains and section leaders failed to notice that they were hitting the masts and rigging and not the *Saratoga*'s hull and deck.[39]

The American gunfire close to the waterlines of their respective opponents began to have a telling effect. Several holes in the sides of the Royal Navy's vessels admitted water faster than the carpenter and his crew could plug them. The men on the pumps found themselves working at a failing effort. In the *Linnet* the water rose nearly a foot over the lower deck and the wounded had to be placed on the tops of chests and cables to keep them from drowning.

Twelve shots hit the *Confiance* between wind and water, one driving out a seven-foot plank through which water poured. With both pumps working and constant bailing through the main hatchway, the ship was kept afloat. To keep them from drowning, wounded men had to be moved. Most of *Confiance*'s masts were disabled, and much of its standing rigging was shot away. Still, both served as anchored floating gun platforms capable of delivering deadly fire into the *Saratoga* and *Eagle*.

Things seemed to be going reasonably well for the Americans until Henley decided he needed to change the *Eagle*'s position. Finding its starboard guns disabled, Henley tried to turn the *Eagle* on its cables, but the spring line had been shot away making such a move impossible. Despite the efforts of Lieutenant Smith to install a new spring line (during which time he was wounded), the *Eagle* could not be rotated to utilize its port guns. Henley ordered its cable cut, sheeted home its topsails, and ran down the American line to a position between and slightly inshore of the *Saratoga* and *Ticonderoga*. From this location he began firing at the *Confiance*, providing a fresh larboard battery's fire on the British flagship. At the same time, it exposed the *Saratoga* to raking fire from the *Linnet*. Macdonough was not pleased with this unauthorized change in position.

The situation on the American flagship grew increasingly desperate. With the action now well over an hour and a quarter old, its starboard guns one by one became disabled either by enemy fire or by overcharging. Finally the last usable carronade flew off its carriage and fell down the main hatch. There was nothing left to fire from that side of the *Saratoga*. The time had come to test whether Macdonough's pre-battle preparations for such an emergency would work.

Letting go of the stern anchor and cutting the bow cable, Macdonough sought to use the leverage gained from the two kedge anchors and their hawsers to turn the vessel 180 degrees. His tars hauled the starboard kedge hawser to the vessel's stern and then hauled the *Saratoga*'s stern to the kedge. As its stern became more and more exposed to the *Linnet*'s guns, Captain Pring loaded his remaining guns and waited patiently for the opportune moment to rake the American ship. Knowing this would happen, Macdonough moved as many men as he could to the forecastle. *Linnet* fired, and the *Saratoga* absorbed the hit. Soon the first guns of the American ship would focus on the *Confiance,* but before the American guns could be brought to bear, *Saratoga* refused to budge any further. Then, in a beautiful lesson in physics, Macdonough ordered the larboard (port) kedge hawser hauled under his vessel's bow and carried aft to the starboard quarter. Hauling on this cable, the crew wound the ship around and unleashed a fresh broadside into *Confiance.*

During all this Lieutenant Robertson on HMS *Confiance* tried desperately to increase his firepower by bringing the vessel's unengaged side into the action. But it had lost the anchors and spring lines necessary for such an effort early in the battle. Frantic efforts to install a new spring line to its starboard anchor failed, and without the necessary fulcrum to accomplish the task, the British flagship soon hung suspended with its head to the wind. The *Saratoga's* broadsides wrought a terrible cost on the *Confiance.* Were this not enough, it found itself facing the fire of the *Eagle, Ticonderoga,* and the gunboats that had heretofore remained rather reluctant to engage any vessel. The *Confiance's* crew refused to fight an obviously losing battle. Robertson struck its colors. Macdonough undoubtedly smiled as he saw the famous red-crossed ensign of the Royal Navy flutter down. But there was more work to be done.

Pring, who had fought the *Linnet* so well, found himself in a hopeless position. Throughout the engagement he had ignored the pesky but damaging fire of the five northernmost gunboats, instead focusing his attention on the *Eagle* and *Saratoga.* Taking on water, unsupported by any of the British gunboats, two of his principal consorts having surrendered and the third aground, he now faced the full wrath of *Saratoga* which Macdonough brought to bear by hauling farther inboard with the starboard hawser. Pring sent his first lieutenant to the *Confiance* and learned upon his return of Downie's death. Finally Macdonough's guns began firing. The *Linnet* was helpless, but Pring fought on for several minutes before ordering its colors hauled down. It was now about 1135.

The Royal Navy gunboats fled the scene with their American counterparts in pursuit. Macdonough ordered them back. There was too much work to be done in Plattsburgh Bay. The wounded had to be tended, ships had to be saved, and prisoners had to be secured. Furthermore, the nation had to be notified of the achievement. Before sunset, Macdonough composed and dispatched to Secretary Jones the news: "The Almighty has been pleased to Grant us a Signal Victory on Lake Champlain in the Capture of one Frigate, one Brig, and two sloops of war of the enemy."[40]

The news of this "signal victory" reached the summit of Monticello, where Thomas Jefferson effusively wrote President Madison that "the destruction of a second hostile fleet on the lakes by McDonough" meant that the British would "be stung to the soul by these repeated victories over them on that element on which they wish the world to think them invincible." The former president extravagantly concluded, "We have dissipated that error. . . . We can beat them gun to gun, ship to ship, and fleet to fleet."[41]

Seldom has a victory had more immediate and far-reaching tactical and strategic consequences than that of Macdonough's squadron at Plattsburgh Bay. For reasons that will never be fully explained, the British Army had not attacked General Macomb's position in south Plattsburgh when His Majesty's naval ensigns fell to the water. Royal Navy advocates argued that Prevost's failure to take the American fortifications and their guns cost the navy its victory. British Army veterans of the Peninsula campaign felt the American position would have been easily taken even after Macdonough's victory. But one must be careful in accepting these assessments. The American defeat at Bladensburg, Maryland, notwithstanding, the U.S. Army and its militia ran up a string of victories against British regulars that summer of 1814 that should make any observer wary before assuming an easy British success in such an attack. The battles at Chippawa, Lundy's Lane, Fort Erie, and Baltimore witnessed a new American military capability that reversed the image of unpreparedness and ineffective leadership that led to the defeats of the previous years.

It is highly doubtful that had an attack by Prevost begun at the time the naval battle started it would have been terminated before the British squadron struck their colors. It is even more problematic that a victory on land would have forced Macdonough out of Plattsburgh Bay before the naval outcome had been determined. Once the American naval victory was known, Prevost correctly determined to withdraw. A tactical victory in south Plattsburgh would not have been strategically useful to the British without naval superiority on the lake. Isolated in an unfriendly country with a tenuous line of supply and communications to Lower Canada, Prevost would have had to evacuate the post anyway before winter set in.

While Macdonough's tactical victory operationally forced the retreat of British ground forces from the western shores of Lake Champlain, its strategic impact was even greater. Combined with the American victories at Fort Erie and Baltimore, the failure of the Lake Champlain campaign contributed significantly to the British decision to end the war status quo antebellum. The British and their Native allies dominated much of what are now the Upper Peninsula of Michigan and the state of Wisconsin as well as the Penobscot region of Maine. But American mastery of the critical Detroit River region, much of modern southwestern Ontario, and parts of the Niagara frontier compensated for these losses. With the western end of the Niagara portage in American hands and the critical straits of Detroit theirs also, the British were in poor position to make demands upon the United States for territorial readjustment. Thus, after over two and a half years of fighting, neither side could claim territorial gain.

The *Times* of London called the Lake Champlain defeat "more disastrous" than that suffered on Lake Erie a year earlier. This assessment was correct. It was obvious that the British would have to accept another year of warfare if they were going to continue to press for the terms they assumed would be easily achieved just a few weeks earlier. Any enthusiasm for such a task soon disappeared in the mind of the British public. Moreover, Parisians only reluctantly accepted the restored Bourbon monarchy imposed upon them and the possibility of a restoration of Napoleon loomed. Finally, the Congress of Vienna designed to resolve the problems of a post-Napoleonic Europe seemed about to collapse in a whirlwind of conflicting demands for territorial aggrandizement among the victors. News from Federalist informants in America found that the Chesapeake invasion had not brought down the Madison government but had instead united many of the president's opponents into a defense of national honor and territory. Thus events in Baltimore, Fort Erie, and Plattsburgh combined with problems in London, Paris, and Vienna to convince the British government to lessen their demands to the American delegation in Ghent.

One can never fully assess the exact proportion Macdonough's victory had in the final diplomatic equation. Secretary of State James Monroe forwarded instructions to the United States negotiators not to press for the cession of Upper Canada. For a while the British cabinet desired a treaty based on *uti possidetis,* the territory actually in control of each nation. During the summer and early fall, their delay tactic in Ghent seemed to justify this stance based upon expected victories giving them territorial gains. But the situation known in mid-October made such a position less tenable. Moreover, a desire to send the Duke of Wellington to replace Prevost found the Iron Duke reluctant. Wellington hesitantly accepted the proposal to send him across the Atlantic, but at the same time he rejected the idea of *uti possidetis* and urged the acceptance of the American position of status quo antebellum. Such a policy objective by the proposed commander in chief doomed any cabinet desire to continue the war. On 21 November 1814 the British administration confirmed its decision to settle on the basis of status quo antebellum. It took over a month to draft the concluding documents. The various diplomats signed the Treaty of Ghent on Christmas Eve. Whatever relative importance Macdonough's victory provided the diplomatic solution, it was without doubt significant.[42]

The War of 1812 seemingly ended where it began, but the United States that emerged therefrom was transformed economically, politically, diplomatically, and militarily by the events that transpired in this conflict.[43] Thomas Macdonough's life, career, reputation, and status entered a new phase.

Carl von Clausewitz argued that a strategy decides "the time when, the place where, and forces with which the engagement is to be fought."[44] Using this definition Macdonough demonstrated an exceptional ability as a strategist. He used his persuasive and managerial abilities to keep sufficient force on the lake to maintain naval superiority for almost the whole of his tenure on Lake Champlain. He and Macomb determined the site for the confrontation with the British invasion force. While certainly the exact timing of the battle had much to do with British decisions, Macdonough's mere presence on the lake forced them into a much later move toward Plattsburgh than they would have made had he not been there with his forces.

That the United States had a fleet sufficient to fight the Royal Navy force was largely due to Macdonough's efforts. In less than two years he had built a squadron from virtually nothing. He exhibited leadership traits involving a variety of skills. As an administrator he coordinated with the highest naval authorities in Washington concerning the construction, maintenance, and expansion of the Lake Champlain squadron. There can be little doubt that his insistence on construction of the *Eagle* provided the margin of firepower necessary to win the victory. The young commodore established close relations with departmental officials in New York, Boston, and Newport, who provided him with necessary supplies and manpower. Civilian contractors from Albany to Vergennes dealt successfully with him in providing a variety of equipment, transportation, and supplies. Above all, he knew when to delegate responsibility to contractors such as the Brown brothers, whose acclaimed skills as shipbuilders required only limited supervision. He demonstrated extraordinary patience when he found his legitimate needs were not fully met by those with an incomplete understanding of the strategic problems faced on this critical frontier.

Macdonough demonstrated particular skill in conducting joint operations with a variety of army commanders operating out of Burlington and
Plattsburgh. No other naval officer in this war worked more closely with
his military counterparts. One searches in vain to find an army officer's
complaint of his lack of cooperation. And he found this support recipro-
cated. In the spring of 1814 it was the army that supplied the bulk of artillerymen and militiamen to defend his Vergennes construction site.
Regular army soldiers and militiamen provided the necessary manpower to
man his tiny squadron. However reluctant army commanders were to support his manpower requests, in the final analysis Macdonough did not fail
for a lack of crewmen. Throughout this war an absence of such mutual interservice support hampered American operations in other theaters.

Although Macdonough's obligation to suppress the illicit trade with
Lower Canada proved difficult to achieve, he had some notable successes,
the most important of which were the achievements of his subordinates in
interfering with the shipment of masts and spars to Île aux Noix.
Macdonough's success in suppressing some of this trade demonstrated another leadership trait that characterized his career: he willingly utilized
subordinates to conduct operations requiring skill, daring, and enterprise
not expected from persons of modest rank. In other words, he developed
in many a sense of responsibility that did much in the advancement of the
squadron's mission. Certainly Lt. Samuel Smith's role in the loss of the
Eagle and *Growler* in the Richelieu River in 1813 showed what happens
when a subordinate failed to live up to Macdonough's expectations. On the
other hand, the activities of Cassin, Vallette, and Abbot exhibited the
pluck, skill, and audacity Macdonough anticipated in these junior officers.
That he inspired such officers and their men to undertake so many risks in
various enterprises says much about Macdonough's leadership style and
how much Stephen Decatur's example in the Mediterranean influenced
him. If military leadership is a process by which one influences others to
accomplish the unit's mission, then Macdonough clearly motivated his
men in this regard,

Most important, Macdonough exhibited the skills of a combat leader
that will forever make his name one of fond memory to the United States
Navy. First and foremost, he trained his men to the tasks they would face.
Only the *Eagle* did not have sufficient time to develop the unit cohesion
necessary for combat success. Because they had been together for some
time before the battle, the Saratogas, Ticonderogas, and Prebles exhibited
the unit cohesiveness that is the hallmark of operational success. One

might question the leadership on the *Preble,* but not the crew's effective-ness. Even the Eagles fought well, particularly when one understands that many of them had been army prisoners just a few days before the engage-ment in Plattsburgh Bay.

As a tactician Macdonough effectively positioned his vessels to receive the enemy and forced that foe to attack him at anchor. He took every ad-vantage he could of his battle position. In particular he understood the im-pact that Cumberland Head had on wind characteristics to any squadron attacking him, and he deployed his ships to take full advantage of such knowledge. He understood the necessity of preparing for every contin-gency and of having multiple options available as the tactical situation changed. In this he exhibited the skills in seamanship, gunnery, and tactics characteristic of notable naval commanders. The commodore effectively communicated his desires and objectives to his subordinates and inspired them with not only an effective battle plan but also the broader objective: "Impressed seamen call on every man to do his duty."

Above all, Macdonough exhibited strength of character. Throughout the two years on Lake Champlain he possessed that self-control, steadi-ness, perseverance, and imagination that inspired those around him. Without significant combat experience on his own part and with even less among his junior officers, the young commodore hid behind the "mask of command" all the insecurities, apprehensions, and fears that disquieted him. On the day of battle he faced a superior foe without the first lieu-tenant he expected, he accepted the loss of his most senior subordinate without flinching, and he withstood being thrown to the deck twice with-out ever going below. More important, at the moment of supreme crisis he confidently directed the winding of his vessel so that it might remain the decisive weapon in this engagement. He exhibited a sense of personal re-sponsibility, the desire to do all in his power to accomplish his mission, an essential component of effective naval leadership. In that most irrational of situations—combat—Macdonough's steadiness under stress, understand-ing of the situation, and example of courage motivated his officers and men. For all this, he was to receive the accolades and rewards of a grateful nation.

Chapter Six

Life Ashore

Macdonough, and thy gallant bands!
Fit guardians of thy native lands,
    Where every wrong's redress'd;
O haste, and free from war's alarms,
Within thy plausive country's arms,
    Find GRATITUDE and rest!
—A brighter chaplet ne'er hath been,
    Nor e're to latest time shall be,
Tho' ages rise and roll between,
    Than that which Fame entwines, from them and thee!
    "Ode on Commodore Macdonough's Victory," 1814

SOMETIME SHORTLY after the Battle of Plattsburgh Bay, Commodore Macdonough opened his copy of the Book of Common Prayer and turned to the section containing forms of prayer to be used at sea. There on the morning of the battle he had found the prayer in anticipation of combat. There also he must have turned to the collect after a victory which read in part, "O Almighty God, the Sovereign Commander of all the world, in whose hand is power and might, which none is able to withstand; we bless and magnify thy great and glorious Name for this happy victory, the whole glory whereof we do ascribe to thee, who art the giver of victory."[1] Ferocious in combat, Macdonough became gracious in victory. When the surviving British commanders presented their swords to him, he allowed them to keep them as recognition of their valor. A few days thereafter he allowed the surviving senior officer, Daniel Pring, a parole to return to the British lines.

Macdonough also discovered that victory did not end the burdens of command. There were vessels to be repaired, prisoners to be secured, wounded to be succored, messages to be composed, and congratulations to be received. Moreover, he needed to prepare his much-enlarged squadron for winter and for an expected renewal of the contest for Lake Champlain the following spring. In addition, the tension between himself and Master

Commandant Robert Henley revived itself almost immediately after the smoke cleared.

He would spend most of the remainder of his life ashore. In 1818–19 he commanded the USS *Guerrière,* and in 1824–25 he commanded the USS *Constitution.* Otherwise, upon relinquishing his Lake Champlain billet, he commanded the Portsmouth Naval Station and the USS *Ohio,* which never left its New York port.

Aftermath of Victory

First Macdonough had to prepare a full report of his activities to Secretary of the Navy Jones. Most of his report dealt with the activities on board the *Saratoga.* He gave only brief attention to the actions of subordinate vessels, beginning with, "The *Ticonderoga,* Lt. Commt. Cassin, gallantly sustained her full share of the action." He noted that the sloop *Chubb,* opposed to the *Eagle,* capitulated early. Of the American brig he added that at 1030 the "*Eagle,* not being able to bring her guns to bear [on *Linnet*], cut her cable and anchored in a more eligible position between my ship and the *Ticonderoga,* where she very much annoyed the enemy, but unfortunately leaving me exposed to a galling fire from the enemy's brig." While he did not discredit Henley's performance, neither did he use the accolade "gallantly" in referring to his senior subordinate. All other honors are given to the *Saratoga's* officers. Lt. Peter Gamble ("a gallant young officer...who, I regret to inform you, was killed early in the action"), Acting Lt. Elie Vallette, Sailing Master Philip Brum, Purser George Beale, Master's Mate Joshua Justin, and Midn. Lawrence Montgomery received special mention. In addition, Midns. Walter Monteith, John Graham, Charles Williamson, Charles Platt, Samuel Thwing, and James Baldwin "all behaved well and gave evidence of their making valuable officers."[2] Since being mentioned in dispatches was particularly important to career advancement, Macdonough's failure to mention Lieutenant Budd of the *Preble* and any of the junior officers on any other vessels undoubtedly caused some anxiety among these young men.

Macdonough's failure to fully document the conduct of the officers of his subordinate vessels reflected a narrowness of vision that undoubtedly hurt their prospects of early promotion. This was a common problem with after-action reports from senior officers during the War of 1812, and it often resulted in postwar acrimony. Certainly Macdonough could have been more explicit regarding the performance of more of his junior officers, who often went to the lakes reluctantly and deserved a mention in the report to the Navy Department.

Henley understood he would not fare well in Macdonough's official report on the battle. Apparently he wrote two letters to Macdonough on the twelfth. One gave a detailed account of the action and accorded exceptional credit upon the officers and petty officers in his command; it was assumed Macdonough would relay this information in his report to the secretary of the navy.[3] The other merely stated that his officers and men "acted bravely, and did their duty in the battle of yesterday." Henley abruptly said that he would "have the pleasure of making a more particular representation of the respective merits of my gallant officers" to the secretary. This second message Macdonough forwarded. Presumably Henley knew what Macdonough would say in his report to Jones. That Henley's conduct left the *Saratoga* "exposed to a galling fire from the enemy's brig" would not redound to the *Eagle* captain's credit. While it was somewhat presumptuous for Henley to make such a private report to Washington, he doubtlessly felt Macdonough should have waited for all reports from officers before filing his message to the secretary. Henley properly felt that he and his officers deserved more credit for the victory than Macdonough was willing to give. A special wartime promotion depended as much on the secretary's good opinion of an officer's conduct in battle as on seniority. Many of the officers on the other vessels probably felt left out by Macdonough's failure to mention them and by his not forwarding letters of the subordinate captains describing their behavior. Moreover, by this time Henley probably knew that Macdonough had given Cassin the distinct honor of carrying the captured enemy flags to the nation's capital. Cassin, the son of a navy captain who had given Henley a poor efficiency report, was not the messenger the *Eagle*'s captain desired.[4]

Henley's solution to his problem was twofold. First, he wrote Secretary Jones his own version of the battle in which the *Eagle* played a dominant role. In Henley's version not only did the *Eagle* force the *Chubb* to surrender, but it fought off the *Linnet* and *Confiance* simultaneously. Filled with falsification and exaggeration, Henley's report then attached the long letter he wrote to Macdonough. At least his officers would now receive the notice they deserved.

At the same time Henley played his second card: he requested leave to proceed to Washington where he might obtain a furlough from Secretary Jones for the purpose of "paying attention to my health which is so necessary for its reestablishment." Macdonough refused permission, so Henley secured a letter from his surgeon that the *Eagle's* captain's "health is extremely inform & delicate & that this climate is very injurious to persons in his situation." Macdonough did not respond promptly. He probably thought that Henley, who had served only a few weeks on the lake, did not deserve special treatment on account of health when compared with long-serving officers such as Smith, Cassin, and himself. The now-desperate Henley resigned his command on 17 September because of "extreme ill health." The next day he left his vessel.

The casualty reports reflected the intensity of fighting during the battle. The *Saratoga's* list included 28 killed and 29 wounded, the *Eagle's* toll was 13 killed and 20 wounded, the *Ticonderoga* had 6 killed and 6 wounded, *Preble* lost 2 killed and none wounded, the gunboat *Borer* had 3 killed and 1 wounded, and the gunboats *Centipede* and *Wilmer* each had 1 wounded. The grand total for American casualties were 52 killed and 58 wounded. British losses were more difficult to determine. Officially they include 41 killed and 40 wounded on the *Confiance*, 10 killed and 14 wounded on *Linnet*, 6 killed and 16 wounded on the *Chubb*, and 4 wounded on *Finch*. British losses on their four largest vessels therefore totaled 57 killed and 74 wounded. This figure does not reflect the losses on the British gunboats, which should include 9 killed and 3 wounded among the French Canadian militiamen plus those in the Royal Navy and Royal Marines. The official losses reported for the four captured vessels may include only the Royal Navy seamen, not the soldiers and militiamen serving thereon. There were 27 officers and petty officers among the British prisoners along with 387 seamen.[5]

Macdonough grew increasingly suspicious of Henley's casualty report and sent his own surgeon to the *Eagle* to investigate. Surgeon John Briggs reported that only nine, not the twenty-seven Henley initially reported, were wounded seriously enough to merit hospitalization. Most of the so-called officer and petty officer wounds were slight, none keeping them from duty for more than a month.[6] From the commodore's perspective, Henley padded his casualty list in order to make it appear that he had undergone more serious fighting than actually had occurred. At the same time, the *Saratoga's* casualty list included only those crewmen whose wounds required hospitalization.

Commodore Macdonough's final word on this affair came in his autobiography written around 1822. He remained "decidedly of opinion" of *Eagle's* duty "to remain in the station assigned her as long as it was possible for her to maintain it. Her list of killed and wounded would show what necessity she was under to change her station, and even that evidence of her disability was made up of the names of wounded men, in part, who had only been so scratched or slightly hurt as not to merit the name of wounded."[7] Macdonough remained unforgiving of Henley's performance in Plattsburgh Bay.

An onerous duty of any combat commander is the writing of letters of condolence to the parents of those lost under his command. In this most difficult of tasks Macdonough composed sympathetic letters to Maj. Thomas Gamble and Brig. Gen. Tobias Stansbury informing them of the deaths of their sons, Lts. Peter Gamble and John Stansbury, during the engagement on Lake Champlain.[8]

Equally important were the necessary preparations of Macdonough's command for caring for the wounded and prisoners and preparing his enlarged squadron for winter quarters. The fleet remained in Plattsburgh for weeks after the battle. The seriously wounded went to the Crab Island hospital; the prisoners (with the exception of Daniel Pring and 47 of the British wounded sent to Canada on parole) went south on 15 September. The squadron itself spent weeks repairing the damage to ships and boats before heading for winter quarters in Whitehall, New York.

In early November Macdonough received orders to command a new steamship in New York Harbor and permission to return to Middletown for reunion with his family. Before leaving, he wrote the senior officer, Lieutenant Budd, directions for his conduct that constitutes a model of a commander's guidance to a subordinate. First Budd was to "be particularly careful to guard against any enterprise of the enemy" on the lake and to protect the "Public property, the Citizens, or their property" from any raids the enemy might make. The commodore emphasized the necessity of caution when at the far northern end of the lake not to be induced into action unless in accompaniment of a superior American land force. Second, Budd was to take the squadron to Whitehall, New York, where the vessels would be "farthest from the enemy land forces during the winter." At this location at the southern end of the lake he was to arrange the vessels so as to best protect their position, to coordinate with the commanding general regarding possible enemy threats, and to remain vigilant at all times.

Third, the commodore cautioned Budd not to make any financial commitments without coordinating with the local purser and the naval agent in New York City. He and his officers and men were to be protective of the government property under his control from theft and fire. In this respect Budd was to see to the maintenance of the sails, vessels, and other government property. Finally, Budd was to adopt those measures necessary to promote the best welfare of the men under his command (especially trying to prevent the "fatal consequences" of intoxication) and to provide against the possible mischief his men might make against local citizens.[9] This long, explicit epistle is a fine example of just how competent Macdonough had become as an senior executive concerned not only with his naval mission but also with his obligations to the welfare of government property, his officers and men, and the local community.

Macdonough's caution about finances was well advised. The national treasury was bare; the nation's credit was nonexistent. Merchants refused to honor charges to the accounts of various federal agencies, including the Department of the Navy. As triumphant as Macdonough might have been, he was unable to cash drafts on the navy because merchants said they would not be paid. Even apothecaries refused medicine to the surgeons caring for the sick and injured among the crews.[10]

At the same time, the squadron's sailors pleaded with Purser Beale for their prize money. "Sailors," Beale wrote in a friendly letter to his commodore, "are not reasonable beings—they know nothing of the wants of the Treasury or of politicks, nor do I believe they care—they ask simply for what they are entitled to and should they be once deceived, it will be a matter of astonishment to me if they ever again re-enter" naval service. Their expectations were great. The final tally of the value of the British squadron was $329,000, of which Macdonough was to receive $22,807—the largest single day's prize awarded during the War of 1812. The commodore could wait for his treasury to be filled; sailors could not. Congress moved faster than the prize courts and specifically authorized the purchase of the British vessels at the value determined by the Navy Department, not the courts. This gave the officers and men of the squadron more money at a faster rate than the courts would allow.[11]

Were this not enough, Lieutenant Perry plagued Macdonough with solicitations for inclusion in the squadron's prize money list. As noted earlier, he was absent from the squadron on the day of the battle as the consequence of illness. When Perry questioned Beale and Macdonough concerning his non-inclusion on the prize list, Macdonough wrote that he had excluded Perry's name because he recalled that the lieutenant had been released from his command and ordered to report to the Department of the Navy for further assignment before the battle. Perry eventually proved that he had been formally assigned to the *Saratoga* until 4 February 1815 and therefore was entitled to prize money. Beale, however, continued to deny him the funds because he was not on the list. On the recommendation of his brother, Commodore Perry, Lieutenant Perry employed the services of noted Norfolk, Virginia, attorney Littleton W. Tazewell to commence action against Beale for the $2,012 he was entitled. Perry eventually received his prize money.[12] If he had not heard of him before, Macdonough would remember Tazewell's name when he found need of a leading practitioner of maritime law.

Macdonough's willingness to acknowledge his mistakes and to see that they were corrected was only one example of the commodore's honesty with himself and others. The case of Acting Lieutenant Drury constitutes an important example of Macdonough's compassion and willingness to give a subordinate another chance. Drury, readers will recall, commanded a patrol that accidentally killed a Vermont tavern keeper. When it appeared state authorities would criminally charge Drury, he fled to Washington, D.C., and secured a reassignment away from the clutches of Vermont law. Macdonough wrote that he thought the death was purely accidental and that Drury should "lay your hand on your heart and acquit your Conscience and feelings to God of being intentionally, directly or indirectly instrumental in the unfortunate occurrence." Should he do so, he would find "the Almighty whose attribute is all goodness . . . [would] forgive one of his children when asked in a humble manner with a heart penitent for the offence." Macdonough promised to bring Drury on his next cruise should he so desire.[13] There is little in his surviving correspondence that so manifests the commodore's deep religious commitment and concern for the well-being of others as this letter does.

As a newly promoted captain and a national hero, Macdonough's former shipmates besieged him for assistance in their careers. Even as Lieutenant Perry sought prize money, he was not too proud to solicit the commodore to write the secretary suggesting he be given command of one of several schooners of war being fitted out that winter. "My Brother," he beseeched, "says in his last letter to me—'Comd. Macdonough can procure you the command of one of these Vessels.'" Purser Beale pleaded for Macdonough to solicit a position on his next ship for himself. All he had to do was to indicate his desire to the secretary and then "just step to the desk of the Chief Clerk and say 'you will write orders for Mr. Beale the purser on Lake Champlain to join my ship'!! The Clerk will write them and hand it to the Secy. For his Signature and the business will be fixed."[14] He would face such requests for the remainder of his career.

Rewards of Victory

For the next several months Macdonough's life would be filled with banquets, toasts, portraits, poems, congratulatory letters, and gifts of real estate, silver, swords, and pistols. Undoubtedly the two he most preferred were the promotion to captain and the prize money.

Cassin also received promotion, to master commandant, but Henley would not obtain what he desired most, advancement to captain. Instead, Cassin would be right behind him on the list of master commandants. Congress ordered that all three have gold medals struck in their honor, a most unusual tribute. Previously there had been two separate gold medals, one issued to Commodore Perry and the other issued to his second in command, Jesse Duncan Elliott, for their action on Lake Erie. Obviously Congress thought Cassin's conduct deserved a singular honor, and Henley could not be ignored.[15]

For Macdonough the next several weeks were filled with congratulatory dinners and laudatory toasts. Poetic praise filled the pages of the national press and numerous flattering articles appeared. The *New York Columbian*'s article on "Our Naval Character" was typical. While the victories of American frigates and Perry's on Lake Erie were the product of American broadside superiority, Macdonough's triumph was one where British preeminence could not "be denied, evaded or misconceived." "Every thing connected with this affair renders it great beyond its scale of action," wrote the *Columbian,* "and it will receive a lustre from the records of time, which can alone do justice to noble achievements."

Gifts of property came his way from grateful cities and states—Albany gave him a lot on Washington Square, New York state awarded him a tract of land in Cayuga County, and Vermont deeded him a tract of land on Cumberland Head that remains in family possession today. New York also provided a sword; Delaware commissioned a portrait by Thomas Sully and awarded him a sword and a gift of silver plate. Of the latter he wrote with a wry sense of humor to his longtime supporter, former congressman Caesar A. Rodney, "Mrs. Macdonough is quite anxious to get the plate into her possession and is fully as much gratified with the present as myself. I believe there is a little competition among our many ladies who can show the most plate." Even antiwar Connecticut belatedly awarded its adopted son a brace of pistols to commemorate "their preservation from imminent public danger."[16]

In his home state the *Delaware Gazette* provided a brief biography which ended with the note that "in a very gloomy moment he answered the hopes of his countrymen, and in a radiance of glory dispelled the menacing storm. But it was not he! It was the Lord of Hosts who stooped to show an offending nation, in a moment of despondence, that he will listen to the prayers and nerve of the arm of a Christian Hero." It is clear that Macdonough's religious emphasis received considerable support in the nation at large. Macdonough reinforced that perception when, at a dinner in Albany, he acknowledged the praise of the mayor and citizens by graciously commenting that the victory was the consequence of the "individual exertions and conduct of my brave companions in arms, under Divine Providence."[17]

Equally important to the emerging Macdonough symbolism was the famous cock that crowed in the *Saratoga*'s rigging during the battle. The *Naval Monument* recorded the event thusly: "In the hottest of the action, a cock in the commodore's ship flew into the shrouds, and crowed three times! The crew seized the happy omen, and shouted *victory!* This little incident must have had a powerful effect on the seamen." At a celebration in Middletown, one of the decorations was a gilded figure of a cock, which according to the local newspaper had "crowed undauntedly throughout the action."[18] This fighting cock became a recurring theme in the mythology accorded the Lake Champlain victory.

Family Life

On 10 December 1814, Macdonough returned home to Middletown, where he found Lucy Ann with their six-week-old son Thomas Nathaniel. This was her second childbirth. The first died shortly after his birth in 1813. Thomas N. Macdonough lived only until 26 June 1815. "Two sweet boys have I now lost in less than two years," the commodore wrote his sister Lydia. Lucy Ann (Shaler) Macdonough went through nine pregnancies during her twelve-year marriage and delivered ten children. Of those, five died before they were three. The five survivors were James Edward (1814–1849), the surviving twin Charles Shaler (1818–1871), Augustus Rodney (1820–1907), Thomas (1822–1894), and Charlotte Rosella (1825–1900).

Most of the sadness of the loss of children lay in the future. At this point the young couple could be optimistic about their fortunes. They had spent much of their first two winters together in Vergennes, where she found society much less cultured than in Connecticut and the mud so deep one could not be sociable if one desired. The lack of suitable accommodations for a lady of her background, her first pregnancies, and the commodore's need to devote full time to naval duties ("his public duties are the first and nearly all with him," she wrote her mother) resulted in Ann's going to Middletown for the summers and her confinements. Now they could renew their union with less interference—or so it seemed. But to a naval officer of Macdonough's sense of duty, public service that meant separation from his spouse was a part of his obligation. The unfortunate loss of his first two children wrote John McDonough to his brother, "is the work of the Lord. He had given you and he has taken away from you. You have confidence in Him and consequently fortitude to bear trials of that description."

The apprehensions of a navy wife at having to go through childbirth without a husband's presence were tenderly expressed in a letter Ann wrote her longtime friend Abbey Hortense Chew in 1816: "Having twice passed through this painful scene in his absence, I feel particularly solicitous to have him with me [this third time]. The horrid idea of leaving the world without bidding him farewell increased my suffering greatly...and now I feel as if I wanted him here to receive my adieu—or to welcome my little stranger." Macdonough came to Middletown for the birth of the third child and reported with satisfaction back to a friend in Portsmouth that she "has a fine son who with herself are doing well." As Ann feared, her last pregnancy ended with the birth of their only surviving daughter and with her death a few weeks later without his being present.[19]

Although the commodore lacked enthusiasm for an assignment to command the world's first naval steamship, *Fulton First*, a posting in New York would probably mean that the couple would be together and be close to her mother's Denning relatives in that city. There Macdonough also would be commanded by one of the navy's most respected officers, Stephen Decatur. Before this could happen the national command authority received notice that new dangers threatened the squadron in Whitehall. The British desired to make an over-the-ice raid on the squadron. Macdonough urgently went northward, found that the threat had passed, and returned to Middletown. In a letter to Secretary of the Navy Crowninshield, Macdonough stated he desired not to be placed in command of the lake. This appeal reflected a growing concern with his health that begins to appear in his correspondence with the Navy Department.[20]

Although Macdonough desired a sea command, he did not receive one. Instead, relieved of the *Fulton First* assignment, he took command of the navy yard in Portsmouth, New Hampshire, in July 1815. Shortly thereafter the Macdonoughs moved into their newly completed official residence.

They also began their long support of various family members through financial difficulties. In 1815 he had stopped by the Trap en route from Washington to Middletown. There he met with family and friends for one of the last times in his life. But he never forgot their welfare. In particular, he lent his brother John McDonough of Queen Anne's County, Maryland, over $2,000 in 1815–17 that Thomas did not expect to be returned "unless [John] should become rich." He admitted to his older sister Lydia Roberts that he was "almost as much a stranger to the situation of the younger parts of our family as a man would be who had never heard of them." Yet from 1818 to 1823 he took extraordinary care and expense to educate James Thomas McDonough, son of his deceased brother Samuel, at one of Connecticut's premier boarding schools. This young man he found to be "a smart boy, looks well, and learns well. I hope he will make a good and capable man." The expenses amounted to over $600. Concurrently, Ann looked after her siblings. In one instance she assumed a debt of $331 from her brother William D. Shaler.[21]

The time in Portsmouth should have been among the more enjoyable years in Macdonough's career. He and Ann resided in comfortable quarters and should have enjoyed each other's companionship during a lengthy shore assignment. Instead, the death of his father-in-law and Ann's "continued ill health" required her to return to Middletown and compelled him to spend much of the summer of 1817 in Connecticut. Although he returned to Portsmouth that fall, he was in Middletown on a leave of absence again in December. While he was stationed at Portsmouth, Thomas and Ann began building a home in Middletown on property acquired from her father's estate. For the rest of their lives this commodious edifice remained their permanent residence.[22]

With money and time, the Macdonoughs in all probability began seriously collecting a large library. The diversity of their intellectual curiosity was significant. They particularly liked the history and travel literature relating to the places to which he was going. Thus, they owned Charles Rollin's six-volume *Ancient History* in one of the several English editions of this famous French work and Rollin's Roman history in French. Other histories included Oliver Goldsmith's *History of Greece* and Edward Gibbon's *Decline and Fall of the Roman Empire*. It is highly probable that the "History of the Reformation" on the estate list was an edition of Anglican Bishop Gilbert Burnet's *History of the Reformation of the Church of England*. Travel literature included Thomas S. Surr's three-volume *Winter in London* (1806), Robert Southey's equally long *Letters from England* (1808), and John Moore's *Residence in France* (1794).

There were numerous volumes of poetry and literature. Sir Walter Scott was a favorite of the Macdonoughs. Their library included his poetic *Marmion* (1808), *The Lady of the Lake* (1810), and *The Lord of the Isle* (1815) as well as his novel *Guy Mannering* (1815). Another British novel was Daniel Defoe's *Robinson Crusoe*. Two early American novels graced their collection, Hugh Henry Brackenridge's *Modern Chivalry* (1792) and James Fenimore Cooper's *Lionel Lincoln* (1824). The couple regularly subscribed to the *North American Review*. These tomes were part of a long list of literary works, including three poetic volumes by Alexander Pope plus his translation of the *Odyssey*, and the poems of Elizabeth Denning (one of Ann's cousins), Richard Glover, John Milton, William Sotheby, and William Thompson. In addition there were such titles as *English Bards*, *Arabian Nights*, John Dryden's *Fables Ancient and Modern* (1700), and Samuel Johnson's dictionary and his *Lives of the Most Eminent English Poets*. Particularly unusual was James Macpherson's purported translation of the third-century Gaelic poet Ossian. They owned several editions of Greek, French, and Italian grammars and dictionaries. They admired the classics and owned editions of the works of Homer, Euclid, Virgil, Plutarch, and Juvenal. It is interesting that no volume of Shakespeare appeared in the inventory; perhaps they used the one owned by her father.

There were the assorted professional volumes. One of the more prominent was Thomas Smith's six-volume set, *The Scientific Library, or, Repository of Useful and Polite Literature: Comprising Astronomy, Geography, Mythology, Ancient History, Modern History, and Chronology* (New York, 1818). The nautical books included one of James Ferguson's astronomy texts, U.S. Navy surgeon Usher Parson's *Sailor's Physician, Elements of Drawing*, one of Richard Brookes's *General Gazetteer* volumes, and an edition of James Walker's geographic atlases. Government documents included copies of naval regulations, laws of the United States, Richard Radcliffe's edition of President James Monroe's speeches titled *The President's Tour* (1822), and a reprint of Connecticut's famous 1650 *Blue Laws*.

Religious writings were prominent in the Macdonough collection. These included an edition of Richard Baxter's *Saints Everlasting Rest*, William Law's *Practical Treatise upon Christian Perfection* (1726), John Smith's *Triumph of Religion Over Infidelity* (1813), Lindley Murray's *Power of Religion* (1818), John Flavel's *Navigation Spiritualized*, and books on Newtonian philosophy, plus several Bibles and prayer books. Their interests went beyond Church of England divines. The collection contained an English edition of French bishop John Massillon's sermons, English dissenting minister Philip Doddridge's *Rise and Progress,* and John Bunyan's old reliable *Pilgrim's Progress.* Two volumes of the works of North Haven's Congregational minister, the Reverend Benjamin Trumbull, graced their shelves. Religious periodicals included volumes of the *Christian Observer* and *Christian Journal.* The family received from Ann's brother-in-law, the Rev. Edward Rutledge, a copy of his *History of the Church of England* (Middletown, Conn., 1825). Given the deaths of half of their children, Thomas and Ann sought solace in Edward Young's *Night Thoughts on Life, Death, and Immortality,* which had been published in many editions over the previous seventy-five years.[23]

This was the library of an inquisitive young couple. Its very breadth and depth testified to the cerebral concern fostered in them by Ann's father and continued throughout their married life. With little formal education, they educated themselves liberally and chose an intermixture of belle lettres and practical readings reflecting great credit upon themselves. This partial list dramatizes their wide-ranging curiosity and acquaintanceship with the intellectual life of their day surpassing that of many of those whose schooling was more extensive. Their collection exhibited an eclectic choice of volumes ranging from contemporary literature to classical utilitarianism to Christian ethics and professional development. No wonder that Macdonough evidenced a stoicism, self-confidence, and determination that distinguished him from many of his fellow officers.

Moreover, the young couple understood that their children needed a broad education, and they fostered that interest in Macdonough's young relatives. Even though both parents died before their children reached their teens, the commodore hoped to provided them with "as good an education as I am able to." In 1822 Macdonough described with typical parental pride his four surviving sons as "smart, intelligent, well-behaved children." The next year he sent his son Edward to boarding school with Hezekiah Case of Simsbury, Connecticut. The final determination in the education of his children lay with the Middletown Probate Court. That court placed the children in the care of Ann's sisters and their husbands.[24]

Throughout the decade after the War of 1812, the couple faced serious health problems. Both seem to have contracted chronic tuberculosis, which the family blamed on the long tour the commodore underwent on Lake Champlain. However, it may be that he contracted the disease at the time he had yellow fever in Havana. Puberty is a period of low resistance to the bacillus, and Macdonough was a teenager at this time. The description of the Havana "hospital" where he stayed indicates that this might have been the most environmentally contagious time of his life. The infection could have remained largely in remission until reactivated by the environment and stress imposed by his command on the northern lake. Unlike many infectious diseases, the tubercle bacillus does not produce immunity to it. Instead, exposure at an early age often leads to relatively high mortality rates in middle age. Crowding increases chances of an infection, and the disease was especially prevalent among seamen who lived in crowded conditions. On the other hand, urbanization does not appear to have been an important factor in tuberculosis mortality rates. Instead, sparsely populated rural areas with substandard living conditions often have greater incidence of the disease than urban ones. Thus it may well have been the conditions around frontier Lake Champlain where quarters were primitive and crowded and might have been a factor in their acquiring the disease. Poor nutrition plays a key role in the etiology of the disease, but it is hard to imagine that this middle class couple suffered from malnutrition. We have no record as to whether Macdonough smoked, something which would have aggravated his condition. While climate was long considered a factor in the disease's pathogenesis, recent studies find that temperature, humidity, and other climatic factors do not influence either its risk of development or its course.

Tuberculosis was common among eighteenth- and nineteenth-century seamen. A detailed study of its impact has not been made of U.S. Navy personnel, but studies of Russian and Finnish sailors dying in Britain indicates it was the most common cause of death among enlisted men. Physician Sir Gilbert Blane (1749–1834) argued that tuberculosis was on the increase to such a degree that it had become as widespread as the scourge of seamen as scurvy had been. Since most American officers dying of the disease presumably were on shore leave at the time of their death, its incidence afloat was not as high has one might expect. Historian J. Worth Estes indicates that over 20 percent of all navy personnel dying at Portsmouth, New Hampshire, and Boston between 1801 and 1820 were tubercular.[25]

Commodore Macdonough suffered from the most common form of the disease, pulmonary tuberculosis, or consumption as it was called at the time. Its most prevalent symptom is a frequent and violent cough producing sputum often streaked with blood. Other manifestations include fatigue, lethargy, chills, sweating, and low-grade fevers. His condition may have been intensified by his bout with yellow fever during his first year of naval service. Tuberculosis often has a progressive phase followed by periods of quiescence. This appears to have been Macdonough's experience. In its subsidence phase the recovered portion of the lung walls off the infected area. Stress or other factors can cause the walled off area to open up and the disease spreads again.

The disease is transmitted normally by the inhalation of droplets coughed or sneezed into the air by persons, like the commodore, with pulmonary tuberculosis. Assuming Thomas had the disease first, Ann may have contracted it from him. Undoubtedly her continued pregnancies had a debilitating effect upon her health. Childbearing lowers the resistance to infection and therefore induces or aggravates the disease. Tuberculosis in infants occurs almost always after birth by contact with the mother or another adult with the disease. Thus the early deaths of some of their children might be attributed to the presence of tuberculosis in the household.[26] Whenever the disease entered the family, it had a tremendous impact on the remainder of the Macdonoughs lives and contributed to their relatively early deaths.

Portsmouth Navy Yard Commander

News of the peace brought Macdonough a new assignment as commander of the Portsmouth Navy Yard. He arrived there on 3 July 1815 and found the post undermanned and the exact nature of his duties uncertain. He held this post for three years.[27]

At Portsmouth he relieved Isaac Hull and immediately plunged into the varied and numerous duties of the commander of such an installation. With him were several veterans of the Lake Champlain campaign—Joseph Smith, Walter Monteith, and Joel Abbot. His marine commander was Capt. Archibald Henderson, soon to become a famous commandant of that corps. Most of the duties there were routine and mundane but necessary matters that confront those in such a position. They included condemning 191 barrels of rancid pork sent from Norfolk to Portsmouth because of the "manifest inattention on the part of some person." Another issue involved problems of paying the carpenters of the yard. A third concerned the charges for iron work on the USS *Washington,* a new seventy-four-gun vessel currently being fitted out in his yard. Still another problem involved securing blocks for the *Washington* in Boston when they were unavailable in Portsmouth. And so it went through 1815, 1816, 1817, and into 1818.[28]

While in this post, Macdonough constantly found himself confronting pleas from former members of the Lake Champlain squadron or their families. In 1816, for instance, he recommended Midn. Joseph L. Cannon for promotion to lieutenant. In 1818, he gave advice on how to secure a pension for the widow of one of his officers in that campaign.[29] One of the most poignant supplications came from Elizabeth Brum, widow of Philip Brum, the *Saratoga*'s sailing master. Her solicitors begged Macdonough to intercede for a pension for his widow because of an injury received in the battle. Unfortunately, at the time it was considered too insignificant to classify as a wound, so Mrs. Brum was deemed ineligible for a pension. Macdonough replied immediately with a statement that Brum received a blow from a splinter during the action and Macdonough asked him if he was much hurt. The sailing master replied faintly that he hoped not too much and shortly thereafter returned to his duties. However, Macdonough subsequently heard him complain of the injury and claim that he was "fully of the opinion that he was entitled to a pension."[30]

During his tour at Portsmouth, Macdonough frequently made trips for the government to various locations. These included an 1816 inspection tour of Lake Champlain to assist the U.S. Army Corps of Engineers plan for fortifications for that lake's defenses. His efforts contributed to the decision to build Fort Montgomery at Rouses Point, New York. Much of the concern over northern defenses abated after the Rush-Bagot Agreement of 1817, which limited naval armaments on the inland seas. The squadron Macdonough constructed and captured slowly rotted away in the harbor at Whitehall.[31]

All of these reflected the normal duties of a senior officer assigned to command a shore station. There was no military glory in such routine responsibilities, but much professionalism develops in the successful performance of these charges.

Following Macdonough's cruise on the *Guerrière* discussed in the following chapter, Macdonough spent most of 1820–24 in command of the USS *Ohio*, a vessel that never went to sea during his posting. Therefore he spent most of this time in Middletown. There were, however, frequent trips on official business, among them a December 1822 journey to New York City for a court of inquiry regarding Capt. Samuel Evans and a March 1824 trip to Norfolk, Virginia, to sit on a court-martial.

By this time the commodore's investments, especially in Bank of the United States and in Middletown Bank stock, were paying handsome dividends. At the end of 1821 he had cash assets amounting to $5,321.85. Prior to his departure on the *Constitution* in 1824, he settled his accounts with the Navy Department and most of his creditors. His meticulous account books recorded detailed expenses and receipts. He carefully accounted for each day's expenses down to the penny. There must have been a certain smile on his face after debiting his wife's account $200.00 to purchase furniture in New York for their Middletown house and then noting eight days later her return of $14.35 in an unexpended balance.[32]

During these latter years there are indications that the couple and their growing family took vacations to escape the humid summers in Connecticut. For instance, in 1820 the Macdonoughs summered at Saratoga Springs, New York, and Lake Champlain. In the fall of 1822 he toured western New York to Niagara Falls, crossed Lake Ontario, and descended the St. Lawrence to Quebec. He took great pride in negotiating the rapids of that river in a bateau.[33]

The decade following the battle witnessed Macdonough's growing commitment to Christ Episcopal Church in Middletown. Twice he represented the congregation at the diocesan convention. In 1820 he made a temporary loan of ninety dollars to the churchwardens, which they repaid two months later. When a destructive hurricane hit Middletown in September 1821, Macdonough headed a committee to replace the spire of the church, which had collapsed into Main Street. Presumably the vestry felt that someone who knew how to raise a mast would know how to replace a steeple. After many debates over whether it should be a tower, dome, or cupola, they substituted the fallen steeple with one of lower height.[34]

Perhaps the best description of Macdonough's piety came in the funeral address for him: "His religion was not a garment to be assumed or laid aside as *taste* or *convenience* might dictate. It was not an air of solemnity that pervaded him only when in the society of the Good: It was not a current feeling which commenced and terminated within the precincts of the Sanctuary: But it was an essential part of his character; an indispensable in his very being: he appeared on no occasion without it."[35] Few could ask that more be said about their religious beliefs.

The commodore's concept of religion was one of moderation, not abstinence. Nowhere was this better noted than in an exchange in 1822, when Commo. Thomas Tingey at the Washington Navy Yard forwarded through Purser Thomas I. Chew a barrel of "Old Columbia" for "our old friend Captain Macdonough." Macdonough paid Chew twenty-six dollars for the whiskey.

At another time his youthful prank with the church bell in New Castle, Delaware, caught up with him. James Booth and Henry Colesberry wrote Macdonough in early 1822 as representatives of a committee of Immanuel Episcopal Church soliciting funds for its maintenance and expansion. In particular, they made reference (without any allusion to Macdonough's participation in the incident) to a need for a new bell—"that which formerly belonged to the church having been broken many years ago and never replaced." The wardens and vestry of the parish authorized this committee to solicit a contribution from nonmembers, and they wrote him "being a native citizen of this State." We do not know if he petitioned others involved in the bell's destruction, but Macdonough's account book notes that he sent thirty dollars to the committee.[36]

More important, command of the *Ohio* laid up in ordinary in the Brooklyn Navy Yard frustrated a man of Macdonough's professional temperament. He desired sea duty. In January 1822 he wrote the secretary of the navy, "I consider myself too young to remain so long inactive on shore. I have seen but little [sea] service of late . . . and am desirous of employing myself in the arts of my profession." He sought command of the *Constitution* on its next rotation. Knowing that that rotation took place the following year, in September 1823 he wrote again: "I have long since considered it a point of duty an officer owes his country to keep in exercise and a state of improvement his professional faculties in order that he may the better perform such services as may be required of him." Finally, eight months later, he received orders to report to New York and take command of the most famous frigate in the navy, the USS *Constitution*. Despite his declining health and Ann's ninth pregnancy he took up the responsibilities of command with enthusiasm; a sailor should go down to the sea in a ship.[37]

The years ashore from 1814 until Macdonough took command of the *Guerrière* in 1818, and from the time he returned from that cruise in 1820 until he went to sea with the *Constitution* in 1824, were particularly important in the lives of Thomas and Ann Macdonough. During this time their family grew and shrank; tears often followed their joys. Their fortunes rose with his promotion, his prize money, and the gifts of land combined with her inheritance to provide a generous livelihood for the young couple. They built a large home in Middletown and participated actively in church and community life. They demonstrated a Christian charity toward numerous relatives. Their intellectual horizons expanded. Thomas's naval reputation and Ann's relatives' status opened doors to the highest levels of government and society.

But a cloud of chronic illness loomed over them. Despite their relative youth and social position, they both declined in health during the decade following the Lake Champlain victory. The commodore and his family hoped the tour to the Mediterranean would help him recover his health. It was a gamble, but one Macdonough willingly undertook.[38]

Chapter Seven

Cruise of the Guerrière

Columbia! Though thy cannon's roar
  On inland seas prevail,
And there alone—while round each shore
  Outnumbering ships assail.

Yet deed with deed, and name with name
  Thy gallant sons shall blend,
Till the bright arch of naval fame,
  O'er the broad ocean bend!
    "Battle of Plattsburgh, and Victory on Lake Champlain"

THROUGHOUT THE PORTSMOUTH assignment, 1815–18, Macdonough's family worried not just about Lucy Ann's health but also about the commodore's continuing physical decline. They urged him to secure a command in a warm climate, and the Mediterranean was thought to be the most desirable. Accordingly, he obtained orders (25 April 1818) to command the almost new forty-four-gun frigate *Guerrière* at Boston. The vessel's initial assignment was to deliver the American ambassador to Russia to St. Petersburg. Later it was to join the U.S. Mediterranean Squadron.[1]

Preparing the Guerrière for its Cruise

Named for the French-built, Royal Navy–captured vessel that the USS *Constitution* defeated and burned during the War of 1812, the new *Guerrière* was a fine frigate of 1,507 tons carrying four hundred officers and men. Its one previous cruise was as Stephen Decatur's flagship in the Mediterranean. A London paper described the *Guerrière* as having equipment "most complete and effective for the purpose of defense or aggression. . . . She is remarkably clean but nothing appears to be made for mere show. Her bits are extremely large and every rope is led through a separate block; each has its own belaying pin." On *Guerrière's* main deck were mounted "thirty long twenty-four pounders, on the quarterdeck fourteen forty-two pounder carronades and two long twenty-four pounders, and on the forecastle forty-two pounder carronades and two long twenty-four pounders."

(Like many American warships of the era, it carried more armament than it was rated as having.) British admiration continued with remarks that the "tackles are rove through various large sheaved blocks, which considerably lightens the labor and renders the guns capable of being worked much quicker than in our ships. The trucks of the gun carriages are of larger diameter and the axle-trees are much longer, and effectually prevent the guns from upsetting."[2] In giving its command to Macdonough, the navy had awarded him one of the prime vessels on its list. Such an assignment was indeed a compliment to his reputation.

This assignment also gave Macdonough an opportunity to reward those careers he hoped to further. In particular, he wanted Joseph Smith as his first lieutenant. He had promised Smith such a posting if it became available and he hoped to have him assigned over Lt. William H. Allen, who was currently on board. Besides Smith, he requested Secretary of the Navy Benjamin W. Crowninshield order a series of lieutenants, sailing masters, a surgeon, surgeon mates, and midshipmen whose promise he thought merited such an assignment. Crowninshield granted a substantial portion of this request, four of six lieutenants, eight of fourteen midshipmen, and the surgeon from Macdonough's list. Five of the officers had served at Lake Champlain: Smith, Lieutenants Vallette, Abbot, and Conover, and Midn. Charles T. Platt.

Vice President Daniel D. Tompkins, the wartime governor of New York, prevailed upon the Navy Department to warrant his son as a midshipman and to ship him on the *Guerrière*. And the department's chief clerk, Benjamin Homan, could not forego urging Macdonough to take his nephew along as clerk. Homan concluded that if the *Guerrière's* captain accepted his kin, he would be under "very Great obligations" to Macdonough for the favor.[3] While such solicitations were normal, that the vice president would trust his son and the senior civilian in the Navy Department his nephew to Macdonough's ship said much about the Hero of Lake Champlain's reputation in the highest levels of the government.

While acquiring officers and midshipman was easy, securing the vessel's blue jackets proved a difficult task. Macdonough received forty men from the *Independence*, but those sent him by Capt. David Deacon he found to be "worse than they had been reported to be." These included "one, two or more negroes from the states Prison well calculated to keep the ships company...in disorder, the master at arms, [was] to all appearance a confirmed drunkard, a disorderly Irishman." With Capt. Isaac Hull he quarreled over the assignment of a boatswain who was an aged and "habitual drunkard."

Still, by 9 July Macdonough had 350 sailors and 45 marines. On the whole he found the men to be "light and an unusual number of them boys."[4]

Even so, Macdonough turned his attention to instructing them in their duties. He ordered each midshipman to have a quadrant, case of instruments, and a book in which to keep their computations and observations. Except when on watch, midshipmen were to attend the classes of the chaplain, Philander Chase Jr., from 1000 hours until noon and from 1400 until 1600. A year later he told the midshipmen that his intention toward them had been "the improvement of your knowledge in the duties of your profession." Such devotion required them "to devote all your leisure hours when not on Deck to the study of such books as relate to your profession, & when on deck to the duties going forward there, so as to make yourselves well acquainted therewith." He hoped they would all eventually "hold the highest rank in the service gained by industry, virtue and sobriety." Finally, he urged them to "keep aloof from the many temptations which you are exposed to, take care of your constitutions, . . . improve yourselves in all usefull and, in your professions, all necessary learning, and in some future day you will hold a conspicuous ground in the affections of your country."[5] It is doubtful that there were any officers more concerned than Macdonough was about the education and welfare of the "young gentlemen" in his crew. From Macdonough's point of view, the selection of young Chase proved most fortunate. After a year on board the *Guerrière*, Chase left the vessel to return to the United States and a career as an Episcopal minister. Before he departed, Macdonough heaped praise upon his performance as clerk and schoolmaster. As chaplain, his "discourses and example" provided a model of Christian responsibility the ship's captain proudly asserted. Macdonough knew most naval commanders lacked appreciation of chaplains, but he felt Chase's religious efforts gratified all the Guerrières. As for his instructional achievements, Macdonough knew that someday the young gentlemen would with fond remembrance recall Chase's "mathematical labours towards them, with feelings of great regard." "Our Sundays," concluded Macdonough, "I fear, will be differently passed, and like others, we shall forget the good and endearing customs of our native land." The *Guerrière*'s captain had every reason to be proud of his selection of a chaplain who met his every expectation for excellence. Following ordination, Chase went south to seek a healthier climate. He died a few weeks before his twenty-fifth birthday in 1824 and was buried in St. Michael's churchyard in Charleston, South Carolina. Macdonough's brother-in-law, the Rev. Edward Rutledge, preached the funeral oration.[6]

Several records of the *Guerrière's* cruise survive. The journal of Surgeon Parsons and the autobiography of Midn. Charles Wilkes (who would later become famous as the leader of an Antarctic exploration expedition) are among these. Unfortunately the Parsons journal is less useful than it was when he was with Perry on the Great Lakes and in the Mediterranean. He left blank pages for "Remarks &c. on Russia" but never filled them in, and most of his Mediterranean observations concern medical facilities. Midshipman Wilkes's memoirs are much more beneficial. Wilkes found himself assigned to the *Independence* in Boston Harbor and requested a transfer to the *Guerrière*. At first abruptly dismissed by Commo. William Bainbridge when he submitted his request for transfer, Wilkes later found himself invited to sip a soda with the commodore in Boston at which time Bainbridge wrote out an order reassigning him to Macdonough's command. He left a memoir concerning both the voyage and the controversies in the U.S. squadron.

A third journal is that of young Chase. The nineteen-year-old chaplain's journal provides the most detailed description of the journey from an individual who had particularly close ties to the Macdonough family. The Reverend Philander Chase, the elder, had trained Macdonough for confirmation and an intimate friend of the younger Chase was the Reverend Edward Rutledge, who was married to Macdonough's sister-in-law. While his father was moving westward, where he became the first Episcopal Bishop of Ohio, the younger Chase finished his courses at Harvard College and secured the position with Macdonough. That a religious leader of Bishop Chase's reputation should allow his son to go to sea under Macdonough's command says much about the reputation of the *Guerrière's* captain. Unfortunately, the Chase journal describes none of the internal politics of the ship that one finds in the Wilkes account.

Constantly on Macdonough's mind as the commander of a warship were preparations for combat. The lieutenants commanding gun divisions were to exercise their crews twice daily, and there was to be a general exercise of guns three times a week. Even so, in November Macdonough grew anxious about the state of the *Guerrière's* gunnery. He wrote his first lieutenant what for the taciturn Macdonough was a long letter discussing his views on the importance of this facet of seamanship:

> The desirable qualities of a man of war are the management of her Guns with celerity and precision and of her sails with regularity and alertness. These qualities give her the character of efficiency in battle and of reputation as a smart ship, and can only be attained by pride, practice and close attention on the part

of those, whom, placed as the chiefs of divisions, and on the quarter Deck, have the immediate execution of those duties respectively. The time of peace is the time to prepare for war, then when it arrives all is ready. I cannot therefore too urgently recommend minute attention to the Guns by the Divisional officers, in learning the men the nature and effect of them; it will at any rate be very usefull to our Navy generally on some future day, which is our duty to look to & which is a matter of no small consideration as in its reputation we are all intimately concerned. Our Guns are, I believe, worked very well, but this is not all; I fear the men have not that knowledge of their direction which is much to be wished and also in working both sides at the same time.[7]

This attention to naval proficiency was the hallmark of Macdonough's command style.

As was normal under such circumstances, Macdonough received numerous letters from parents either soliciting a position on the ship or hoping that the errant individual might be released from naval service. For instance, Justus Robbins of Rocky Hill, Connecticut, pleaded that his fifteen-year-old son be placed in some capacity on board and under the captain's "immediate Eye, Care, & Protection." The widowed mother of landsman John Frost advised through a friend that his "warrant officers . . . observe his conduct; and not . . . place any confidence in him until he shall be found to merit it" because he previously exhibited habits of intemperance and relished low company. On the other hand, Elizabeth Glaiser of Portland, Maine, pleaded that her son Beamsley be discharged, as he was her only support for the family. These were the typical solicitations for a commanding officer.[8]

Macdonough also sought to expand his knowledge of the region to which he was being sent. We are not privy to when or where he purchased a *History of Russia*, the author of which is now unidentifiable, and what was probably Pavel Petrovich Sviniin's *Sketches of Russia* (London, 1814). However, their very presence in his library indicates the depth of his intellectual curiosity. One easily imagines he purchased them either in Boston or in England.[9]

Cruise to St. Petersburg

By 30 June 1818 the *Guerrière* was ready to sail, but the American ambassador to Russia was not on board. Macdonough grew impatient. He soon became irritated at the ambassador and his entourage. Ambassador George Washington Campbell's party contained his wife, three small children, and servants. In addition the government sent Dr. Samuel L. Mitchell and "other scientific Gentlemen . . . [plus] sundry articles as presents to the Emperor of Russia" including a plough. Campbell politely requested Macdonough provide "supplies of every kind, wine etc." and two milk goats (for his children) be laid on his account which would be paid on his arrival in Boston. But when the ambassador finally arrived, he paid only eight hundred dollars of the two thousand Macdonough had spent. He said eight hundred of the remainder would be paid by the State Department. The remaining four hundred dollars Macdonough billed to his own account. Three years later the eight-hundred-dollar bill Campbell said would be remitted by the State Department remained unpaid. Neither the State Department nor Navy Department would reimburse Macdonough for Campbell's expenses. An exasperated Homan wrote Macdonough that "an honorable man would shrink into a nutshell rather than have" this deficiency "explained to the world." The only other recourse was to expose Campbell by a suit in the court to "expose his meanness." The tangled outcome of this all lay in the future. Meanwhile, Campbell's party came aboard, crowding officers and midshipmen even more than normal and making for a very tense situation. Finally, Silas E. Burrows of the State Department joined the vessel en route to Sweden with dispatches.[10]

The *Guerrière* at last left Boston on 24 July and soon exhibited a disposition to crank—a tendency to threaten to overturn when carrying too much sail caused by a lack of ballast. Although the Charlestown Navy Yard had reportedly installed 130 tons of ballast, Macdonough found there was "no shingle ballast in the ship." The problem persisted throughout the voyage to St. Petersburg. He ordered *Guerrière*'s guns housed inboard as much as possible in order to keep it balanced. Macdonough improvised ballast by sending casks of seawater and two 24-pounder cannon from the forecastle into the hold. He concluded that some of the "iron ballast was taken out at Charlestown and either taken for some other vessel, otherwise disposed of in the yard." One wonders why neither Macdonough nor Smith discovered this situation before their vessel left port. While in Russia, Macdonough had forty tons of iron ballast loaded on board to correct the problem.

Naval regulations required that a ship's crew go to quarters whenever it met a foreign warship. The waters of the English Channel, North Sea, and Baltic were particularly crowded with such vessels. One night the drummers beat to quarters for the first time after dark and confusion reigned: "No lights in the battle lanterns, no tubs & casks for the gunners, and the gratings & powder boxes, match tubs, shot racks & the extra articles required were no where to be found." Midshipman Wilkes admired Macdonough's coolness under the circumstances. The commodore's only words were, "By zounds this must not happen again. We must be prepared for such events." Soon such nighttime exercises became commonplace and the time required to go to quarters went down from five minutes to fifty seconds.[11]

Beginning 8 August the ship faced strong breezes from the north; these so-called Chops of the English Channel precluded an easy journey into Spithead off the coast of southern England. Ambassador and Mrs. Campbell became ill from the ship's motion. Finally they anchored off Cowes on the twenty-first, and the ambassador and his wife went ashore to recoup. From his view on the quarterdeck, Chase described the country through which they sailed—"the county of Hampshire on the north—the beautiful town and church of Christ Church, Poole Harbour, the Hurst Castle on the left and on the bow the high bluff of the Isle of Wight with its light." He later observed the towns of Portsmouth and Spithead "with the English fleet lying there at anchor" which "formed a prospect truly grand."[12]

While in the Spithead roadstead for four days, *Guerrière* received a number of distinguished guests, including Adm. Sir George Campbell, commander in chief at Portsmouth, Lord Spencer, formerly of the admiralty, and the Marquis of Buckingham. Undoubtedly these individuals wanted to view the new and highly acclaimed American frigate as well as meet the captain who had beaten one of their squadrons. Chase indicated that the *Guerrière* "swarmed with company. . . . English officers of the Army and Navy of every description, Gentry, Nobility, Commonality, & rabble continually thronged our decks." The crew went ashore on the Isle of Wight and took a quick tour of Portsmouth Harbor, during which Nelson's Trafalgar flagship, HMS *Victory*, was anchored. The famous vessel made little impression on Wilkes. Upon leaving Spithead, the *Guerrière* found good southwesterly breezes and the ship moved quickly past the cliffs of Dover, up the North Sea, and through the Cattegat Strait to Elsinore, Denmark, where it anchored in the sound with a view of the famous Cronenburg Castle on 30 August. One wonders if visions of Hamlet flew through Macdonough's head as he gazed on the edifice. The next day they anchored in Copenhagen, gave a nineteen-gun salute, and the ambassador's suite went ashore. Before they left Chaplain Chase went ashore and found to his surprise that the ladies of Denmark were lovelier than those in America. "Happily," he recorded, "I fell in love with none of them."[13]

In Copenhagen *Guerrière* picked up a Baltic Sea pilot named Peter Hee who would be an important augmentation to the crew during the next phase of the cruise. The Baltic was new to Macdonough, numerous vessels sailed the often-dangerous waters, and the potential for fog remained high. When *Guerrière* entered the Gulf of Finland the fog "became so thick that we could hardly see from stern to the bow of the ship." Macdonough appreciated having Hee aboard. Running a course through the middle of this gulf, sailing past Revel (Tallinn, Estonia), *Guerrière* arrived at the Kronshtadt anchorage on 13 September 1818. Chase's conclusion must have been echoed by all on board: "The navigation of the Gulf is most dreadfully difficult. The winds change so suddenly and the shoals so numerous that it requires all the skill of the most experienced pilot to keep a vessel afloat."

During their brief stay, the crew took the steam ferry from Kronshtadt to St. Petersburg. The city's architecture and wide streets impressed Wilkes and Chase, but they found the community lacking vitality because there was little commercial and residential life. "Each block of houses has its guard house and guard as a police & these are constantly alive turning out the guard for any and all officers who may happen to pass, and this gives a kind of military despotism feeling to the stranger," wrote the young midshipman. Even the market "savored of despotic or imperial will, and there did not appear that liberty of trade which in all Marts gives life and activity to the Scene." Capt. Lyman Kellogg, the marine commander on board, confirmed his reputation as "an eccentric character, very vain and punctilious in all he did." Kellogg put on his dress uniform with a very long feather in his hat, hired a barouche, and rode around the city causing the guard of each block to be turned out for what appeared to a high-ranking official from some strange country.[14]

As expected, there was much ceremony in St. Petersburg. When the ambassador left *Guerrière*, Macdonough had manned the yards with the crew and fired a salute on the envoy's departure. Of course, Macdonough visited the commander of the Kronshtadt naval yard and he entertained a number of visitors aboard his ship, including Prince Labanoff, an aid to the Emperor Alexander. In the capital city itself, the Russians honored Macdonough with a review involving ten thousand exceptionally well dressed and disciplined soldiers. With the diplomatic personnel gone, the crew could now repair to their normal quarters. The officers' living conditions would be more comfortable for the remainder of the cruise.[15]

In a strange twist of circumstances, sailors in a navy that had just fought a war with the United Kingdom to secure sailors' rights now deserted the

Guerrière to join the Royal Navy. This is exactly what happened in Kronshtadt. Macdonough found that seven of his men when on liberty had deserted to the British Navy because they felt that Mediterranean service would compel them to serve longer than the term for which they enlisted. He commended a British admiral's and Russian officials' cooperation in attempting to apprehend the deserters but feared they had already been "secreted" on the English ships and would not be returned.[16]

When the *Guerrière* left Kronshtadt on 2 October, Macdonough demonstrated to all his stern attention to regulations and his high expectations of performance by leaving behind two officers who did not meet his standards. Along with Lt. Charles Crawly and Midn. Egbert Shaler, Surgeon's Mate Nathaniel W. Miller and Midn. Augustus A. Nicholson went ashore the last evening to attend a ball. They knew Macdonough wanted to leave early the next morning should the wind be fair. Crawly requested that Miller and Nicholson (who went "to visit some friends" or, as Macdonough put it, to "prolong their amusements") be at the mole at sunrise, when the ship's boat would arrive. Crawly and Shaler were on time, but Miller and Nicholson missed the scheduled boat and somewhat pompously sent a message requesting the ship send another to pick them up. Macdonough was anxious to depart. The tide and wind were right for departure. Ice was forming in the bay, and the channel was narrow, requiring delicate maneuvering for a ship of *Guerrière's* draft. Macdonough inquired if there were commercial boats capable of taking the two men and learned there was. Miller and Nicholson refused to lower their dignity and come by other than an official boat. "By zounds," exclaimed Macdonough, "then they may stay there." He ordered the boats hoisted and the anchor raised and the ship left without the two. They had to return by merchant vessel to the United States. This episode left a lasting impression on all. Wilkes noted that it "was a mere matter of pride of these officers who took it into their heads that it was or would be unbecoming in them to procure a passage in a shore boat to the ship, and were determined, as they thought, to force the Ship's boat on shore for their accommodation. In this they were disappointed." Wilkes, a New Yorker, took no little satisfaction that the two Virginians had their pride deflated.[17]

To avoid a recurrence of this event, while in Gibraltar on 14 November 1818, Macdonough issued orders that regulated the use of boats when in harbor. He directed that a boat be sent at sundown for all liberty men and midshipman that would wait fifteen minutes for all to board, another would be sent at 2000 hours for the lieutenants and wardroom officers that would wait the same length of time. The captain's gig would operate at such times and remain as long as "I may find it necessary to direct."[18]

The return trip through the Baltic was uneventful. In Copenhagen the *Guerrière* dropped off Mr. Hee, the ship's pilot on that sea. Macdonough was so impressed with his services that he wrote a rare personal note in the ship's journal: "Mr. Hee is an excellent Pilot for the Baltic & Gulf of Finland. We had much foggy weather & much to do with the Gulf in the night, he was quite at home, well acquainted and has conducted the ship with my aid in perfect safety & to my entire satisfaction." In Copenhagen they encountered the USS *Hornet*, Capt. George C. Read, but the rough waters meant there was little contact between crews. Shortly thereafter Macdonough took ill, and at Elsinore he hired another pilot to negotiate the narrow Cattegat Strait into the North Sea. This man proved incompetent, and the ship nearly foundered before making the open waters.[19]

Strong headwinds from the southwest and southeast made the cruise to Cape St. Vincent rough, but thereafter the crew went on to Gibraltar with fresh breezes on their larboard quarter. They arrived in Gibraltar on 13 November and departed three days later. Macdonough had his sailors busy "making every preparation for joining the squadron up the Mediterranean." At Syracuse on 6 December, *Guerrière* found its squadron: the *Franklin, United States,* and *Erie.* By this time both Parsons and Sailing Master Hixon had become so ill that they requested permission to leave the ship. Macdonough and Chase went ashore together, where they toured a Capuchin monastery. Chase was courteously received, even though the monks, he recorded, "knew my character as a heretic chaplain and thought me a priest."[20]

Winter in Sicily

During their brief stay in that Sicilian port an incident occurred that undoubtedly grieved Macdonough. His young brother-in-law, Midn. Egbert Shaler, became embroiled in an argument with his messmate, George P. Upshur. The argument had something to do with rivalries between Shaler's New England pride and the equally trivial Virginia conceit of Upshur. In the resulting duel, Shaler received what at first was believed to be a mortal wound. Fortunately, he recovered; shortly afterward young Shaler left the navy. Upshur continued a naval career that eventually included the superintendency of the new naval academy. Thomas Macdonough despised duels but did not discipline the participants on this trip the way he would on his next cruise.[21]

The commodore of the Mediterranean Squadron was Charles Stewart, one of the navy's most senior captains. Stewart had a distinguished career. He commanded the *Syren* during the raid at Tripoli that saw the burning of the *Philadelphia*. Commodore Preble consulted him on the other assaults on Tripoli. Late in the War of 1812 he commanded the *Constitution*, escaped the British blockade of Boston, and took the ship to the eastern Atlantic, where he scored one of the most dramatic naval victories of the war over HM sloops *Levant* and *Cyane* on 20 February 1815 (the battle was fought after the war was officially over, as neither side knew of the Treaty of Ghent). Stewart's victory was one of the most tactically brilliant of those achieved by the American frigates in the conflict. For all his heroism, Stewart had a reputation for quarrelsomeness. During the Tripolitan blockade, Stewart and Preble became embroiled in a petty argument over the assignment of a sailing master to the *Syren*. Also, on his last *Constitution* cruise his first lieutenant had been Henry Ballard, who tried to quell sailors' discontent with Stewart's placing the crew on reduced rations.[22] In 1818 Ballard commanded the *Erie* in the Mediterranean and would serve on the court-martial that eventually led to his relief along with Macdonough's.

Perhaps the most controversial aspect of Stewart's career was his return to Boston in 1814 after a three-month cruise with the *Constitution* that netted few prizes and ended long before the Navy Department expected. Secretary of the Navy Jones demonstrated his outrage when he ordered a court of inquiry into Stewart's conduct. The secretary did "not perceive, in the reasons and motives assigned, a satisfactory cause for the premature termination of the cruise of the U.S. Ship *Constitution*" when under Stewart's command. In particular, Jones could not comprehend Stewart's decision of "returning to be Blockaded during the Summer, in preference to continuing the cruise, or running the risk of being Blockaded in a foreign port...as a motive for [Stewart's] return." Although the court concluded that Stewart "did not neglect his duty" by returning early, it noted that he "might have remained, in obedience to his sailing orders and instructions sometime longer at sea." His decision to return was an "error of judgment," not malfeasance.[23] Regardless of the court's decision, it was a case known to the navy's officer corps, and one not reflecting positively upon Stewart's reputation.

Nonetheless, Stewart was the officer selected to replace Isaac Chauncey as commodore of the Mediterranean Squadron. Many senior officers in the navy considered the squadron to be in a state of near mutiny and insubordination. Stephen Decatur reportedly told Stewart he had to "reduce to subordination and discipline" this ill-disciplined and insubordinate group.

In doing this, Stewart was to "exercise with the greatest caution and discretion" the responsibilities of command.[24]

Commodore Stewart removed his squadron, consisting of the ships *Franklin, United States, Erie,* and *Guerrière,* plus the brig *Spark,* from Syracuse to the smaller port of Messina, where the squadron anchored from mid-December 1818 until mid-April the following year. Chase found the town presenting "no objects of curiosity and nothing of any particular note." Even the local nobility impressed the chaplain as "a poor, gambling, degraded sort of people," and the girls, he noted, were "most horribly ugly." Except for a small theater and opera house with its casino rooms, little existed to amuse the Americans. The officers received cards of invitation to both the gambling hall and the weekly dances. Macdonough encouraged his midshipmen to attend the dances but to avoid the billiard and rouge et noir tables. At the former Midshipman Wilkes found there to be "a large collection of Really beautiful Girls" with whom the officers "readily secured partners." However, it was not the casino balls but the great gambling rooms that were the attraction to all too many: "At the tables were usually native[s], the old lady dowagers, who were betting their small sums, [and] the Bankers occupying one side with large piles of gold & silver before them." Macdonough "interdicted" many of his officers making for the gambling rooms. Still, the lure was too much for many to keep from "taking the fly." When they did so, they maintained a careful watch lest the captain should see them and quarantine them to the ship.

In gambling they followed the example of their commodore, Stewart, who "generally took a Seat at one of the tables & betted largely." Officers from other ships in the squadron did not chafe from the supervision of their captains, as did the Guerrières. Wilkes reported the ship's officers resented the distinction in comportment they were expected to present in contrast to that of the other naval officers. "Although this surveillance did not prevent [gambling] entirely, it made the officers of our ship very circumspect" in their behavior, often going to smaller gambling establishments where they rejoiced when they could break the bank.[25] One can only speculate whether their contrasting life-styles created tensions between Stewart and Macdonough. Did Stewart find Macdonough sanctimonious? Did Macdonough deplore Stewart's licentiousness? Did the winter in Messina contribute to the mutual animosity between the two that would erupt a few months later in the shadow of Mount Vesuvius?

The Messina winter also contributed to disaffection among the various crews. According to Wilkes, "The discipline and morals of the Squadron suffered greatly; in fact little attention except on board the *Guerrière* was paid to keep it up. The crews were intoxicated almost daily and at night the 'Brig' was generally filled and very many in double irons." Macdonough sought to stop this and pledged to punish any officer, even the petty officers, who allowed alcohol to come aboard. Things quieted down for a while, but soon the intoxication resumed. The officers could not determine the source of the liquor until one of the oranges regularly brought on board happened to break open and Wilkes discovered a bladder inside that contained the *aqua delecte*. But the oranges had already been distributed, and shortly thereafter the ship became "a drunken brothel."

Among those participating in the bacchanalian reveries was "Old Murray, the Quarter Master, who became exceeding intoxicated & uproarious." Macdonough had him confined in double irons. A favorite of the junior officers, they hoped the quartermaster's white hair and twenty years' service might spare him the captain's wrath. They did not. Macdonough vowed no mercy for anyone. He disrated Old Murray and sentenced him to twelve lashes. Murray came forward, had his shirt removed and his hands tied to the rigging. The lashes cut into his back. "There was scarcely a dry eye among the officers. The captain's voice almost failed him, but he could not well escape when he had shown such an example, and, if let off, the law would not have been carried out with Justice." When taken down, Murray said it was a justifiable punishment but this was the first and would be the last time the cat-o'-nine tails would be administered to his back. Macdonough reinstated Murray's rank. Afterward the rest of the accused, almost a third of the crew, came forward to receive their punishment. It was a bloody, heart-rending scene, but it had the desired effect. Drunkenness ceased on the *Guerrière* for as long as Macdonough commanded her.[26]

The tough administration of justice sometimes found Macdonough recoiling at what he had to undertake. Seaman Thomas Wilson received a court-martial sentence of three hundred lashes, and after the first one hundred had been administered, he found himself on the surgeon's report as too ill to receive the next one hundred. Macdonough requested Wilson receive Commodore Stewart's "further mercy." Stewart remitted the remainder of the sentence on account of the "state of Thos. Wilson's health and the severe punishment he has already received for his misconduct." However, the following October, Wilson accused several officers of the *Guerrière* of lying at his earlier trial; only "Captain Macdonough and Commodore Stewart knew you were all perjured & therefore he let me off," he declared.[27]

Undoubtedly the *Guerrière's* captain prevailed upon Chaplain Chase to preach a sermon on Palm Sunday, 4 April 1819, hoping to restore some sobriety, some conciliatory behavior, and civil language among the crew. Using nautical terms Chase sought to warn them of the consequences of misbehavior: "You all know very well, that before you sail upon the bosom of the wide ocean, if you be not well prepared for the voyage before you set out, if the ship is not in a fit condition, or your stores and support inadequate, that the voyage will be dangerous to you—and probably fatal." If preparation is necessary for the journey across the sea, so also is it needed for the eternal voyage. "Death will soon launch you forth upon that eternity of which the sea is but a figure and emblem, and you may depend that the wreck of your soul will most certainly follow if you have not taken care now while you are upon earth to do your duty in laying out a preparation for this interminable voyage." Such sentiments undoubtedly pleased Macdonough; that many of his crew followed them is doubtful.[28]

Before he returned to the United States due to chronic illness, Purser James M. Halsey of the *Guerrière* wrote Macdonough a letter of praise: "In this climate, where so many of our officers have yielded to its luxuries, influences & live its habits, so entirely unsuited to those of our own country: permit me, Sir, to felicitate you in the undeviating example of moral rectitude you have so uniformly shown to the officers under your command."[29] Surely Macdonough hoped these sentiments reflected a common attitude among his officers. However much that might have been the case, Chaplain Chase recognized that his situation was "different from that probably of any other chaplain in the service." The reason for this situation was obvious: "the character of our Commander and that of the officers of the ward room."[30]

Relief from Command

As the senior captain in the squadron after Stewart, Macdonough served frequently that winter on courts-martial and courts of inquiry. For instance, when Midn. David R. Stewart claimed Lt. Robert F. Stockton of the *Erie* had conducted himself in an "unofficerlike, ungentlemanly" manner, observed "scandalous and immoral conduct," and used "abusive & provoking language," Macdonough's court of inquiry concluded there was insufficient evidence to warrant a court-martial.[31] In most of these cases Benjamin F. Bourne, purser on the *Erie* and a member of the Massachusetts bar, served as judge advocate. Macdonough increasingly relied on Bourne's legal advice in these delicate matters.

On 13 April 1819 the American squadron left Messina for Palermo; from there it went for Naples, where they arrived on 13 May. In many ways it was an uneventful cruise. The *Franklin* received a visit from the King of Naples and Emperor of Austria and the *Guerrière* manned its yards during this inspection of the flagship. The daily entries indicate the routine of the ship— "crew variously employed," "beat to quarters for inspection," "performed divine service and mustered ships company," and so on. Then, on 28 May, came the brief entry that did not forewarn of the consequences: "At 9.45 made signal for court martial—at 10 the court convened."

Commodore Stewart convened the court to try the case of Pvt. Robert Sloan, USMC. The court consisted of Macdonough, president, with Master Commandants Henry Ballard and Joseph J. Nicholson, and Lts. John Gallagher and Benjamin Page Jr. as members. Bourne served as judge advocate. Both Ballard and Nicholson were midshipmen on the *Wasp* when Macdonough was its first lieutenant. The court convened on the *Guerrière* in Naples Harbor. While in Palermo on 1 May, Sloan allegedly illegally procured "certain wines & spirits, other & more than his legal allowance and made himself drunk therewith" and was thereby unfit to perform his duties. According to the charges, when Lt. Joseph L. Kuhn, USMC, ordered him to be confined, Sloan resisted arrest and took a bayonet and stabbed Cpl. Archibald Campbell and tried to stab Cpl. John E. Lloyd, USMC. Campbell was slightly wounded and, along with Lloyd, finally subdued Sloan and put him in irons. It was a fairly open-and-shut case, and the court quickly convicted Sloan of three of the four charges against him and sentenced him to "one hundred lashes with the Cat-of-nine-Tails upon the bare back." Following a reading of the sentence the court adjourned until 1500 hours the next day at Bourne's quarters in the Sun Tavern in Naples, where the court received the official transcript of the trial. There the "record having been read over by the Judge Advocate in the presence & hearing of the Court, and having finished all the business before them," the court adjourned "without day"—that is, sine die.[32] The proceedings were forwarded to Stewart. It is interesting that Sloan's sentence for assault was one-third of what Thomas Wilson had received for drunk and disorderly conduct.

At this point, Stewart could have accepted the court's proceedings and ordered the sentence administered. Instead, on the morning of Monday, 31 May, the *Franklin* signaled for a court-martial. A somewhat confused Macdonough immediately went to the flagship and confronted Lt. William A. Weaver, the commodore's aide and signal officer. Macdonough asked what court-martial was to take place.

"The one in being," Weaver responded. "You know there is no other. It is not dissolved."

Macdonough replied, "I know it is not. The Commodore has not dissolved any court that I have sat on in this sea. Where is the court to be held?"

"On the *Guerrière.*"

"Then why," questioned Macdonough, "did you not make the signal respecting the ship on board of which it was to sit?"

"If the signal is not understood, I will designate your ship," Weaver answered, which he did. At no time during this exchange did Commodore Stewart leave his cabin. Macdonough knew something was amiss, and he recorded this encounter as a memorandum in his own hand in his letterbook. Macdonough repaired to the *Guerrière,* and at 1100 hours the other members of the court and Bourne joined him. Once convened, the court admitted Lieutenant Weaver, who presented Macdonough the following message from Stewart:

> The Commander-in-Chief of the squadron, in consideration of the foregoing proceedings of the Court, being illegally held on the last day of the meeting, of the said Court in the City of Naples, where the United States of America have no jurisdictions and it being there held in violation of the order, contained in the warranted dated May 26 1819, directing the same to be held on board the U.S. Frigate *Guerrière,* directs the Prisoner to be released, and considers the proceedings as null and void. The Commander-in-chief presuming this to have arisen on the part of the Court through inadvertence, is willing to pass it over without further notice, but recommends to the Court more caution in future, that culprits deserving punishment, may not escape justice to the prejudice of the Public Service.

Considering the final sentence of this letter, the court could have adjourned and let the matter end. Clearly the court felt itself maligned and its independence insulted as well as its character impugned by the final sentence. Rather than letting Stewart's decision stand, the court resolved to reconsider the proceedings of the trial then in the possession of the commodore. Macdonough wrote a letter to Stewart requesting the record. Instead of his normal "Respectfully etc.," Macdonough closed his letter with "I have the honor to be with great consideration, Sir, your obedient servant." The court adjourned until 1500 hours the same day when Lieutenant Gallagher produced the record he had received from the *Franklin.* In complying with Macdonough's request, Stewart implied that the court's proceedings were legal.

Stewart's leadership style at this juncture comes into question. Why did he not consult with Macdonough individually or with the court corporately about the matter? Could he not inform the group of his belief that the court acted contrary to the law and provide it with legal opinions to justify his stance? Or why did he not dissolve the court and thereby remove it from any legal justification for its subsequent actions? Did he have to release Private Sloan without any punishment when the court might have reconvened on the *Guerrière* and merely followed Stewart's format of meeting where it should have? One wonders if Stewart were not deliberately laying a trap for the sometimes self-righteousness Macdonough. That no private discussions were held and all intercourse between the court and the commodore was through written, legalistic communications indicates the degree of tension that existed among the commissioned officers of the squadron.

Bourne advised the court that the session in Naples was legal. Then the court learned that a signal from the *Franklin* ordered them to put to sea at 1700 hours, and it directed Bourne to "reduce his opinion upon the legality of their sitting to writing & submit it to their consideration hereafter." It then adjourned to meet upon a signal from the *Guerrière* "as soon as the public service shall allow it." (It appears Stewart did not deliberately signal the sailing in order to break up the court, because he had issued a general order on 28 May that the squadron would sail on the thirty-first.) Before their departure, Macdonough wrote the commodore that the court-martial "resolved to adjourn without day in consequence of the squadrons putting to sea." As the ships sailed toward the rock of Gibraltar, Bourne had plenty of time to draft a detailed opinion regarding the legality of the meeting at the Sun Tavern. On 17 June the *Franklin, Guerrière, Spark,* and *Erie* arrived at Gibraltar Bay and anchored at Algeciras on the Spanish side.

Stewart had been sent to command the Mediterranean Squadron because of the serious disciplinary problems that supposedly existed there. He found he needed to assert his authority by disciplining senior subordinates. Stewart clearly wanted to forbid the assault upon subordinates by his officers. No case caused greater problems than that of Gunner's Mate David Vestry of the *Erie*. When Lieutenant Stockton refused Vestry's request for liberty at Messina, the gunner's mate acted disrespectful and insolent. After being repeatedly told to leave the lieutenant's presence and not doing so, Stockton struck him down. When the court sentenced Vestry to reduction to seaman and fifty lashes, Stewart disapproved the sentence and remitted it on the grounds that Stockton's conduct constituted a flagrant "violation of the Law, order, discipline & humanity" and the trial placed Vestry in double jeopardy for being twice tried and punished for the same crime. Even more inflammatory was Stewart's decision to direct that his disapproval of the sentence be read in front of all the officers and midshipman of the squadron. Lieutenant Stockton was outraged that Stewart "wantonly exercised the great powers" of his office by "punishing a commissioned officer, in a mode expressly disallowed and forbidden, by the Act of Congress" by having him "publicly reprimanded . . . upon the Quarter Deck of this ship in the presence of all the Lieutenants and Midshipmen of the Squadron." Stockton admitted having struck Vestry "under the grossest provocation of insolence," but this error, he contended, "was deserving of reproof only." Stockton wrote Capt. John Rodgers, president of the Board of Navy Commissioners in Washington, that he was "hurt but not humbled, and excited but unimpassioned, at this illegal attempt that seemed intended to crush me."

Naval officers were not inclined to accept criticism of their conduct and to be publicly reprimanded in front of their subordinates. Dissent rose among Stewart's senior officers. Master Commandant Ballard, captain of the *Erie*, wrote Stewart, regretting the commodore had "found occasion on the trial of [Petty Officer David] Vestry to reprimand me as in the wrong." For this reason, Ballard requested permission to return to the United States "in the hope that with the Government I may be able to put myself in the right." Stewart denied the request.[33] It is clear that there was considerable resentment against Stewart among such men as Ballard and Stockton, the former of whom was on the Sloan court-martial board with Macdonough. For these officers the Vestry court-martial represented the arbitrary interference with officers in the administration of their office, even if that meant using corporal punishment to achieve the due discipline they sought. Stewart, on the other hand, determined to assert control over the use of physical punishment by officers.

Deteriorating discipline among the officers became evident in the frequent outbursts and duels between Americans and between them and British officers. In the years following the War of 1812 the antagonisms among the junior officers of the two countries rose to such an extent that numerous challenges and duels resulted over trivial affronts to what were deemed national or personal honor. A most belligerent American officer was Stockton, who along with Bourne, Surgeon Alexander M. Montgomery of the *Erie*, and Purser A. G. Humphreys of the *United States* became involved in a series of encounters with British officers, mostly from the Sixty-fourth Regiment of Foot. In April 1819, Stockton and Bourne engaged in duels at St. Michael's cave and at the neutral ground (located near the site of the modern Gibraltar airport). Wilkes described Bourne as "a very proud and cross-grained man of high mettle but extremely conce[i]ted." The situation became so strained that Lt. Gov. George Don of Gibraltar ordered the *Erie* to leave that port. Soon it became commonplace for the English squadron to depart Gibraltar when an American vessel arrived.

When he arrived at Gibraltar Bay in June 1819, Stewart anchored his ships at Spanish Algeciras rather than British Gibraltar. He had each vessel's commander issue a general order similar to the one that Macdonough did for the *Guerrière:* the ship was to be ready to depart at all times; the officers and men could not go ashore in Gibraltar, six miles away, in the evenings. There was one final directive: "All personal communication with the Garrison of Gibraltar is strictly forbidden." Even this was not enough to stop the problems.

The squadron was in Algeciras only two days when Macdonough wrote Ballard and Gallagher that they should come on board the *Guerrière* for a court of inquiry. The court, which was to inquire into the duels earlier in the year, sat from 21 June to 3 July. Macdonough forwarded its conclusions to General Don. During a brief absence of the *Franklin* while on a trip to Cadiz, Macdonough was the senior American officer present and he conducted correspondence with General Don.[34] What is significant is that at the very time the Sloan court-martial controversy was going, Macdonough, Ballard, and Gallagher were members of a court of inquiry into the roles of Stockton, Montgomery, and Bourne in the breach of "the peace of the Garrison of Gibraltar" earlier that spring. In other words, the dispute that arose between Stewart and the Sloan court-martial board had nothing to do with the competence of the latter's members to perform their duties, even duties of a legal nature.

As was customary, at noon on 4 July the squadron's vessels fired a twenty-one-gun salute for each of the states in honor of Independence Day. This bit of patriotism was a lull before the storm. The next morning Macdonough ordered the court-martial signal flags raised. All the squadron's ships took notice thereof, including the *Franklin*. Stewart made no attempt to annul the session either by adjourning the court or by canceling the meeting. Macdonough wrote another memorandum in his journal that the *Franklin*'s officer of the deck sent a midshipman to notify the commodore of the message. It is clear Macdonough wanted an accurate, written record of the commodore's knowledge of his signal.

The court began by receiving Judge Advocate Bourne's lengthy, convoluted opinion justifying the session at Sun Tavern. The essence of his argument was that if a sovereign allows a foreign vessel to conduct trials aboard ships while within his territorial waters, there existed an "implied permission, or consent" to conduct such courts ashore. He concluded, "If Court's-Martial may be legally convened on ship-board adjournments to the shore are by necessary and inevitable consequences legal." Undoubtedly Bourne's implied powers doctrine would have made the late Alexander Hamilton quite happy. It was not going to set well with Stewart, however, who was clearly Jeffersonian in dealing with such niceties of the law.

After "maturely" considering the contents of Stewart's note of 31 May, the court prepared an intemperate response. The influence of Bourne probably pushed the court beyond what would be a suitable address to its convening authority. Macdonough should have known better than to endorse the statement that the court forwarded to Stewart.

It began by arguing that the court's adjournment to Naples was done "for good & sufficient reasons of which this Court were alone competent to judge." In this case they contended it was Bourne's "infirm health" that required them to come to his onshore residence. But the question remains: Why was the judge advocate well enough to come aboard the *Guerrière* the day before?

Second, the court boldly declared that once constituted as a judicial tribunal, they ceased to be under the commander in chief's "control," and that to allow them to be "controuled by the express or implied will of the Commander-in-Chief would be to allow the existence of an influence, subversive of the independence of Court's-Martial, indispensable to the ends of military law." What they sought was to avoid what is today called "command influence" over court-martial proceedings. They were about 130 years ahead of their time. It would not be until the passage of the Uniform Code of Military Justice in 1949 that serious attempts would be made in this direction. However, the tone of this clause was clearly an affront to Stewart's perception of his command authority. The independence of courts-martial is the key issue around which the whole controversy revolved.

Third, in a very condescending tone, the court said it would "forbear expressing a doubt of the Commodore's right, to declare their proceedings null and void." It went on to "lament the apparent want of confidence in their ability or integrity which they apprehend is betrayed, in not submitting to their reconsideration, that share of their proceedings, which have been seized upon with abundant alacrity, as sufficient to vitiate and annul the whole." The court is correct here. Stewart did not have to annul the whole proceedings to have the events at Sun Tavern canceled.

Finally, the court approved a long paragraph that could only elicit Stewart's outrage:

> This Court owe too much respect to the Commander-in-Chief, and are too conscious of their own infirmities to venture an attempt at expressing the feelings excited, on finding him, or any other authority presuming on their inadvertence, as an apology to himself for overlooking any alleged or imagined misconduct or erroneous proceeding on their part; and most especially in an instance when the whole error is found to consist in having conducted their proceedings according to their own deliberate convictions, instead of his peculiar notions of their duties; and the Court can only regret that the Commander-in-Chief, has deemed it expedient to make use of them as an example to the Squadron and the Navy; that he will forgive as inadvertence in them what he has neither the right nor the power to punish even if wilful; but they will cheerfully endure the reproach of having furnished the first extraordinary instance in which a Tribunal sitting in judgment has been told that their errors are to be past over, because they are presumed to result from inadvertence. And finally that this Court are made deeply sensible of the Commander-in-Chief's superior discretion in his obliging admonition to them, to be more cautions in future and they beg leave most respectfully to tender to him, the only suitable return in their power by reminding him, that it has always been a reproach to trials at law, that after a plodding and laborious enquiry by a Jury of men, laying claim to no more than common sense, it often turns out to be labour in vain, for the superior sagacity of the judge will display itself, in picking out a flaw in their proceedings, just large enough to let the culprit escape.

According to Wilkes's memory, Macdonough relied "more upon the judgment of Mr. Bourne . . . than on his own." If this was the case, Macdonough imprudently followed the judge advocate's legal advice and his draft of the response. The reply the court approved could only excite the commodore to a most drastic reaction to such an assault upon his person and position. When one places this episode in the light of the other instances of insubordination occurring among the Mediterranean Squadron's officers over the previous few years, Stewart may have felt it necessary to make the decision that would follow this address.[35] The insolence of the court's conclusions, combined with the growing discontent with his administration of the squadron evidenced in Stockton's appeal to Rodgers, undoubtedly contributed to his conclusion that the time had come to assert the prerogatives of his office.

But this gives the commodore the largest benefit of doubt. Stewart may have considered Macdonough a sanctimonious prig who excited contempt of his conduct at the gaming tables in Messina. He may have been envious of Macdonough's combat record and the huge amount of prize money won by the commander of the Lake Champlain squadron. There might have been a case of jealousy of the admiration heaped upon Macdonough by both ordinary citizens and naval officers that had been denied him because his victories in the war came too late to make him the recipient of popular adulation. But Stewart had every right to be upset at the insubordinate tone of the court's conclusions regarding his conduct in the Sloan court-martial. Was the necessity to assert his position as commodore enough to justify his suspension of the captains of three of his squadron's four ships from the performance of their duty?

Obviously the dispute between Stewart and Macdonough had nothing to do with the competence of the latter to perform his duties. Both men allowed the situation to get way out of hand. Both had missed opportunities to gracefully avoid this encounter. Stewart determined to take drastic action. On 8 July he sent to each board member a message similar to that received by Macdonough: "*Sir;* You will be pleased to transfer to the officer next in command to yourself on board the *Guerrière* all general orders, rules and regulations, and all orders appertaining to the service to you addressed which remain to be executed wholly or in part, and consider yourself suspended from your office and the duties thereof until further orders."[36]

This was an extraordinary decision. Relief from command is unusual in peacetime service. To relieve four commanding officers of a squadron was unparalleled in U.S. Navy history. Ballard, commander of the *Erie;* Nicholson, captain of the brig *Spark;* John Gallagher, flag captain of the *Franklin;* and Page, also of the *Franklin* received similar letters. Stewart placed the safety of his ships and men under the command of very inexperienced junior officers. Ironically, Bourne received a promotion. He became purser of the *Guerrière,* which was a larger ship than the *Erie,* replacing a purser who departed because of illness.

To justify such a drastic disciplinary measure, Stewart immediately wrote two letters to Secretary of the Navy Smith Thompson. One enclosed the transcript of the court-martial of Private Sloan and charged that the "self-convened Court" met on 3 July on the *Guerrière* and again on the *Erie*. The former's log indicates a meeting on the fifth, not the third. Does this mean there were meetings proceeding the one on the fifth, or was Stewart merely mistaken? In the other letter Stewart sought to explain his rationale for the relief. He called the court "a self-created" body that existed "contrary to law; illegal from the want of authority." (He did not explain the absence of efforts to impede their assembly or to dissolve the court.) The court's proceedings constituted "insubordination towards, and disrespect for the position & power of the Commander in Chief of the Naval Forces employed in the Mediterranean Sea." In the final analysis these proceedings tended "to bring the said Commander into contempt, to impede him in the exercise of his duties, & to shackle his impressions & opinions in the free use of his understanding, & comprehension of such subjects as may come before him for the exercise of his judgement."

At "the head of this combination of the officers under my command" was Macdonough, "to whom the Country owes so much for his distinguished services in the cause, & who has contributed so largely to the high standing and brilliant character of our infant Navy has acquired in its late struggle with the Leviathan of the deep." Moreover, Stewart acknowledged, Macdonough otherwise served under his command "with reputation to himself, & perfect satisfaction to his superiors." Stewart requested that replacements be sent immediately so that "the objects of the Government may not be delayed, & the discipline relaxed for a longer period than necessary." He noted that he was sending them home under arrest in order that they might be brought "before such Tribunal, as [the government] may deem proper, for the investigation of this their conduct."[37]

The five suspended officers immediately undertook a defense of their actions. After reading Stewart's letter to the secretary, they wrote a joint letter to Stewart declaring that they "firmly" believed themselves to be a duly constituted tribunal. They disavowed "most clearly & explicitly any spirit of defiance of Law or of your authority, of insubordination or of disrespect for the person or powers of the commander in chief of the naval forces employed in the Mediterranean." In particular, they wanted to distinguish their opinions as a court from their willingness as officers of the squadron to obey his directives. At the same time, Macdonough wrote the secretary a note stating that "the commodore had no reason to suppose me unwilling or even not desirous to do my duty in all respects in obedience of his orders."[38]

As one might suspect, the impact of this suspension by the commodore did not set well with Macdonough's officers and men. He immediately sought to soothe their tempers and to direct them in their duty. He thanked them for the support received in a letter of appreciation. Then he noted that "the time is not far distant when the accusations against me will appear to have resulted from angry passions and not to subserve the ends of Justice." He ended with a prophetic note: "I have no doubt but my command will speedily be restored to me." Such an outcome would not come as quickly as he hoped. Already he had misgivings about his conduct. While waiting at the quay of Gibraltar, Macdonough struck up a conversation with Midshipman Wilkes concerning the affair. "By zounds," concluded the captain, "I do not know how it will end."[39] Macdonough also wrote the distinguished Norfolk, Virginia, attorney Littleton W. Tazewell asking his opinion regarding the dispute.[40] The reply would not be received until after his return to the United States.

None of the squadron's ships were scheduled for immediate rotation, and Stewart had no desire to send five officers under arrest on a commercial conveyance. So for the next several months the squadron sailed the Mediterranean with the officers in quarters on the various vessels. Stewart considered the five to be prisoners-at-large who could either stay on board their respective ships or go ashore. The *Franklin, Guerrière, Erie*, and *Spark* sailed for Leghorn, Italy, on 21 July and arrived there two weeks later. At this port the *Guerrière* received Capt. Charles Thompson, who became the vessel's commander. Thompson and his wife were vacationing in Europe at the time and he had no uniforms when he came on board. The *Guerrière* returned to Gibraltar and Macdonough spent some time in lodging ashore. Finally the five arrested officers sailed back to the United States on board the *Erie*. Commanded by Stockton, that vessel made a somewhat unusual winter crossing of the Atlantic and arrived in New York on 21 January 1820.[41]

Commodore Stewart was about to receive a complete surprise regarding the navy's response to his suspensions. There is reason to suspect the department felt Stewart did not "exercise with the greatest caution and discretion" the responsibilities of command that Decatur admonished him to do. The long list of complaints against Stewart did not set well with either the Board of Navy Commissioners or the secretary. They had to uphold some of his conduct, but were obviously dismayed by the consequences of his actions and the suspension of three vessels' commanders over an incident having nothing to do with their fitness to command. Very quickly upon his return, Macdonough secured from Tazewell the requested legal opinion. That document sustained Stewart's right to annul a court-martial decision. Macdonough then wrote the secretary an apology for his actions, which had been based upon Bourne's opinion. He placed "full confidence" on this new opinion and regretted not having it when in the Mediterranean. "I now see this affair in some respects in a different light," he wrote, "and I solicit either orders or permission to go to Washington and have with you a personal interview on the subject." Permission received, Macdonough journeyed to the capital for the conference with the secretary of the navy. He wrote another letter of apology in which he recognized a court could not act in a place other than "that designated by the authority constituting it." The court's opinion "arose from an impression that Courts Martial were as absolutely independent as those of civil jurisdiction." As a consequence, Macdonough acted under the perception that he "was maintaining the just rights & independence of Courts Martial; with a single eye to the public good and the advancement of the naval service." This misperception of the court's independence led to what he acknowledged was an error. At first this conclusion might create the impression that Stewart was fully vindicated.[42]

On the contrary, the administration's response was highly favorable to Macdonough. Secretary Thompson reported that President Monroe had read his letter and commended the "candour & magnanimity" of Macdonough's acknowledgment of his error. This, continued the president, was "a course which might be expected from an honourable and high minded man, and a pledge that your future conduct will be such as to sustain the high character you have hitherto held in the estimation of your Country." Under these circumstances, the president authorized the secretary to restore Macdonough to the command of the *Guerrière*. Such a decision was a direct insult to Stewart, who expected the insubordinate five officers to be disciplined, not returned to duty. Instead, not only was Macdonough rehabilitated in the eyes of his superiors, but the other four also continued on careers that would lead to all being eventually promoted to captain, the navy's highest rank before the Civil War. Macdonough was not about to serve with Stewart again and both he and Thompson knew that such service was not in the best interests of the navy. Under these conditions, Captain Macdonough requested assignment ashore due to the "present bad state of my health." He subsequently received command of the seventy-four-gun ship-of-the-line *Ohio*, then under construction in New York.[43]

Such a reward, changing from a forty-four-gun to a seventy-four-gun command, could not help but be seen as a slap in face of Commodore Stewart. More such indignities would follow. Perhaps the most galling had to be the response of the men of the *Guerrière*. Somehow the blue jackets gathered approximately three hundred guineas and bought Macdonough a specially designed sword from one of the world's greatest swordsmiths in London. According the *Guerrière*'s purser, the crew forbid any commissioned or warrant officer to contribute to their secretly collected fund. They required the sword be "for use & not for show . . . with no jewelry—but gold and steel and nothing else." Purser Bourne, who handled the transaction for the crew through the counsel general in London, expressed his amazement that the ship's tars thought so much of their captain that they would forgo a major loss of income to make such a presentation. "It is without example in naval history," he declared, and reflects a relationship subsisting "betwixt a ships company and their Captain that was never heard of until now." According to the Bourne, "The crew are to a man cordially attached to him & were quite as much hurt at this temporary degradation of their Captain as he was himself." Lieutenant Conover delivered the gift to Macdonough in Middletown, expressing the esteem with which his crew held their captain. Macdonough replied, "It is to me a most pleasing circumstance to receive so handsome an expression of the good feeling of the crew of the United States frigate *Guerrière*, a crew distinguished for their activity and good conduct when I had the honor to command that ship." The sword was described as being "beautifully and heavily mounted in gold, the mounting showing exquisitely wrought symbols of peace and war." One side of the scabbard contained an etching of "the battle of Lake Champlain, with the famous cock perched in the rigging of the *Saratoga*." On the other side was the inscription "The Crew of the U.S.S. *Guerrière* to Captain Thos. Macdonough, 8 July 1819." The beautifully etched blade bore the motto "No Impressment" on one side and "Maintain Your Rights" on the other. It was considered such a fine specimen that some viewed it as an example of what ought to be done for Andrew Jackson, the hero of New Orleans.[44]

The novelty of this expression of gratitude from the enlisted men, who served under him and were subject to severe discipline by him, is particularly telling. In a brief pamphlet published a few years after Macdonough's death, a biographer wrote, "There is a good share of sagacity in the common sailor; he sees through the character much clearer than we generally think he does. . . . There are few so ignorant that they cannot discover moral worth, when connected with professional ability; and none so bad, as not to approve of it." Throughout his career Macdonough seems to have garnered this type of admiration from the American tars.[45]

Many in the navy and in the general public seemed to favor Macdonough in his dispute with Stewart. Gov. Oliver Wolcott of Connecticut wrote him a supportive letter. In the midst of the whole contretemps, Thompson conveyed Macdonough the congressional gold medal for his victory on Lake Champlain. Lt. Joseph Smith noted good press on Macdonough's behalf and requested duty with him on the *Ohio*. In particular, he congratulated Macdonough on the resolution of the issue with Stewart and commended the "promotion" from a frigate to a ship-of-the-line command.[46]

What is clear is that Stewart and Macdonough held widely divergent views on how to rectify the indiscipline among the Mediterranean Squadron's officers. Stewart assumed what was needed was stronger direction from the commodore and rigorous disciplinary measures taken against officer misconduct. Macdonough, on the other hand, thought that court-martial independence from the commander in chief's influence was the key to remedying the situation.

Commodore Stewart would not be disciplined for his conduct in this affair. Later he would take the *Franklin* on a Pacific cruise and would be court-martialed upon his return. The charges against him included unofficerlike conduct, disobedience of orders, neglect of duty, and oppression and cruelty. Although he would be exonerated by the court-martial (which had Stephen Cassin as a member), it is clear that his administration of the Pacific Squadron attracted as much discontent as it had in the Mediterranean.[47] As he had so often in his career, Charles Stewart was unable to get along with his subordinates.

Macdonough emerged from this affair somewhat chastised and embarrassed, but with his reputation as a champion of sailors' rights vindicated. The blue jackets of the *Guerrière* knew he was the man who flew a signal at the battle of Lake Champlain proclaiming "Impressed seamen call on every man to do his duty." Surely his appeal to the cause of court-martial independence championed their resistance to arbitrary authority over the enlisted men and junior officers in a commodore's command.

When it was all over, one of Ann's brothers wrote of Macdonough's "troublesome judicial functions" and hoped that such scandalous spectacles would cease. Courts-martial, he concluded, "have ruined the credit of the army and the navy seems inclining to the same extravagance."[48] Undoubtedly this reflected the sentiments of large numbers of the general public that was appalled not only at the courts-martial but also at the petty quarrels that brought all too many officers to the dueling grounds.

In the midst of this affair, a minor episode in Macdonough's life reflected on a particular part of his personal temperament and sense of professionalism. While in Washington in 1820 he was one of several officers who refused to serve as Stephen Decatur's second in his forthcoming duel with Commo. James Barron.[49] This decision not only reflected Macdonough's abhorrence of dueling but also demonstrated his reluctance to become deeply involved in the petty infighting that characterized the postwar leadership of the U.S. Navy. He and Ann lived, and associated with those who lived, mostly outside the conspiratorial waters of Washington, Philadelphia, New York, and Boston. There is little correspondence of his in the papers of the more involved senior officers of the postwar navy. There is a reason for this: his concept of naval professionalism did not require him to work behind the scenes in behalf of personal agendas.

Chapter Eight

Life's Final Cruise

Green be thy grave, MACDONOUGH!
A nations' tears have wet it.
Undying be thy glory,
Thy country'll ne'er forget it.

"Thou has not liv'd in vain!"
Columbia's annals tell—
Thy death was that the righteous die—
Lamented Shade! Farewell.

Middlesex Gazette, 30 November 1825

THE USS *Constitution* arrived in New York on 20 May 1824. In early June, Commodore Macdonough took command from Capt. Jacob Jones. Jones had been a midshipman on the *Philadelphia* with Macdonough and had undergone the trial of imprisonment that Macdonough escaped. Now they exchanged commands. Jones also had the reputation of running a loose ship. Macdonough needed to change this situation and to return the vessel to its traditional distinction as one of the country's most disciplined and orderly men-of-war.

Fitting Out Old Ironsides

Immediately Macdonough began assembling officers and crew. As his first lieutenant he secured Vallette, who as a midshipman and acting sailing master had so gallantly assisted him on the *Saratoga* just a decade earlier. Macdonough chose him from the middle of the lieutenants list. For Vallette it was a career-enhancing opportunity in a professional life that eventually earned him an admiral's flag. Vallette secured permission from the secretary of the navy to void his orders as the first lieutenant of the *Ontario* so that he might join Macdonough again. He was the only officer on the *Constitution* that had served on Lake Champlain with the commodore. He also served on the *Guerrière* cruise. Macdonough and Vallette sought to create the type of crew that best fit their concept of naval professionalism.

As was normal, Macdonough sought his own preferences for the most senior and sensitive billets. Of his 12 June request to the secretary of the navy for six lieutenants, Vallette, Thomas W. Wyman, and Josiah Tattnall received billets on the *Constitution*. Macdonough desired to have a number of officers who had previously served with him, including Lieutenant Platt of the *Saratoga* and *Guerrière* and Lieutenant Page, who had served on the Sloan court-martial board in 1819. Platt did not receive the assignment, and Page had to decline due to ill health. In the latter's place the commodore sought and secured Joseph Cross of the *Guerrière* as the sixth lieutenant. Subsequently, when the commodore found out that Cross had "become very intemperate" he sought to have his assignment revoked.[1] It was not. On the whole, the *Constitution* received a very high percentage of the lieutenants its commander desired.

While Vallette concerned himself with the enlisted members of the crew, Macdonough bombarded Secretary of the Navy Samuel L. Southard with letters concerning the other officers. He requested James M. Halsey, formerly purser of the *Guerrière,* and was denied. Similar results came after initial requests for a surgeon, sailing master, several midshipmen, and gunner. When John W. Mooers and Richard R. McMullin applied to him for midshipmen berths, he forwarded their desires to the secretary with the comment that "these young gentlemen are available & intelligent & I should like to have them in this ship." Mooers received a billet but proved unsatisfactory and was sent home for dueling.[2]

Several of the Navy Department's proposals for officers proved unacceptable to Macdonough. The case of the surgeon provides a good example. Of one candidate Macdonough wrote that in "the abilities of that gentleman, I must say, I have not much confidence." When Southard pressed him on the issue, Macdonough bluntly told the secretary that "the moral qualifications of this gentleman are unexceptionable, & . . . I entertain sentiments . . . in regard to his professional abilities, that I cannot, notwithstanding my friendship for him, divest myself." At Macdonough's suggestion he received Dr. William Turk, longtime surgeon with the postwar naval establishment on Lake Champlain. He had known him at least since 1820, when he returned to that lake while on vacation. But because of Turk's "delicate" health, Macdonough wanted an especially good surgeon's mate. The first one suggested was noted for his "habits of intemperance, & therefore one little to be desired on board ship, particularly in the character of a Physician."[3]

A similar situation developed with the choice of chaplain. Macdonough found the character of one suggested individual to be unacceptable since he had been told "that he is intemperate, & that he is utterly regardless of the sanctity of his profession." But Secretary Southard did not accept Macdonough's suggested candidates. As late as 2 October he noted to the secretary that "in the multiplicity of business with which you are surrounded, it may have escaped your notice that this ship is yet without a Chaplain." Twenty days later the Reverend John McCarty reported for this office. McCarty had serious family problems—an ailing wife and small children—and he went with the expectation that he would be allowed to return home long before the cruise was over.[4] And so it went for position after position as Macdonough sought his preferences for critical billets. Also on board was Macdonough's almost four-year-old son, Augustus Rodney Macdonough, known as Rodney to his family.

Two other issues complicated personnel problems. One involved a contretemps between Midshipman Augustus Barnhouse and Purser John B. Timberlake. Macdonough suspended the midshipman from duty "for a flagrant breach of discipline" when he claimed notes from Timberlake were a payment for a debt owed by the purser rather than a debt owed by the midshipman. Moreover, the commodore found "this young man's conduct towards myself, has been indecorous." The exchange of letters between Macdonough and Barnhouse and between Macdonough and Secretary Southard regarding this affair is by far the most lengthy in the period leading up to the ship's departure. In the end, Macdonough counseled both Timberlake and Barnhouse and concluded to the secretary that the midshipman was finally "sensible of the offence he committed against the discipline of the service, which I trust will be a useful lesson to him in the future."[5] As we will see, it was not as useful a lesson as the commodore hoped.

At the last moment another issue arose. The master at arms desired to take his wife with him. The gunner made a similar request. Macdonough preferred that no women be allowed aboard ship. "Women are frequently serviceable with the sick," he noted, "but I have seldom known them to be on board without producing difficulty among the men, & being otherwise troublesome."[6] No women sailed on this cruise.

While he importuned the secretary for personnel, he also wrote Commo. John Rodgers, president of the Board of Navy Commissioners, regarding equipment for the *Constitution*. He called for replacing the standing rigging and cables.[7]

Slowly but surely all the minutiae of preparing a ship for a major cruise came to a close. Macdonough knew that thoroughness was essential for effective leadership. With personnel, rigging, sails, cables, provisions, and stores, the successful commander was the one who saw to each of these with particular care. The old adage "The devil is in the details" applied to military preparations as well as to matters of civilian life. The commodore sought to exorcise this demon with careful attention to the particulars that bedevil any commander. In late August he moved the crew of the *Constitution* on board the ship, and on 16 October he informed the secretary that the "ship is ready to receive your instructions to proceed to sea." The instructions arrived on the twenty-fifth.[8] The commodore and the crew paid their final farewells.

Mediterranean Service

On 29 October 1824 Macdonough hoisted his star-spangled, swallowtail, broad blue pendant, and the *Constitution* sailed out of New York Harbor for the Mediterranean. It was a gallant and proud vessel. Known as a "crack ship," it could be compared with other vessels to "what a nice, tidy, fashionable gentleman is among men." In 1826, one new crewman described it as being in fine order: "every part . . . under excellent regulation; her crew . . . thoroughly disciplined, and her officers well trained." Such a comment was a tribute to Macdonough and Vallette's professionalism and attention to duty. The *Constitution* was exceptionally large, fast, and lethal for its rate as a forty-four-gun frigate. It was 175 feet between perpendiculars with an extreme beam of 44 feet, 2 inches. Its mainmast rose 200 feet. It carried thirty 24-pound long guns on the main deck, two 24-pound gunades, and eighteen 32-pound carronades on the spardeck and quarterdeck. In total it held fifty guns; like most American vessels, it carried more guns than its rate.

Launched in 1797, *Constitution* had the most impressive combat record of any sailing vessel in the navy. Four of its former commanders won gold medals from Congress for their distinctive combat leadership on this frigate—Edward Preble, Isaac Hull, William Bainbridge, and Charles Stewart. Thomas Macdonough received such a decoration for his service on Lake Champlain, and he, Hull, and Stewart were awarded silver medals for duty under Preble in the Mediterranean. The *Constitution* carried a few mementos of its victories: enemy balls indented some of its cannons, and a row of muskets at the cabin door carried the mark "G.R." and the royal crown. Its heritage was such that it remains in commission today and no other ship in the navy's history has borne its name.[9]

In previous postings the commodore was a tall, dignified, and commanding figure. His complexion, hair, and eyes were light. He had always been thin but muscular in body frame. He normally displayed such firmness and steadfastness in his gaze that he immediately commanded the attention of all. But the man who now paced the windward side of Old Ironside's quarterdeck was wan, stooped, and sickly in appearance. The vessel's surgeon wondered if he would survive the voyage. Undoubtedly similar thoughts crossed Lieutenant Vallette's mind, as he found himself faced with more responsibilities than normal for an executive officer.

As usual, the captain and first lieutenant had to bring the crew into the daily routine of warship life. At dawn the reports of the night guns of the sentries, fired at the first tap of the reveille drum, disturbed the slumbers of the sailors. Then the boatswain, stationed on the gun deck, gave a long pipe echoed by similar ones from his mates and followed by the cry "All hands, ahoy." Following another long pipe, came the cry "All hands up hammocks, ahoy." Springing from their hammocks, the men lashed them and carried them to the deck for storage in the netting. All this took twelve minutes.

Thereafter the boatswain and the officer of the berth deck reported to the lieutenant of the watch. Afterward the starboard watch spread over the spar deck and the larboard watch over the main deck. Sailors pumped water onto the decks and the men then took a hoe-like instrument called a "squill-gee" with a wooden head covered with leather to push away much of the water. Following this, the crew violently slapped the deck with mops, called "swabs," to remove more water. (From time to time they began the work by scouring the wet decks with sandstones called "holystones." The large ones, used on the main part of the decks, were called "Bibles," the smaller ones, used in the corners, were known as "prayer books." The Bibles were fastened in the middle of a strong rope, which six men drew backward and forward across the deck while another sprinkled sand. This was followed by swabbing.) Soon the decks took on a smooth, even surface, appearing almost white. Meanwhile, the carpenter's gang scraped the hatches and grating and the quarter gunners cleaned the match tubs, shot boxes, gun carriages, and guns.

This done, a brief interval of leisure followed until six bells (seven in the morning), when the boatswain piped the crew to breakfast—tea, a biscuit, and cold meat. Finally the officers appeared, having been roused at six bells. Their hammock boys lashed their beds and stowed them on deck. While the officers promenaded the deck, the crew cleaned their quarters.

Normally the first lieutenant made the daily inspection. However, at about 1000 on some days, Lieutenant Vallette reported to Captain

Macdonough that the ship was ready for inspection. With the first lieutenant behind, the commodore first inspected the gun deck. As they
passed, each man lifted his hat or, if uncovered, tipped a lock of hair. They
then descended to the berth deck. The master-at-arms, in charge of this
deck, ordered, "Stand by your places men." Each cook stood by his chest
with hands crossed before him. On their own chest they stacked a pyramid
of kitchen utensils, each with a Bible on top, an obvious appeal to the commodore's reputation for piety. Macdonough wore white gloves and often
rubbed them against the whitewashed beams and the gleaming cauldrons
and copper pots to see if they were clean. Then Macdonough and Vallette
went to the storerooms, steerage, cockpit, and wardroom. Each was inspected with the same attention to order, neatness, and cleanliness.
Following inspection the various groups of men began their various tasks:
carpentry, coopering, shoemaking, barbering, tailoring, cooking, black-
smithing, sailmaking, and learning in school.

After dinner with its grog at midday, the men swept the decks again and
returned to work. After grog and supper (evening meal) the decks were
again swept and the remainder of the day found the crew on its own except for routine duties. Men dispersed around the deck, told tall tales,
played checkers, and listened to music from the forecastle. At sunset the
drummers and fifers beat to quarters and the band struck up "Hail
Columbia" as the colors were lowered. The petty officers passed out the
hammocks by number and most turned in, but a few continued to listen to
yarns about "witches and hobgoblins, battles and shipwrecks," many rival-
ing the Arabian Nights in their flights of fancy. Eventually the cry "Put out
all fires, lights, pipes, segars, and everything that can make a light; except
the sentry's light, and the match in the galley" was heard, followed by the
reply, "All out, sir." The *Constitution* settled down for the night. When in
port, "by ten o'clock, the tread of the officers of the watch, is the only
sound heard; except the occasional hail of a boat, or, at every half hour, the
striking of the ship's time, answered by sentries above, with 'all's—well,'
'all's—well.'"[10]

On Sundays the crew went through the same inspection ritual, but this
time they dressed in better uniforms, and at 1100 the cry "All hands to
muster, ahoy" went out. Chaplain John McCarty used the capstan as a pul-
pit. Behind him stood two long lines of very stiff marines with Lieutenant
Henry B. Tyler at their head. Only when the lieutenant gave the word
"Rest" did they relax. To his front were the officers and midshipmen, and
abaft of them the crew. When all was ready, Lieutenant Vallette descended

to the captain's cabin and brought Macdonough to the quarterdeck. As soon as he appeared the commodore raised his hat and everyone else returned the salute. The ship's band played sacred music to start the worship service then read from the Book of Common Prayer. After the Gloria Patri they played again. The chaplain gave a sermon, and the band played at the conclusion. All was orderly, and afterward, when they were in port, the officers clamored, "Who's for going ashore?" On shore they played billiards or monté or went to balls. On Sundays in port there was no required work unless there was an emergency. After grog and dinner the men dispersed about the ship, napped, read, talked, danced, and otherwise amused themselves. After grog and supper there was music and bed. Occasionally, groups of men visited other ships in port or secured permission to go ashore.[11]

Of course the main difference between the *Constitution*'s purpose and that of the great American commercial vessels that plied the world's waters was that it was a man-of-war. Its mission was to be prepared for combat. Macdonough's emphasis on gunnery reflected a doctrine expressed six years earlier: "The time of peace is the time to prepare for war, then when it arrives all is ready."[12]

With what must have seemed monotonous regularity, the crew exercised the guns. Each gun and the one opposite it on the same deck had a dozen men assigned to it. Eight to ten guns made a division, supervised by a lieutenant and one to three midshipmen. The three divisions on the main deck each had five gun crews operating ten guns each. The fourth division was on the forecastle and the fifth on the quarterdeck where the carronades and gunades were located. The typical gun crew consisted of the first and second captains, first and second spongers, first and second loaders, two shot and wadding men, first and second train and tackle men, first and second crowbar and handspike men, fireman, and powder boy.

The divisional lieutenants began the exercises, but the gun captains largely conducted them. The crew ran in the gun, practiced loading and priming, ran the piece into battery, pointed it toward an imaginary target, and then fired. In the exercises there was, of course, no explosion; it was a dumb show. Over and over again they repeated the drill. Once the routine became commonplace and every gun crewman knew the duties of the others, they practiced firing broadsides and sequential firing as an imaginary target came into range. Eventually each division conducted live fire exercises against empty-barrel targets towed by boats being rowed by other crewmembers. Now the crewmen heard the din of battle, saw the flashes of gunfire, smelled the acrid odor of burning gunpowder, and found themselves partially blinded and their bodies and clothing blackened by the smoke. They witnessed the shrieking recoil of the gun as it strained on the ropes while it raced inboard. The hands, stripped to the waist, avoided the recoiling gun carriage and sponged, loaded, and rammed home the charge, then ran between one and two and a half tons of metal back into battery for the next firing. The men reacted with spirit as their aim improved and the barrels disintegrated when the shot blew them apart.

The commodore paced the quarterdeck observing the speed and accuracy of his various crews. It was this routine of both exercises and live firing that made American naval gunnery the most feared in the world during the War of 1812. Macdonough and Vallette were determined to maintain this reputation. They knew that if a crew had an intimate conviction of its moral and technical superiority over its opponents it would confidently go into an engagement. At the decisive moment all this training would positively affect the outcome.[13]

The Atlantic crossing went well, and the *Constitution* arrived in Gibraltar after a fine passage of twenty-five days; Macdonough was pleased with the competence of his crew. There was little time for leave as the ship departed six days later with the corvette *Cyane*, Capt. John O. Creighton commanding, accompanying it. At sea it encountered the sloop *Ontario*, Master Commandant John B. Nicolson commanding, which joined the small squadron. Macdonough then detached the *Cyane*. After a four-day stay in Tunis, where they deposited new consul Charles D. Coxe and family, the two-ship squadron arrived in Syracuse.

En route to Sicily Macdonough may have felt a sense of foreboding when one of his black seamen, John Norman, died of consumption. The same illness that affected him had taken Norman's life. Norman's body was brought on deck, covered with a flag, and guarded by a member of his mess. Toward noon on 19 December 1824 the cry "All hands bury the dead, ahoy" went out. The corpse, sewed into a hammock with a cannon ball at the feet, was laid on a board and brought to an opened gangway. All the men uncovered their heads, and Chaplain McCarty read the service for the burial of the dead at sea from the Book of Common Prayer. When he came to "We therefore commit his body to the deep," the messmates raised the head of the board and the body plunged into the blue waters of the Mediterranean. Such a ceremony caused the men, and especially Macdonough, to contemplate their own mortality.[14]

The *Constitution* and *Ontario* stayed in Syracuse and were joined there by the sloop *Erie,* Master Commandant Deacon commanding. While there the commodore's broad pendant flew from the *Constitution's* main skysail masthead, during the day and at night a light on the mizzen top distinguished it from the other American vessels. The other two vessels could not beat to quarters, strike a bell, or fire their evening guns until the flagship did so. The *Erie* and *Ontario* found their every movement subject to the *Constitution's* bidding. On 15 January, while at anchor, the *Constitution* and *Ontario* swung out of phase and the *Ontario* fouled the flagship, carrying away its jib boom. On 5 February the *Constitution* and *Erie* sailed for Messina, where they spent the rest of the winter conducting typical overhaul. The *Ontario* and *Cyane* subsequently rejoined them there.

The stay in Sicily must have brought back memories both good and bad of the 1818–19 winter spent there. How much control did the commodore have over his officers and their desires to visit the gaming tables in Messina? We do not know for sure, but the disciplining of his junior officers emphasized that Macdonough's zeal for proper behavior had not burned out. He demanded the resignation of Midshipman Barnhouse for "ungentlemanly and unofficerlike conduct"—he cheated at cards. Macdonough returned to the United States Midn. Gray Skipwith, who intended to resign. Macdonough ordered a court-martial for Midn. Edward M. Vail of the *Ontario* and, following his conviction for disobedience of orders and treating his superior with contempt, returned him to the States. He ordered Lt. John H. Bell, first lieutenant of the *Erie,* to trial and subsequently had Bell publicly reprimanded before being restored to duty. For unknown reasons, Macdonough did not forward a record of this somewhat unusual trial of a vessel's first lieutenant to the Navy Department. In this instance Macdonough appears to have chosen the path of leniency. Perhaps his greatest outrage occurred when Midn. James B. Glentworth made "unfavorable aspersions against a brother officer." Macdonough sent Glentworth and John W. Mooers, Henry W. Morris, and Samuel Swarthwout, all of the *Constitution,* home because of their parts in a duel involving Glentworth. Before this disciplinary bloodbath ended, Macdonough had eliminated six of the seven most junior midshipmen from the flagship along with officers from other vessels in his command.[15]

What Macdonough did not know was that Secretary Southard had grown increasingly upset over sending such young men home for what he considered minor infractions. While Macdonough was engaged in these disciplinary enterprises in the Mediterranean, Southard wrote Commodore Rodgers of his displeasure at the conduct of Macdonough's predecessors who had similarly ordered men back to the United States because of disciplinary infractions. In compliance with this policy, Commodore Rodgers would subsequently note his displeasure at Macdonough's sending Midshipmen Morris, Glentworth, Swarthwout, Mooers, and Vail home from Gibraltar without providing them with any funds for a merchant passage. "I cannot conceive of any offence which, they [Morris and Vail, who were ill] could commit against the laws and discipline of the service that would justify their being turned on shore among Strangers in a foreign Country without funds to carry them home," Rodgers wrote the secretary of the navy. The young men had to prevail on the American consul for funds to return to the United States.[16]

Rodgers and Macdonough disagreed on the nature of punishment for minor infractions. It would appear that Macdonough felt that the iron hand of the seniority system could only be tamed by imposing severe disciplinary measures on errant midshipman who were not yet under its provisions. As noted, in 1818 Macdonough left two delinquent officers at the dock in Russia and compelled them to use consular funds to return to the United States during the *Guerrière* cruise. A few months later Macdonough secured his brother-in-law's resignation from the service after he became involved in a duel. Macdonough was a stern taskmaster and demanded a standard of behavior among his midshipmen that Southard thought excessive. In a twist of fate, Rodgers would compel the dying Macdonough to go home on a merchant vessel rather than a naval one.

Despite his best efforts, Macdonough could not restore the taut discipline he hoped to have in the Mediterranean Squadron. Rodgers wrote Secretary Southard that "bickerings and bad feelings" prevailed throughout the squadron, particularly on the *Cyane*. Rodgers, who had not been to sea for several years, attributed the lack of "harmony and subordination" among the officers to "an excess of indulgence." He found that the *Cyane*'s officers spent too much of their time in Messina not in pursuit "of useful information but of pleasures neither calculated to benefit their constitutions, improve their morals, or enlarge their minds, but to lead them into acts of extravagance." It is hard to believe that "indulgence" describes Macdonough's standards on the *Constitution,* but it is clear that on some of the other vessels in his command there was great leniency concerning midshipmen's conduct ashore.[17]

From time to time Macdonough invited the lieutenants and midshipmen to his cabin for splendid breakfasts and dinners. Here he taught them the proper decorum of gentlemen officers that he had learned, years earlier, under similar circumstances. The conversation was respectful, and from it the commodore gained an understanding of his lieutenants and midshipmen's abilities and promise.

On a happier matter, Macdonough's health improved over the winter. It seemed the change of climate had a positive effect on his well-being.

That winter Macdonough learned lessons never taught on board a ship. There was no school for senior command, there were few examples of it in American naval history, and Macdonough had never served on a squadron flagship. He had captains under him, each of whom was God Almighty on his quarterdeck but had to obey the slightest whim of a commodore. Macdonough had no choice in who they were. When sailing together or when in port, they and their ships were at his beck and call. At this Sicilian port Commodore Macdonough reached the pinnacle of his naval service and prestige. But developments in Washington were about to change his command status.

The Aegean Interlude

The United States had sought, and failed, to conduct formal diplomatic relations with the Ottoman Empire for years prior to the War of 1812. After the conflict the Americans renewed these efforts. With the outbreak of the Greek independence effort, attempts by Commodore Bainbridge to conclude such an agreement in 1820–21 resulted in failure. Stories about the atrocities of Turkish soldiers and years of schooling on the ancient Greek democracies helped to foster an enthusiasm on behalf of the Greek Orthodox Christians and against the Turkish Muslims. Former presidents Madison and Jefferson urged the Monroe administration to work with the British government in fostering Greek independence. Support for an independent Greece abounded in the United States. Towns from Ithaca, New York, to Athens, Georgia, to Ypsilanti, Michigan, received names honoring the ancient city-states and modern independence heroes. Greek revival architecture swept the country. Such devotion did not set well in Constantinople. Nonetheless, in 1824 the Monroe administration sought to reach an Ottoman-American accord. To mediate these negotiations Monroe and Adams decided to send the country's senior naval officer—John Rodgers, the chairman of the Board of Navy Commissioners.

The choice was an astute one. Rodgers had limited diplomatic experience during the Barbary Wars and extensive knowledge of the attitudes of President Monroe and Secretary of State John Quincy Adams regarding the situation in the Middle East. Macdonough had none of these qualifications. Adams instructed Rodgers "to ascertain in what matter a Treaty of Commerce, founded upon principles of reciprocity, and by which, access to the navigation of the Black-Sea, should be secured to the commercial shipping of the United States."[18] Although the decision to send Rodgers to the Mediterranean came before the *Constitution* sailed from New York, Macdonough never received notification of Rodgers's expected arrival time.

Rodgers commanded the *North Carolina.* Rated as a 74-gun vessel, it was one of the first completed of five ships-of-the-line built for the U.S. Navy. Pierced for 102 guns, it actually mounted 94. Carrying a crew of 960 men, its officers included Capt. Daniel T. Patterson as captain of the fleet and Master Commandant C. W. Morgan as ship's captain. Rodgers boarded the vessel in Norfolk on 18 December 1824 and raised his broad pendant over it. He did not receive final instructions from the president and secretary of state until 27 March 1825, and he sailed to Gibraltar in thirty-three days. Macdonough sent *Ontario* to Gibraltar on 7 March, and it returned without learning of Rodgers's pending arrival.

Greatly disappointed at not finding Macdonough and his vessels there, Rodgers wrote a damning letter to the secretary of the navy. "If Captain Macdonough was officially apprised" of my coming, he said, "as I presume he was previous to his departure from the United States, that I was to command in the Mediterranean, I shall feel it my duty to remove him from the command of the *Constitution* for not meeting me here or apprising me where I might find him."[19] Rodgers's hasty and intemperate remarks may reflect a friendship with Commodore Charles Stewart who had disciplined Macdonough previously.

Macdonough did not learn of Rodgers arrival in Gibraltar until late May, at which time the *Constitution*'s flags ordered the squadron (*Ontario, Erie,* and *Cyane*) to raise anchor and head immediately for the Rock. Meanwhile, the petulant Rodgers went to show the flag at Málaga, Algeciras, and Tangier. When he arrived at the British Crown colony on 12 June, Macdonough first learned of Rodgers's whereabouts. The new commodore arrived shortly thereafter, and Rodgers learned that the victor of Lake Champlain had not been made aware of his coming. Macdonough took offense at the tone of a letter from Rodgers, which must have been similar to the message he sent the secretary of the navy.[20] It says much for Macdonough's character that he displayed no ill temper at Rodgers's false accusation and instead calmly reported the situation. There were none of the harsh words and recriminations that characterized the Stewart-Macdonough exchange of six years earlier.

During this stay in Gibraltar Macdonough sought to enhance the welfare of his officers and crew. For instance, he improved the circulation below deck by removing some of the bulkheads. In addition, he urged Secretary Southard to promote acting boatswain John Ball to permanent status in that office. When a promotion cost him an acting master of the ship, he recommended Rodgers to promote Midn. John Pope to that post. When Purser Timberlake complained of the quality of beef recently brought on board, Macdonough had it condemned. He followed Surgeon Turk's advice to discharge a seaman from duty because he was "unfit for service," and he reluctantly approved Chaplain McCarty's release from duty and his return to the United States. Thus at the very time Macdonough's own physical condition required some spiritual consolation, he was without a chaplain.[21]

After replenishing themselves with supplies in Gibraltar, the vessels sailed to the eastern Mediterranean. A brief stop in Tunis preceded a tour in the Aegean Sea. For Macdonough's fast frigate, maintaining a slow enough pace to remain in formation with the slow-sailing *North Carolina* and the squadron's other vessels proved annoying. The *Constitution*'s historian writes, "What a frustrating time it must have been for her watch officers, harnessed with the responsibility of staying with a plodding liner."[22] The American squadron visited Ausa on Paros Island, the Bay of Smyrna (presently called Izmir), Turkey, and the delightful and easily defended port of Napoli de Romania (now Nauplia), Greece, in the Gulf of Argos. The latter place was the capital of the struggling Greek independence movement. The American squadron was operating in a delicate situation in the midst of the Greek revolt against the Ottoman Empire while at the same time trying to negotiate with the Turkish naval minister. Their efforts nevertheless brought them good will from both combatants.

While in Smyrna a fire began to spread through the town. Rodgers sent his officers and men to assist the residents in extinguishing it. Both the foreign merchants in the city and the local citizens expressed their gratitude for this assistance. Despite the abuse heaped on the Sultan in America, the locals treated the squadron's officers and seamen with respect. However, some ill will arose when members of watering party crews pilfered grapes and figs from nearby orchards.[23] Efforts by Rodgers and American counsel David W. Offley to contact the Ottoman grand admiral in order to negotiate a treaty failed. On the other hand, the Turks who saw the American vessels were quite impressed and a few years later close ties between the Turkish navy and the U.S. Navy began.

The stay in Napoli de Romania had a similar impact on American-Greek relations. Driven to this tiny port in the Peloponnesus, the revolutionary leaders delighted in having representatives of the world's largest democracy visit them. They recognized that the American squadron represented a link to the outside world they desperately needed if there was the slightest chance for their revolt to succeed.

Deaths on Land and at Sea

For Macdonough the Aegean experience must at first have seemed a delight. Here he was in the midst of the waters traversed by St. Paul. Somewhere in the nearby Turkish coast lay the ancient city of Ephesus, and on the Greek coast was Corinth, communities to which the apostle wrote his famous epistles. In the Bay of Argos near Napoli, Agamemnon assembled the famous thousand ships to return Helen from her abductor in Troy. It was an ideal region for someone with Macdonough's interests. But a six-week stay in the Aegean during August and September was not positive for someone in Macdonough's health. In fact, it was not a good time for many in the *Constitution*'s crew. The number of sick more than doubled to forty-two, and four enlisted men died in the first week of September. The heat was oppressive, and Macdonough's condition declined rapidly. To make matters worse, Turk was barely able to assist his patients because of his own ill health.[24]

Unable to find his Ottoman counterpart and faced with growing illness among his crews, Commodore Rodgers ordered his squadron westward on 18 September. They arrived at Gibraltar on 9 October. Bad news awaited Macdonough there.

Macdonough had long known that Ann was in a poor physical state. Two years before her death she wrote a longtime friend that her health was "declining and I must seek all means which God has provided for lengthening a life which I have for many months known could not continue long." Her mother wrote the commodore shortly after his departure in the *Constitution* that his wife was "thin and her spirits are not good. How can they be, with the reiterated losses and a separation so long in prospect from you and our dear little Rodney."[25] Still Ann carried the last pregnancy to term and on 25 June 1825 delivered Charlotte Rosella Macdonough. Her foreboding became a fact when she died on 9 August 1825 at the age of thirty-five.

Shortly after its arrival in Gibraltar, the officers of the *Constitution* learned that Lucy Ann Macdonough had died. Someone had to inform the ailing captain and his young son, Rodney, of her demise. That lot fell on Lieutenant Tattnall. Upon receiving this blow, Macdonough apparently lost the will to live. According to his obituary, from the moment he learned of Ann's death his tuberculosis "made fearful inroads on his already debilitated frame, and in a vain endeavour to return to his country and home where he might repose with the buried objects of his love, he sunk into a sleep of death."[26]

Macdonough requested permission to relinquish his command and Rodgers consented. However, the Mediterranean commander refused Macdonough's request that he be sent home on the *Erie*. Instead Macdonough found himself obligated to secure passage on a merchantman.[27] On 14 October Captain Patterson boarded the *Constitution* and three days later took command of the vessel without any of the customary ceremonies. (There was a special poignancy in this change of command. Three successive commanders of Old Ironsides—Jones, Macdonough, and Patterson—had once been midshipmen together on the ill-fated *Philadelphia*.) On the twenty-second Macdonough, his son Rodney, his personal servant William Green, Turk, and seven invalid *Constitution* enlisted men boarded the merchant brig *Edwin* and were sent home.

The Hero of Lake Champlain never made it home alive. *Edwin* had fair winds and weather most of the voyage, and it seemed the passengers would arrive in the States before death intervened, but this was not to be. Turk did all that was possible to make Macdonough's death easy, and he reported to Ann's mother that the commodore's passing had gone comfortably. Shortly before dying Macdonough made two requests. First, he made a small bequest to Seaman William Green for his "constant and faithful attention" to his dying commander. Second, Macdonough desired that he not be buried at sea but that his body be returned to Middletown for burial beside Ann. On 10 November 1825, he died just a few weeks short of his forty-second birthday.

Shortly after his demise, a storm arose and drove the ship much farther south than its intended New York destination. With considerable irony, the *Edwin* found herself entering Delaware Bay, the very estuary from which Midshipman Macdonough had sailed twenty-five years earlier. There Turk saw that Macdonough's body was preserved and taken to New York, where the Rev. Edward Rutledge, the husband of one of Ann's sisters, met it and young Rodney.

A well-planned funeral dignified Thomas Macdonough's arrival. At first the coffin was brought on board the steamboat *Fulton First*, which the commodore had briefly commanded. Then it was taken to the navy yard where the steamboat *Washington* towed several barges containing the body, dignitaries, and marine and navy bands to the Battery. After a parade up Broadway with seven navy captains acting as pallbearers, the procession visited the city hall and then St. Paul's chapel for a brief service. The entourage then proceeded to the foot of Fulton Street, where the coffin was placed on board the steamboat *Commerce* for the journey to Middletown.[28]

Middletown did its utmost to provide an appropriate farewell ceremony for its local celebrity. On Saturday, 1 December, Macdonough's remains were brought first to his residence and then taken to the local Congregational Church (a larger edifice than the Episcopal one), where the Right Rev. Thomas C. Brownell, Episcopal bishop of Connecticut, read the funeral service. Afterward a procession went to Riverside Cemetery, where the coffin was buried beside that of his beloved Ann in the Shaler family plot. Later in the day the Rev. Henry M. Colton, chaplain of the American Literary, Scientific and Military Academy, delivered a funeral oration outlining the achievements of the commodore.[29]

Eventually the family erected a monument in their memory inscribed in part:

> He was distinguished in the world
> as the Hero of Lake Champlain; in
> the Church of Christ as a faithful, zealous
> and consistent Christian; in the com-
> munity where he resided when absent
> from professional duties as an amiable
> upright and valuable citizen.

For her the inscription read:

> The richest gifts of Nature & of Grace
> adorned her mind & heart, & at her
> death Genius, Friendship & Piety
> mourned their common loss.

For the family, the most critical consequence of these two deaths was the care of the five Macdonough children. As orphans, their welfare became the immediate responsibility of the Middletown Probate Court. The court appointed the Rev. Mr. Rutledge guardian of the children. The rector of the Episcopal church in Stratford, Connecticut, Rutledge and his wife Augusta took responsibility for their welfare for the next several years. He regularly reported to the court on their well-being and the status of their estate from the Macdonough and Shaler inheritances. By 1835 the guardianship changed to Edwin F. Johnson, husband of another Shaler sister, Charlotte. Johnson secured permission to sell the Macdonough house so that the proceeds could be used to provide for the "nurture & education" of the five children. Although at the time this was done the Johnsons lived in Utica, New York, they eventually settled in the Shaler home in Middletown. This, of course, placed the Macdonough and Johnson children under the watchful eye of Grandmother Lucretia Ann Shaler until her death in 1843. It was not until the older sons reached their maturity in 1841 that the Macdonough estate was formally divided among the children.[30]

The Macdonough Legacy

One can never fully document the contributions of an individual naval officer to the institution and nation he serves. Thus Thomas Truxtun's admonitions regarding proper conduct were never codified into regulations, but they may be seen as examples of what was expected of the best of naval leaders. The examples of combat leadership exhibited by Edward Preble and Stephen Decatur never became official policy, but their style became a model of effective command followed by their contemporaries and successors. So also is it difficult to assess Macdonough's legacy and distinguish it from the institutional ideals of naval service. Nonetheless, he illustrated by his conduct many of the best attributes of command that others were to emulate.

Foremost of these characteristics was his technical and tactical proficiency. No one ever questioned his competence in navigation and seamanship. Vessels under his command sailed without significant incident in the North and South Atlantic and in the Indian Ocean and the Mediterranean and Baltic Seas. The attention to detail with which he conducted his every command illustrated a professional competence above reproach. On that fatal day in September 1814 he not only placed his vessels in effective locations to meet their foe but also set an example of gunnery and tactical maneuvering that few could exceed.

Moreover, like most effective commanders, he set an example of personal conduct that few duplicated. In a day when all too many of his contemporaries drank to excess, gambled with abandon, cursed like the devil, and flagrantly disregarded their marriage vows, Thomas Macdonough proved an example of propriety. He not only followed religious morality but also demonstrated Christian charity with family, friends, and shipmates. When others did not meet his standards, he counseled them on proper behavior. When he found subordinates conduct so flagrant that it merited exemplary punishment, he was not above a public demonstration of his disapproval, as in the case of the two young men he left on the pier in Russia or the midshipman he forced to resign for misconduct on his last cruise. His outrage at dueling among subordinates reached a peak between the *Guerrière* and *Constitution* cruises. When asked to second his mentor Stephen Decatur in his famous duel, Macdonough's refusal signified that, for him, personal morality surmounted friendship. Perhaps the most telling indication of his personal integrity was that he was one of a few among his contemporaries never court-martialed or involved in a duel. Macdonough was not given to endless bravado; his deeds were enough—they made his reputation among his peers.

The commodore was not perfect in this regard. His dispute with Charles Stewart demonstrated a tendency to carry a disagreement to excess. He probably should have forwarded more commendatory comments regarding subordinates' conduct during the battle in Plattsburgh Bay. At times he may have been excessively severe. Leaving two young men at the dock in Russia demonstrated a temper rarely displayed. His discipline of midshipmen during the 1825 winter in Sicily indicates a desire to curtail junior officers' activities in a way that offended Commodore Rodgers. Nonetheless, his personal conduct was above reproach, and all that knew him understood this.

Throughout Macdonough's career he sought responsibility and took responsibility for his actions. His taking a furlough to assume command of a merchant vessel was an important step in the direction of learning first-hand the burdens and obligations of leadership. In taking command of the Lake Champlain squadron he assumed a responsibility far above that of someone of his rank and time in service. When he undertook the dispute with Commodore Stewart he understood that he would be held accountable for his conduct and that it could ruin his career. Macdonough's desire for sea service in the 1820s, when he had a virtual sinecure as commander of the idle *Ohio* and lived most of the time in Middletown, demonstrated a sense of professionalism even when his wife's illness and his own made such duty onerous. Thomas Macdonough had an extraordinary sense of duty that undoubtedly influenced those who knew him.

Few of Macdonough's contemporaries exemplified more competently the leadership principle of knowing oneself and seeking self-improvement. His desire for intellectual development both as a professional sailor and as a gentleman, demonstrated by his library, indicates that Macdonough never tired in the quest for expanded understanding of himself and his world. When he sought furlough to command a merchant vessel, he secured advancement in professional experience and geographic knowledge that benefited his naval career. His introspection on the quay at Gibraltar during the encounter with Stewart, when he exclaimed, "By zounds, I do not know how it will end," points to a man who had personal doubts of his own fallibility. His ultimate acknowledgment of error in this affair demonstrated integrity worthy of emulation.

One must recall, however, that Macdonough resisted being ordered to command the steam frigate *Fulton First*. Obviously, he was not one to be an agent of technological innovation. He refused an opportunity in naval modernization. Thus he can be seen as a technological conservative. There were limits to his creativity and sense of what the future of his profession entailed.

Once he found himself in a position of leadership, he assumed the duty of developing a sense of responsibility among his subordinates. Just as Decatur and John Smith had assisted him in his development of leadership characteristics, so also Macdonough mentored those under his command. From the time of his command on Lake Champlain, he looked after and assisted the careers of those he felt deserved more assistance and support in developing their leadership qualifications. Young men like Stephen Cassin, Joseph Smith, Joel Abbot, and Elie Vallette benefited from his support. No one has written books titled *Macdonough's Boys* or *Macdonough's Lieutenants*, as they have for Edward Preble and Robert E. Lee, but during a relatively short career the Hero of Lake Champlain encouraged and provided an extraordinary example for a large number of future captains and admirals.

Perhaps the most famous of these young men was Midshipman Charles Wilkes Jr. of the *Guerrière*, whose leadership of the South Seas Surveying and Exploring Expedition, 1838–42, marked the beginnings of U.S. Navy interest in Antarctica. His often-controversial career included promotion to rear admiral. Other former subordinates of Macdonough who eventually achieved flag rank included Vallette (who changed his last name to LaVallette), Joseph Smith, Hiram Paulding, Frederick Engle, and Charles H. Bell. One can never fully assess the impact of Macdonough or any other naval officer or the navy's institutional expectations on these men's career success; but the Hero of Lake Champlain did provide an example of public service these men continued.[31]

His conduct inspired the enlisted men under his command. From the day Midshipman Macdonough took men into the hold of the *Philadelphia* to the time he aimed guns in Plattsburgh Bay, Macdonough demonstrated a courage and competence that inspired his bluejackets. They remembered his signal on the day of battle: "Impressed seamen call on every man to do his duty." However uneducated they may have been, the typical tar understood when an officer knows his men, their abilities, and their needs. Discipline administered justly was acceptable. The tars accepted hardship and danger knowing that their commander experienced and excelled in similar situations. When they witnessed a senior demonstrating competence their subordination was not resented. Macdonough gained the respect of those men who followed him. The sword from the *Guerrière*'s crew testified to the esteem his conduct incurred.

Above all, Macdonough exemplified an ability to make sound and timely decisions. At critical moments he prudently took risks. An early instance of this occurred in Gibraltar Harbor, when he recovered an American merchant sailor as he was being impressed into the Royal Navy. That he stared down a senior British officer who complained of his conduct shows just how determined he was to justify an action. But perhaps his most famous exhibition of this leadership trait was in Plattsburgh Bay, when he ordered Vallette and Brum to put the anchor hawser under the bow of the *Saratoga* and haul the ship around. Here in the most stressful moment of his naval career he combined his seamanship with prompt and correct decision making to achieve victory.

The ultimate test of naval professionalism involved physical and moral courage. Of course the prime example of this in Macdonough's career involves the combat in Plattsburgh Bay. But he exhibited courage early in his career, and his reputation as Decatur's favorite midshipman exemplified this personal attribute. Suffering from tuberculosis as he was, it took physical courage to assume command of the *Constitution*. Moral courage was an attribute best demonstrated in the quarrel with Stewart. However wrong his case may have been legally, Macdonough manifested a sense of moral outrage at what he considered to be an interference with the deliberations of a court-martial board by his commander. It required great fortitude to dispute the decisions of one's superior. One contemporary wrote, "The great charm of his character was the purity of his principles, and the sincerity of his religion."[32]

Macdonough's reputation has long lived after him, although in relative obscurity when compared to such men as Edward Preble, Stephen Decatur, and Oliver Hazard Perry. Historians of the navy and of the War of 1812 acclaim his leadership on Lake Champlain. Theodore Roosevelt's *Naval War of 1812* (1882) provides the supreme accolade: "His skill, seamanship, quick eye, readiness of resource, and indomitable pluck are beyond all praise. Down to the time of the Civil War he is the greatest figure in our naval history." Sir Winston Churchill praised Macdonough's victory as "the most decisive engagement of the war." James C. Bradford's brief biographical note argues that the battle of Lake Champlain "has often been cited as a model of tactical preparation and execution. Carefully choosing his position and preparing for every possible contingency, Macdonough forced an enemy with superior power to engage him at a disadvantage. His victory is often considered the climatic battle of the war." Capt. Alfred T. Mahan concludes that Macdonough's victory "more nearly than any other incident of the War of 1812, merits the epithet 'decisive.'" Professor Harry Coles concludes that the army-navy triumphs at Plattsburgh were "to the War of 1812 what Saratoga was to the American Revolution. In both cases a major attempt at invasion was foiled and a change in diplomacy resulted." Historian Reginald Horsman describes Macdonough's achievement as a "vital victory" for the United States. In his account of the battle of Lake Champlain, W. M. P. Dunne calls the winding of the *Saratoga* "one of the great exploits of naval history." Yet in their study of the leaders in the navy's age of sail, Leonard Guttridge and Jay Smith conclude that despite the praise heaped upon him, "by all accounts it did not go to his head: humility and modesty remained prominent among his characteristics."[33] There was much more to Macdonough's life and to his naval contributions than the battle on Plattsburgh Bay, but his conduct there epitomized the virtues of this man's career.

Over the years the U.S. Navy honored the Hero of Lake Champlain with four vessels named in his honor. His granddaughter, Lucy Shaler Macdonough, commissioned the first *Macdonough* (Torpedo Boat Destroyer No. 9, DD-9) in 1900. A great-granddaughter commissioned the second *Macdonough* (DD-331) in 1921. A dozen years later another granddaughter, Rose Shaler Macdonough, commissioned the *Macdonough* (DD-351). The latest *Macdonough* (DDG-39), a guided-missile frigate, began cruising in 1961. The latest vessel to honor his famous victory in the War of 1812 was the billion-dollar USS *Lake Champlain* (CG 57), a guided missile cruiser. There are several towns, townships, and counties honoring him, although they are usually misspelled "McDonough."

A recent study of the charismatic dimensions of military leadership describes such commanders as having "exceptionally high levels of self-confidence, a need to influence, with an attendant ability to dominate, and a strong conviction in the moral righteousness of their beliefs." Some studies demonstrate that an untimely death of one's parents often results in a drive to compensate for this loss by personal ambition. Usually such leaders exhibit attributes such as "goal articulation, role modeling, personal image building, extraordinary self-motivation, [and] compassion." The charismatic leader provides his followers with a vision and a sense of mission that gives them faith in the leader's abilities and a desire to abet his objectives.[34] All these are characteristics visible in Thomas Macdonough's career.

Fifty-eight years after the Lake Champlain battle, then–Rear Adm. Joseph Smith, who served under Macdonough not only on that day but also as the first lieutenant of the *Guerrière,* recalled that if anyone "should have been made an admiral, McDonough should have been for his persistence in winding his ship after one side had been disabled & won the victory."[35] This was a magnificent appreciation of his former commander's continuing inspiration to his subordinates.

Another Macdonough contemporary, James Fenimore Cooper, paid the ultimate accolade in his *History of the Navy of the United States of America* (1839):

> Captain M'Donough [*sic*], who was already very favourably known to the service for his personal intrepidity, obtained a vast accession of reputation by the results of this day. His dispositions for receiving the attack, were highly judicious and seaman-like. . . . The personal deportment of Captain M'Donough in this engagement . . . was the subject of general admiration in his little squadron. His coolness was undisturbed throughout all the trying scenes on board his own ship, and although lying against a vessel of double the force, and nearly double the tonnage of the *Saratoga,* he met and resisted her attack with a constancy that seemed to set defeat at defiance. The winding of the *Saratoga* . . . was a bold, seaman-like, and masterly measure, that required unusual decision and fortitude to imagine and execute.

He concluded this summary by noting, "In the navy, which is better qualified to enter into just estimates of force, and all the other circumstances that enhance the merits of nautical exploits, the battle of Plattsburgh Bay is justly ranked among the very highest of its claims to glory."[36]

George Jones became schoolmaster on the *Constitution* shortly after Macdonough's departure. He articulated the characteristics of a successful captain in a series of letters written to a nephew. A ship's commander, he said, "is the connecting link between his own ship and other ships; between his own nation and other nations. In official intercourse abroad, he, of course, appears and his character gives a tone to all such proceedings. To fit him for this, requires an assemblage of qualities seldom found in one man—a mind well disciplined; expanded views of society; thorough knowledge of history, laws and governments; sound judgment; quickness, decision, firmness and intrepidity."[37]

By zounds, this reads much like an idealized Thomas Macdonough!

NOTES

Abbreviations Used in the Notes

ASPNA	*American State Papers: Naval Affairs*
CL	Captains' Letters to the Secretary of the Navy
CLS	Confidential Letters Sent by the Secretary of the Navy
CO	Colonial Office, Public Records Office
HSD	Historical Society of Delaware
LC	Library of Congress
LR	Letters Received
LS	Letters Sent by the Secretary of the Navy
MC	Masters Commandant Letters Received by the Secretary of the Navy
MLS	Miscellaneous Letters Sent by the Secretary of the Navy
MP-Shelbourne	Macdonough Papers, Shelbourne Museum
NA	National Archives
NAC	National Archives of Canada
NHC	Naval Historical Center
PRO	Public Record Office, Kew, England
RG	Record Group
TM	Thomas Macdonough
TMP	Thomas Macdonough Papers, Library of Congress
TMPAB	Thomas Macdonough Personal Account Book
WD	War Department

Chapter 1. Naval Heritage

1. Fowler, *Rebels under Sail,* 303. See also Powers, "Decline and Extinction," and Nuxoll, "American Navy," 28–44; Bradford, "Navies of the American Revolution," 3–25.

2. Good introductions to the international naval history of the war for American independence are found in Mackesy, *War for America;* Dull, *French Navy and American Independence;* Lewis, *Last Campaign of the American Revolution.*

3. *American State Papers: Naval Affairs* 1:497–98 (hereafter cited as *ASPNA,* followed by volume and page number).

4. The best introduction to the navy of this period is Palmer, *Stoddert's War.* See also Elkins and McKitrick, *Age of Federalism,* 643–62; Fowler, *Jack Tars and*

Commodores; Smelser, *Congress Founds a Navy;* and Symonds, *Navalists and Antinavalists.*

5. Palmer, *Stoddert's War,* 25.

6. Stoddert to Barry, 11 July 1798, in Knox, *Naval Documents Related to the Quasi-War* 1:189–91.

7. *ASPNA* 1:58, 74.

8. Shipboard life during the age of fighting sail is best described in such secondary works as McKee, *Gentlemanly and Honorable Profession;* Rodger, *Wooden World,* 82–90; O'Brian, *Men-of-War.* The U.S. Navy copied as closely as it could the routine of the Royal Navy. Naval terminology is explored in Kemp, *Oxford Companion to Ships and the Sea.*

9. Knox, *Naval Documents Related to the Quasi-War* 1:87.

10. *Naval Regulations Issued by Command of the President . . . 1802,* 2, 13. The responsibilities and obligations of the crew are spelled out in detail in these regulations and were only slightly modified during the Macdonough's career.

11. Truxtun to Simon Gross, 30 August 1797; Knox, *Naval Documents Related to the Quasi-War* 1:13–14; Wood, *Radicalism of the American Revolution,* esp. 229–86. On Truxtun's influence in the early U.S. Navy, see Ferguson, *Truxtun.*

12. *Naval Regulations . . . 1802,* 13–15.

13. Ibid., 23–24; *ASPNA* 1:60.

14. O'Brian, *Unknown Shore,* 154.

15. McKee, *Gentlemanly and Honorable Profession,* 47–48, 462.

16. Ibid., 350–91.

17. Goldwsky, *Yankee Surgeon.*

18. *Naval Regulations . . . 1802,* 18.

19. Ibid., 15–16, 18–23.

20. Rodger, *Wooden World,* 27.

21. Millett, *Semper Fidelis,* 4–5, 26–45.

22. This *Register of the Commission and Warrant Officers* is found in John Shaw Papers, Box 2, Manuscripts Division, LC.

23. W. L. Madison to James Madison, 16 March 1810, Rutland and Stagg, *Papers of James Madison* 2:272.

24. *ASPNA* 1:52–53.

25. Hagan, *This People's Navy,* xi.

26. *Naval Regulations . . . 1802,* 8–9.

27. An introduction to tactics and a discussion of the battles mentioned below is found in Tunstall, *Naval Warfare.*

28. Quoted in McKee, *Gentlemanly and Honorable Profession,* 159. The principles of leadership are outlined in U.S. Naval Academy, *Fundamentals of Naval Leadership.* They agree in general with those espoused in U.S. Army, *Military Leadership.* A more general approach to leadership development may be found in Hughes, Ginnett, and Curphy, *Leadership.*

29. McKee, *Gentlemanly and Honorable Profession*, 169.

30. Ibid., 168.

31. U.S. Naval Academy, *Fundamentals of Naval Leadership*, 111.

Chapter 2. Preparation for Command

1. All biographical information on the Macdonoughs comes from *Life of Commodore Thomas Macdonough*, by the commodore's grandson, Rodney Macdonough, and his *Macdonough-Hackstaff Ancestry* unless otherwise noted. On Dr. Macdonough's lieutenant colonelcy in the revolutionary militia, see the Historical Society of Delaware's broadside, "New-Castle, June 2, 1775." Notice of Dr. Macdonough's career for the state of Delaware is found in Bushman, Hancock, and Homsey, *Proceedings*, 283, 479, 531; Thomas Rodney to Caesar Rodney, 1 October 1780, Box 6, Folder 18, Rodney Collection, HSD; HSD, *Governor's Register*, 26.

2. Hoffman, *Spirit of Dissension*, 223–41.

3. Ward, *Delaware Continentals*, 4–89, 486, 492–95, 539. See also Gruber, "America's First Battle," 1–32.

4. On the Trap and related domestic architecture in St. Georges Hundred, see Merman, *Architecture and Rural Life in Central Delaware*, 14–19, 110–15, 151–53.

5. Booth, *Memoir*, v–xi, 14–17, 112; James Macdonough purchased land in St. Georges Hundred in 1748–49 from members of the Huguenot community to which his wife belonged. Carol Garrett, *New Castle County*, 9–10, 85–86; *Delaware: A Guide to the First State*, 337–43.

6. Thomas Macdonough to Lydia Macdonough Roberts, 1 July 1822, Macdonough Papers, HSD.

7. Vandegrift, "Memoir of Commodore Thomas Macdonough," 5.

8. Macdonough, "Paper on Commodore Thomas Macdonough," 16.

9. On the economic development of the state, see Munroe, *Federalist Delaware*, 113–50; Garrison, Herman, and Ward, *After Ratification*; Lindstrom, *Economic Development*; Grettler, "Environmental Change and Conflict," 197–220.

10. On the capture of *L'Insurgent*, see Knox, *Naval Documents Related to the Quasi-War* 2:326–36; Ferguson, *Truxtun*, 160–69. Captain Thomas Truxtun sent Midn. James Macdonough home in March and recommended him for the pension list. Ibid. 2:490. For an enlisted man's view of the *Constellation's* cruise, see Hoxse, *Yankee Tar*. See also Palmer, *Stoddert's War*, 98–103.

11. *Delaware Gazette* reprinted in *Plattsburgh (N.Y.) Republican*, 29 October 1814.

12. Rightmyer, *Anglican Church in Delaware*.

13. Morgan, *Autobiography of Rear Admiral Charles Wilkes*, 64.

14. McKee, *Gentlemanly and Honorable Profession*.

15. For a discussion of professionalization in the American military, see Skelton, "Professionalization," 443–71; Skelton, *American Profession of Arms*; Millett, *Military Professionalism and Officership*; McKee, *Gentlemanly and Honorable Profession*.

16. The list provided is from O'Brian, *Men-of-War*, 38–39, and was similar to that used in the U.S. Navy.

17. Palmer, *Stoddert's War*, 18–24.

18. The inventory of Macdonough's estate is found in Middletown Probate Court, 1824–27, 13:342–46.

19. Fisher, "Gun Drill in the Sailing Navy," 85–92; Tucker, *Arming the Fleet*. For Mullowney's regular gun and small arms drill, see Knox, *Naval Documents Related to the Quasi-War* 5:76. The importance of being a hard drillmaster during training to combat effectiveness is emphasized in Black, "Military Organisations," 884.

20. Knox, *Naval Documents Related to the Quasi-War* 6:17, 92; the Wood quote is ibid. 6:196.

21. Ibid. 6:185.

22. Ibid. 5:475, 481, 517, 564, 567, 568, 576; 6:91, 92, 143. The best introduction to the navy of this period is Palmer, *Stoddert's War*.

23. Knox, *Naval Documents Related to the Quasi-War* 6:163, 164.

24. Ibid. 6:195, 258–59; Macdonough, *Life of Commodore Thomas Macdonough*, 21.

25. Knox, *Naval Documents Related to the Quasi-War* 6:245, 259, 267, 284, 307, 316, 319, 323, 325, 356, 368. On Caribbean diseases and their impact on naval operations, see Kenneth K. Kiple, "Disease Ecologies of the Caribbean," Donald B. Cooper and Kiple, "Yellow Fever," in Kiple, *Cambridge World History of Human Disease*, 497–504, 1100–1107; J. Austin Kerr, "Yellow Fever," in Beeson and McDermott, *Cecil-Loeb Textbook of Medicine*, 100–102; McNeill, "Ecological Basis," 26–42.

26. Macdonough, *Life of Commodore Thomas Macdonough*, 21–22. Pages 20–32 of this book contain a brief autobiography by the commodore.

27. The tradition of Commodore Edward Preble's influence in training the early navy's leaders is developed in Pratt, *Preble's Boys*. The significance of "Preble's Boys" is discounted in McKee, *Edward Preble*. For the decommissioning of *Ganges*, see Knox, *Naval Documents Related to the United States Wars* 1:424.

28. McKee, *Gentlemanly and Honorable Profession*, 37.

29. Knox, *Naval Documents Related to the United States Wars* 1:627, 2:19, 27.

30. Chapelle, *History of the American Sailing Navy*, 128–34, 483; Knox, *Naval Documents Related to the United States Wars* 1:609, 627. The controversy over the design of the *Constellation* and of the vessel of that name in Baltimore harbor today is described in Chapelle and Polland, *The Constellation Question*; Wegner, Ratliff, and Lynaugh, *Fouled Anchors*; Dunne, "Inquiry," 39–55; Dunne, "Frigate *Constellation*," 77–97; Wegner, "Frigate Strikes Her Colors," 243–58.

31. Knox, *Naval Documents Related to the United States Wars* 1:556–58.

32. Ibid. 2:29–40; midshipmen rules on 36. Uniform regulations are found in ibid. 2:255–56.

33. Macdonough, "Journal," 15 March 1802–12 March 1803, HSD.

34. As quoted in McKee, *Gentlemanly and Honorable Profession*, 157; see also Leiner, "Decatur and Naval Leadership," 32.

35. Knox, *Naval Documents Related to the United States Wars* 2:242–43; Macdonough, "Journal," HSD. The standard secondary studies of the North African situation are McKee, *Edward Preble*, and Whipple, *To the Shores of Tripoli*.

36. Knox, *Naval Documents Related to the United States Wars* 2:235, 242, 278.

37. Ibid. 2:306–7, 331, 479, 526–31.

38. McKee, *Gentlemanly and Honorable Profession*, 283.

39. Knox, *Naval Documents Related to the United States Wars* 2:410–11, 419, 482.

40. Ibid. 2:474–77.

41. Ibid. 2:477–78; 3:1–3, 7–11, 80–89, 258. The Moroccan ship's name is variously spelled *Mirboka* or *Mirboha*.

42. Ibid. 3:50; Macdonough, *Life of Commodore Thomas Macdonough*, 23.

43. Letter to his brother quoted in McKee, *Edward Preble*, 181; other quote from Knox, *Naval Documents Related to the United States Wars* 3:258.

44. Knox, *Naval Documents Related to the United States Wars* 3:256–60, 274; Macdonough, *Life of Commodore Thomas Macdonough*, 23.

45. Knox, *Naval Documents Related to the United States Wars* 3:375–77, 413–24, 441–43, 454, quote 414.

46. Ibid. 4:295–98, 345, 347–48, quote 345; the painting is reproduced in black and white opposite page 290; Macdonough, *Life of Commodore Thomas Macdonough*, 24; George Duffield, "Stand up, Stand up for Jesus," v. 3.

47. Knox, *Naval Documents Related to the United States Wars* 4:524, 5:61.

48. Ibid. 5:118. For a discussion of the replacement of Preble, see McKee, *Edward Preble*, 278–81, 306–8. We do not know if Preble made the reassignments of Robinson and Macdonough in order to leave his impress on the squadron in anticipation of Barron's arrival.

49. Macdonough, *Life of Commodore Thomas Macdonough*, 84. The portrait is owned by the Historical Society of Delaware and is reproduced in black and white opposite page 84 of ibid.

50. Knox, *Naval Documents Related to the United States Wars* 6:133, 143.

51. Macdonough, *Life of Commodore Thomas Macdonough*, 24–25.

52. Ibid., 23–24.

53. The discussion of Jeffersonian defense policy is explored in such books as Symonds, *Navalists and Antinavalists*; Smith, *"For the Purposes of Defense"*; Tucker, *Jeffersonian Gunboat Navy*. From James Fenimore Cooper to the present, the standard histories of the navy are highly critical of this Jeffersonian policy. See, for instance, Cooper, *History of the Navy*; Mahan, *Sea Power*; Sprout and Sprout, *Rise of American Naval Power*; and Weigley, *American Way of War*.

54. Dudley, *Splintering the Wooden Wall*, revises the generally accepted analysis of the success of the Royal Navy blockade of the American coastline.

55. Hall, *Middletown*, quote, 11. See also McConaughy, "Maritime Middletown"; Chafee, "Middletown," 12–22; Barratt, "Plan of Main Street," Ephemeral Collection, Russell Library.

56. Adams, *Middletown Upper Houses*, 700–701; Macdonough, *Macdonough-Hackstaff Ancestry*, 81–94; Richter, *Planting and Sustaining the Vine*, 18–21, 32, 41–66.

57. Macdonough, *Life of Commodore Thomas Macdonough*, 89.

58. McKee, *Gentlemanly and Honorable Profession*, xii, xiii, 124, 130, 273, 288, quote 289.

59. Knox, *Naval Documents Related to the United States Wars* 2:33; McKee, *Gentlemanly and Honorable Profession*, 134–35.

60. McKee, *Gentlemanly and Honorable Profession*, 215.

61. Macdonough, *Life of Commodore Thomas Macdonough*, 91–92.

62. Ibid., 94–99; Stagg, *Mr. Madison's War*, 102. Stagg's book is the best introduction to the War of 1812 from the national political viewpoint.

63. Macdonough, *Life of Commodore Thomas Macdonough*, 99; Morgan, *Wilkes*, 51–52, 59–60, 64–70, quote 70.

64. Knapp, *Thomas Macdonough*, 2.

65. *ASPNA* 1:255–56. One of those above him on the lieutenants' list, Robert Henley, would be his subordinate on Lake Champlain.

66. Macdonough, *Life of Commodore Thomas Macdonough*, 101–2. This is one of several letters to and from the commodore that Rodney Macdonough quotes, but which are not available to researchers.

67. Ibid., 103.

68. Richter, *Planting and Sustaining the Vine*, 32, 68–69; Muller, "Commodore and Mrs. Thomas Macdonough," 344–45.

69. Dudley and Crawford, *Naval War of 1812* 1:319–20.

Chapter 3. Lake Champlain, 1812–1813

1. Hill, *Lake Champlain*, 4. For other introductions to the region, see also Palmer, *History of Lake Champlain;* Chambers, *Atlas of Lake Champlain;* and Everest, *War of 1812.*

2. This and subsequent discussions of the war in the Champlain Valley are based upon Everest, *War of 1812;* Stanley, *War of 1812;* Lewis, *British Naval Activity;* Turner, *British Generals;* and Quimby, *U.S. Army.*

3. J. G. Freligh to Michael Freligh, 11 August, 9 September 1812, Freligh Collection, Feinberg Library (hereafter cited as Freligh Collection); Sailly to Mooers, 7 July 1812, Bailey-Moore Collection, Feinberg Library (hereafter cited as Bailey-Moore Collection); Mooers to Tompkins, 8 September 1812, Mooers to Dearborn, 11, 29 August 1812, Bailey-Moore Collection.

4. Dearborn to Eustis, 24 November 1812, Letters Received, WD, RG 107, NA.

5. Mooers to Dearborn, 2 September 1812, War of 1812 Manuscripts, Lilly Library (hereafter cited as War of 1812 Manuscripts); Sawyer to Sec/Nav, 29 January 1813, M148, BC, roll 11, no. 25, RG 45, NA; Mooers to Gov. Daniel Tompkins, 8 September 1812, Bailey-Moore Collection.

6. Lucoes Goes Diary, Lilly Library; Fredriksen, "Letters of Captain John Scott," 66. John Freligh to Michael Freligh, 29 November 1812, Freligh Collection.

7. Von Clausewitz, *On War,* 107, 112.

8. Keegan, *Mask of Command.*

9. Hamilton to TM, 28 September 1812, TM to Hamilton 4, 14, 26 October, 20 December 1812, TM to Jones, 22 January, 1 May 1813, Dudley and Crawford, *Naval War of 1812* 1:319–26, 324–26, 370–71; 2:424–25, 460.

10. Asa Fitch to C. W. Goldsborough, 19 January 1813, M124, Misc. Letters Received (hereafter cited as MLR), reel 53, no. 34, RG 45, NA; Jones to TM, 21 and 23 February 1813, M148, BC, roll 11, vol. 1, no. 76, MLS, vol. 11, p. 203, RG 45, NA; M. C. J. Lewis to Jones, 1 April 1813, MLR, 1813, vol. 2, no. 157, RG 45, NA; TM to Samuel Evans, 6 June 1813, M125, CL, 1813, vol. 4, no. 60½, RG 45, NA; TM to Jones, 1 May 1813, Dudley and Crawford, *Naval War of 1812* 2:460.

11. TM to Jones, 22 January, 1 May 1813, Dudley and Crawford, *Naval War of 1812* 2:424, 460; Jones to George Harrison, 9 February 1813, Jones to John Bullus, 9 February 1813, Bullus to Jones, 23 February 1813, MLS, vol. 11, pp. 187–89, 203, RG 45, NA.

12. Millman, *Life of Charles James Stewart,* 37.

13. Everest, *Pliny Moore,* 22–24, 42–49. For more on commercial intercourse between the United States and Canada, see Mackintosh, "Canada and Vermont," 9–30; Muller, "'Traitorous and Diabolical Traffic,'" 78–96; Alcock, "Best Defence," 73–91. An 1868 memoir of cattle drives into Canada from Orleans County, Vermont, is related in "Smuggling in 1813–1814," 2–26. The broader picture is discussed in Crawford, "Navy's Campaign," 165–72.

14. Quoted in upon Everest, *War of 1812,* 108; Sweetson to Elizha Luce, 5 November 1812, Folder 14, Doc. 96, David Sumner Papers, Vermont Historical Society.

15. Sailly to Macomb, 25 October 1814, Bixby, *Peter Sailly,* 87.

16. Popham to Melville, 8 March 1813, War of 1812 Manuscripts.

17. Dayton to Madison, 30 April 1813, James Madison Papers, Library of Congress (hereafter cited as Madison Papers).

18. Jones to [?], 5 April 1813, U. C. Smith Collection, Pennsylvania Historical Society (hereafter cited as U. C. Smith Collection).

19. Moore to Winter, 16 June 1813, "Maine Troops on Lake Champlain," 39, with other commentary, 34–42; Rottenburg to George Glasgow, 5 June 1813, Dudley and Crawford, *Naval War of 1812* 2:491. Other contemporary commentaries appear in Parker, "Letters," 105–24; *Plattsburgh (N.Y.) Republican,* 4 and 11 June 1813; *Burlington (Vt.) Centinel,* 3, 10 June 1813; Dudley and Crawford, *Naval War of 1812* 2:488–92; Wood, *Select British Documents* 2:221–25; John Freligh to Michael Freligh, 11 June 1813, Freligh Collection.

20. Jones to TM, 17 June, TM to Jones, 11, 22 July, 3 August 1813, Instructions to Murray, 27 July 1813, Dudley and Crawford, *Naval War of 1812* 2:513–16; *Plattsburgh (N.Y.) Republican,* 2 July 1813.

21. "Maine Troops on Lake Champlain," 40–41; Parker, "Letters," 124; Mooers to Tompkins, 13 July, Bailey-Moore Collection.

22. TM to Jones, 3, 4 August, Everard to Prevost, 3 August 1813, Dudley and Crawford, *Naval War of 1812* 2:518–20; *The War* (New York), 10, 17, 31 August 1813; Jones to Madison, 14, 28 August 1813, Madison Papers. See also several letters, 29 July–8 August 1813, Wood, *Select British Documents* 2:226–38; Thomas Parker to David Campbell, 6–8 August 1813, Campbell Family Papers, William R. Perkins Library; Wood to William Barker, 1 January 1814, Eleazer Wood Papers, State Historical Society of Wisconsin.

23. Sheaffe to Prevost, 5 August 1813, Wood, *Select British Documents* 2:233.

24. For general background on these situations, see Malcomson, *Lords of the Lake;* Skaggs and Altoff, *Signal Victory;* Whitehorne, *Battle for Baltimore.*

25. Renshaw to Jones, 18 June, 13 July, Jones to Bullus, 2, 10 July, TM to Samuel Evans, 6 June 1813, Jones to Evans, 7 July, Evans to Jones, 15 July, 10 August, TM to Jones, 22 July 1813, M148, BC, roll 11, vol. 2, no. 142, vol. 4, no. 196, MLS vol. 11, no. 337, 346, M125, CL, vol. 4, no. 42, 60½, 163, 196, vol. 5, no. 88, RG 45, NA.

26. Jones to Madison, 8 September 1813, Madison Papers.

27. John Frelighto Michale Freligh, 8 September 1813, Freligh Collection. Some insecurity is found in Mooers to Tompkins, 8 September, 19 October 1813, and Mooers to Hampton, 3 November 1813, Bailey-Moore Collection.

28. Quimby, *U.S. Army* 1:305. Quimby's discussion of the St. Lawrence Campaign of 1813 appears on 301–48. Other secondary sources of note include Graves, *Field of Glory,* and Stanley, *War of 1812,* 243–65.

29. J. Freligh to M. Freligh, 17 September 1813, Freligh Collection.

30. Mooers to Hampton, 3 November 1813, Bailey-Moore Collection; *Burlington (Vt.) Centinel,* 8 October 1813.

31. Philip Ruiter to Thomas Dunn, 10 December 1813, MG 23 GIII, 3, vol. 1, Ruiter Papers, NAC; Sutterlee Clark to Isaac Clark, 20 March 1814, Separate Collection, Box 1, Folder 55, Isaac Clark Papers, Bailey-Howe Library; Fredriksen, "War of 1812 in Northern New York," 197–98; Pring to Prevost, 5 December 1813, Vol. 731, pp. 167–68, Ser. C., RG 8, NAC; *Burlington (Vt.) Centinel,* 10, 17 September 1813.

32. *Plattsburgh (N.Y.) Republican,* 25 December 1813; TM to Jones, 23 November 1813, Dudley and Crawford, *Naval War of 1812* 2:604; TM to Jones, 23 December 1813, MC, 1813, no. 196, RG 45, NA.

33. *Burlington (Vt.) Centinel,* 1 October 1813; J. G. Freligh to M. Freligh, 22 September 1813, Freligh Collection.

Chapter 4. Lake Champlain, 1814

1. *The War,* 29 March 1814; Tompkins, Address to the Legislature, 25 January 1814, Lincoln, *State of New York* 2:785.

2. Warren to John W. Croker, 30 December 1813, Dudley and Crawford, *Naval War of 1812* 2:307–8. See also Whitehorne, *Battle for Baltimore,* and Dudley, "Without Some Risk."

3. As quoted in Pack, *Man Who Burned the White House,* 166–67; Cochrane to Melville, 25 March 1814, Cochrane to Hugh Pigot, 25 March 1814, War of 1812 Manuscripts.

4. Wellington to Lord Bathurst, 22 February 1814, Gurwood, *Dispatches* 11:525–26.

5. Bathurst to Prevost, 20 January 1814, MG 12, Adm. 2/1379, p. 131; Admiralty to Bathurst, 10 January 1814, MG 11, CO 42, 158, p. 8, PRO.

6. Croker to Yeo, 29 January 1814, MG 12, Adm. 2/1379, p. 131, PRO.

7. Bathurst to Prevost, 20 January 1814, CO 43/23, pp. 140–42; Crocker to Yeo, 29 January 1814, Adm. 2/2379, pp. 130–35, PRO. See also Adm. 1/505, pp. 336–37; CO 42/151, p. 172, and CO 43/23, pp. 133–37, PRO; Malcomson, *Warships of the Great Lakes,* 115–18.

8. Pring to Prevost, C-679, RG 8; Estimate for the cost of a vessel . . . 17 August 1813, C-731, RG 8; Pring to Freer, 7, 18 October 1813, C-731, RG 8; Pring to Simons 7 November 1813, C-731, RG 8, PRO.

9. Bathurst to Prevost, 3 June 1814, reprinted in Hitsman, *Incredible War of 1812,* 249–51.

10. For a brief treatment of the Lacolle "campaign," see Quimby, *U.S. Army* 2:481–84.

11. Madison to Tompkins, 25 January 1814, Madison Papers. See also Armstong to Madison, 24 November 1813, ibid.

12. John Smith to Jones, 5, 17 January, TM to Jones, 17 January, 7, 22 February 1714, MC 1814, 1:14, 15, 48, 63, RG 45, NA; Jones to TM, 28 January, Jones to John Bullus, 10 February, MLS, RG 45, NA. On Browns, see Tucker, *Jeffersonian Gunboat Navy,* 55, 60, 188–89; Gardiner, *Line of Battle,* 79; Chapelle, *History of the American Sailing Navy,* 220, 225, 256–60, 268–72, 298–308, 422; Roosevelt, *Naval War of 1812,* 286–89, 316–19; and Skaggs and Altoff, *Signal Victory,* 70–73, 84–85.

13. It is assumed the construction of the *Saratoga* was similar to that of the *Eagle,* whose submerged hull was found several years ago and has been examined closely by maritime archaeologist Kevin Crisman. For that reason this description follows much of what he describes in *Eagle.* Other secondary accounts that are useful are Longridge, *Anatomy of Nelson's Ships;* Lavery, *Building the Wooden Walls;* Lavery, *Arming and Fitting;* and Lavery, *Nelson's Navy.* For a similar-sized ocean-going vessel, see Goodwin, *20-Gun Ship.*

14. Thomas Perkins to Benjamin Wells, Monkton Iron Company Letterbook, Bixby Memorial Library.

15. TM to Wilkinson, 9 April 1814, WD, LR, Reg. Ser., W-344 (7), RG 107, NA; TM to Jones, 11, 30, April 1814, MC, 1814, vol. 1, nos. 103 and 115, RG 45, NA; Amos Binney to TM, 5 May 1814, no. 41.58, MP-Shelburne; Seelye, *Yankee Drover,* 70–71. On gun weight and its computation, see Tucker, *Arming the Fleet,* 125, 271.

16. Bullus to TM, 15, 30 April, 21 June 1814, Barent & J. R. Bleecker to TM, 22 April, 31 May 1814, Rich. P. Hart & Co. to TM, 19 April 1814, Muller Notes, HSD. This latter collection consists of Muller's typescript duplicates of letters in Vance Macdonough's personal collection. Vance Macdonough of Boston was a great-grandson of Thomas Macdonough. These were notes made by journalist Charles Muller for *The Proudest Day.*

17. Jones to TM, 22 February, 20, 30 April 1814, Letters Sent (hereafter cited as LS); Tompkins to Jones, 10 March 1814, Navy Dept. Papers, NHC Doc no. 01908, NcD; Jones to Tompkins, 10 May 1814, MLS, vol. 12, p. 163; TM to Jones, 30 April, 6, 21 May 1814, MC, 1814, vol. 1, no. 115, no. 121, no. 132; Jones to Bullus, 1 July 1814, LS, vol. 2, p. 107, RG 45, NA. On her construction, see Crisman, *History and Construction.*

18. *The War,* 31 May 1814.

19. Moores to Tompkins, 8 April 1814, Bailey-Moore Collection; Sailly to TM, 6 April 1814, Sailly Collection, Clinton County Historical Society; *Albany Argus,* 8 April 1814.

20. *Plattsburgh (N.Y.) Republican,* 14 May 1814.

21. *Burlington (Vt.) Northern Sentinel,* 8, 15 April, 13 May, 1814.

22. *Plattsburgh (N.Y.) Republican,* 14, 21 May 1814; *Burlington (Vt.) Northern Sentinel,* 20 May 1814; Macomb to TM, 9 April 1814, Box 5, War of 1812 Papers, William L. Clements Library; Pring to Yeo, 14 May 1814, PG8, C Ser., vol. 683, pp. 160–63, PRO; Pring to Lt. Col. William Williams, 14 May 1814, British Military and Naval Records, vol. 683, pp. 164–70, I, C Ser., RG 8, PRO; Davis to Macomb, 17 May 1814, WD, LR, Reg. Ser. I-4 (8), RG 107, NA; Noble, "Battle of the Boquet River," 591–92; Richards, *Memoir of Alexander Macomb,* 7–8. On the Essex County, New York, militia's role in the defense of that state's shore, see the excerpts from various letters of May 1814 published in a story headlined "An Untold Battle," *Troy (N.Y.) Northern Budget,* 13 October 1901, in Henry L. Sheldon Scrapbook, Sheldon Museum; Daniel Wright to Mooers, 15 May 1814, Bailey-Moore Collection.

23. Elisha Jenkins to TM, 23 March 1814, Izard to TM, 24 July 1814, Muller Notes, HSD.

24. TM to Jones, 30 April 1814, MC, 1814, vol. 1, no. 115, RG 45, NA; Jones to Madison, 25 May 1814, Madison Papers. On recruitment problems, see TM to

Jones, 7 February 1814, MC 1814, vol. 1, no. 48, Jones to TM, 17 March 1814, LS, 1814, RG 45, NA; and Seiken, "To Obtain Command," 353–71.

25. TM to Jones, 23 March 1814, MC 1814, vol. 1, no. 89, RG 45, NA. See also TM to Jones 7 March, MC 1814, vol. 1, no. 77, RG 45, NA; Vallette to TM, 17 March 1814, Binney to TM, 8, 28 March 1814, Joseph Smith to TM, 8 April 1814, Muller Notes, HSD.

26. E. A. F. Vallette, to TM, 5 May 1814, no. 41.57, MP-Shelburne; TM to Macomb, 18 May 1814, Izard to Armstrong, 24 May, 10 June, Macomb to Izard 24 May, 1814, LR I-4 (8) and enclosures, and I-21 (8), WD, RG 107, NA.

27. Jarvis to Jones, 9 January 1814, BC, 1814, vol. 1, no. 27, NA; TM to Jones, 11, 20, 30 April, 6, 14 May 1814, Dudley and Crawford, *Naval War of 1812* 3:428–32, 481; TM to Jones, 18 May 1814, MC, 1814, vol. 1, no. 129, RG 45, NA; Richards, *Memoir*, 8; TM to Macomb, 14 May 1814, reprinted in *The War*, 17 June 1814.

28. *Vermont Mirror*, 1 June 1814; Thompson to TM, 1 July 1814, MP-Shelburne; Few to TM, 13 August 1814, 4th Auditor's Accts., Numerical Series, 3529–5290, no. 4125, Dept. of Treasury, RG 217, NA. The transportation charges involved in this account were not settled until 1823.

29. Armstrong to Izard, 25 May 1814, WD, RG 107, NA.

30. TM to Jones, 29 May 1814, Dudley and Crawford, *Naval War of 1812* 3:505; *Burlington (Vt.) Northern Sentinel*, 3 June 1814; *The War*, 14 June 1814; *Plattsburgh (N.Y.) Republican*, 11, 18 June 1814; Samuel Elam Albro to [?], 20 June 1814, in Parker, "Letters," 123.

31. Jones to Madison, 6 May 1814, Madison Papers.

32. TM to Jones, 8 June 1814, MC, 1814, vol. 1, no. 143, RG 45, NA; Gallatin & Bayard to Monroe, 6 May 1814, James Monroe Papers, LC.

33. *Burlington (Vt.) Northern Sentinel*, 19 August 1814; Adams, *History of the United States of America* 2:101.

34. *United States Gazette*, 19 October 1814, quoted in Bailey, *Diplomatic History*, 152; *Albany Argus*, 21 June 1814.

35. For an outline of developments at Île aux Noix, see Lewis, *British Naval Activity*.

36. TM to Jones, 11 June 1814, MC 1814, vol. 1, no. 145, RG 45, NA; Bullus to TM, 30 June 1814, Muller Notes, HSD.

37. TM to Jones, 19 June 1814, MC 1814, vol. 1, no. 246, RG 45, NA; Caleb Nichols to Armstrong, 27 July 1814, WD, LR, Unreg. Ser., N1814, RG 107, NA. See also TM to Izard, 17 June 1814, in Macdonough, *Life of Commodore Thomas Macdonough*, 148–49.

38. Madison to Jones, 3 June 1814, U. C. Smith Collection; Madison Memorandum, ca. 12–30 September 1814, Madison Papers; Armstrong to Izard, 2 July 1814, LS, vol. 7, p. 242, WD, RG 107, NA; two letters, Jones to TM, 5 July 1814, Jones to Messrs. Brown, 6 July 1814, RG 45, CLS; TM to Jones, 13, 18 July 1814, MC

1814, vol. 2, no. 5, no. 7, RG 45, NA; *Vermont Mirror,* 27 July 1814; Brant, *James Madison,* 273–76.

39. Crisman, *Eagle,* contains the best study of that vessel's construction; *Vermont Mirror,* 27 July, 17 August 1814.

40. TM to Jones, 9, 12 August 1814, CL 1814, vol. 5, no. 91, RG 45, NA; *ASPNA* 1:152–53; McKee, *Gentlemanly and Honorable Profession,* 292–94; Crisman, *Eagle,* 46–49.

41. TM to John Rodgers, 6 May 1815, quoted in McKee, *Gentlemanly and Honorable Profession,* 294; Henley to Jones, 19 August 1814, MC 1814, vol. 2, no. 20, RG 45, NA; William M. Fowler, "Henley, Robert," in *American National Biography,* ed. John A. Garraty and Mark C. Carnes (New York: Oxford University Press, 1999), 10:494–595.

42. Jones to TM, 5 July 1814, CLS; TM to Jones, 18 July 1814, MC 1814, vol. 2, no. 7; Jones to Bullus, 18 July 1814, LS, vol. 2, pp. 137–38, RG 45, NA.

43. Bullus to TM, 14, 26 July 1814; T. C. Henry to TM, 12 July 1814; Woolsey to TM, 14 July 1814; J. Walton & Co. to TM, 8 August 1814, Muller Notes, HSD.

44. TM to Jones, 23 July 1814, MC 1814, vol. 2, no. 8, RG 45, NA; Izard to Armstrong, 31 July 1814, LR, I-78 (8), WD, RG 107; "Memoirs of the Hon. Peter Sailly," *Plattsburgh (N.Y.) Republican,* 6 April 1872, p. 3.

45. TM to Jones, 23 July 1814, MC 1814, vol. 2, no. 8, RG 45, NA; *Plattsburgh (N.Y.) Republican,* 16, 30 July 1814; *Albany Argus,* 22 July 1814.

46. Pages 171–73, Joel Abbot Family Papers, Nimitz Library.

47. TM to Jones, 20 August 1814, TM to Drury, 12 November 1814, Dudley and Crawford, *Naval War of 1812* 3:223–25.

48. TM to Jones, 27 August 1814, MC 1814, vol. 2, no. 25, RG 45, NA.

Chapter 5. The Battle of Plattsburgh Bay

1. *Albany Argus,* 9, 13 September 1814.

2. Fisher to Yeo, 30 August 1814, Adm. 1/2737, 183–84, Public Records Office, NAC.

3. *Albany Argus,* 8 July 1814; see also ibid., 1 July 1814.

4. Quimby, *U.S. Army* 2:600.

5. For general background on the British Lake Champlain campaign, see Mahon, *War of 1812;* Hitsman, *Incredible War of 1812;* Stanley, *War of 1812;* Turner, *British Generals;* and Quimby, *U.S. Army.*

6. Provost to Bathurst, 5 August 1814, Wood, *Select British Documents* 3:346.

7. Armstrong to Izard, 28 April 1814, WD, LS, vol. 7, RG 107, NA; Smith to Izard, 22 June 1814, Thomas Adams Smith Papers, Columbia Western Historical Manuscript Collection, copy in Early History Branch, NHC.

8. Nichols to Armstrong, 27 July, 17 August, 1 September 1814, LR Unreg. Ser., N-1814, WD, RG 107, NA; Everest, *Pliny Moore,* 45. For the Izard-Armstrong correspondence, see Izard, *Official Correspondence,* 54–68, 73–76, 100–103.

9. The standard history of this campaign is Everest, *War of 1812;* see also Lossing, *Pictorial Field-Book,* 854–84; Cooper, *History of the Navy,* 404–17; Mahan, *Sea Power* 2:355–82; Roosevelt, *Naval War of 1812,* 337–56; and Fitz-Enz, *Final Invasion.*

10. Daniel Pring's statement, Wood, *Select British Documents* 3:462–63; James, *Naval History* 6:341.

11. One Vermont volunteer's experience is recounted in Jonathan Stevens to Benjamin Stevens, 5 December 1814, "Vermont Letters," 15–20; *Burlington (Vt.) Northern Sentinel,* 9 September 1814.

12. Prevost to Downie, 7 September 1814, Wood, *Select British Documents* 3:466.

13. Downie to Prevost, 7, 8, 9 September, and Prevost to Downie, 8, 9, 10 September 1814, Wood, *Select British Documents* 3:379–83.

14. Coore to Yeo, 26 February 1815, Wood, *Select British Documents* 3:394–96.

15. Taché, "Bataille Navale," 149.

16. TM to Jones, 13 September 1814, Dudley and Crawford, *Naval War of 1812* 3:614–15; Prevost to Bathurst, 11 September 1814, and Plattsburgh Court-Martial, 18–21 August 1815, Wood, *Select British Documents* 3:351, 429–36, 476; Bell's testimony, Wood, *Select British Documents* 3:429–34; *Letter from the Secretary of the Navy,* 15–16.

James Fenimore Cooper merely notes the discrepancy between Macdonough and Prevost without making a decision in the matter. William James says there were ten; *Naval Chronicle,* Benson Lossing, Theodore Roosevelt, Henry Adams, Allan Everest, and Robert Quimby accept twelve; Alfred Mahan, Robert Malcomson, and David Fitz-Enz agree on eleven. Cooper, *History of the Navy,* 407; James, *Naval History* 6:504; *Naval Chronicle,* 32 (August, September 1814); Lossing, *Pictorial Field-Book,* 865; Roosevelt, *Naval War,* 342; Adams, *History of the United States of America* 8:105; Everest, *War of 1812,* 181; Quimby, *U.S. Army* 2:621; Mahan, *Sea Power* 2:377; Malcomson, *Warships of the Great Lakes,* table 41, p. 122; Fitz-Enz, *Final Invasion,* 137.

17. See notes to British Naval Strength table, chapter 5. Prevost to Bathurst, 11 September 1814, shows the British advantage ninety to eighty-three guns and sixteen vessels to fourteen, Wood, *Select British Documents* 3:351. Prevost had a personal interest to show a greater British advantage, just as the Royal Navy wanted to demonstrate something close to parity between the squadrons.

18. Smith to Hiram Paulding, 10 February 1873, Paulding Papers, Archibald Stevens Alexander Library (hereafter cited as Paulding Papers).

19. "Abstract of the Crew of His Majesty's Late Ship *Confiance,*" Wood, *Select British Documents* 3:480–81; James, *Naval History* 6:342.

20. Wood, *Select British Documents* 3:437.

21. James, *Naval History* 6:342.

22. For Great Lakes shipbuilding see Malcomson, *Lords of the Lake,* 229–43, 300–310, and Malcomson, *Warships of the Great Lakes,* 63–133. On gunlocks, see

Downie to Capt. Upton, HMS *Junon*, 1 September 1814, Wood, *Select British Documents* 3:378.

23. James, *Full and Correct Account*, 406.

24. James, *Naval History* 6:343.

25. Wood, *Select British Documents* 3:414, 460, 463–64.

26. Ibid. 3:414.

27. Hill, *Lake Champlain*, 180–82. The biblical verses are James 1:6 and James 3:4. On the famous fighting gamecock, see Lossing, *Pictorial Field-Book*, 867.

28. Macdonough to John Rodgers, 6 May 1815, RG 45, Subject File NI, NA; TM to Jones, 13 September 1814, *ASPNA* 1:310.

29. 5–9 September 1814, Log Book Kept . . . Sloop of War *Surprise*, NA; James Robertson's testimony, Wood, *Select British Documents* 3:474.

30. Book of Common Prayer (1801), sec. 24.

31. Folsom, "Battle of Plattsburgh," 253.

32. The most detailed descriptions of the battle are from the British court-martial testimony published in Wood, *Select British Documents* 3:400–498. Particular attention should be paid to the testimonies and statements of Daniel Pring, 405–6, 436–38, 441–42, 460–65, and James Robertson, 438–41, 468–75. Royal Navy testimony tends to blame the army for the failure to achieve victory and to place the British situation in the worst possible light as compared with Macdonough's squadron. The American side is published in *ASPNA* 1:309–13 and Dudley and Crawford, *Naval War of 1812* 3:607–17. See also Joseph Smith to Hiram Paulding, 10 February 1873, Paulding Papers. One should also consult Macdonough, *Life of Commodore Thomas Macdonough*, 164–200; Mahan, *Sea Power* 2:355–82; and Roosevelt, *Naval War*, 337–56.

33. Wood, *Select British Documents* 3:436.

34. Testimony of Bodell and Seaman Benjamin Cruize, Wood, *Select British Documents* 3:422–29.

35. Wood, *Select British Documents* 3:474.

36. Testimony of gunboat commanders, Wood, *Select British Documents* 3:429–36; Taché, "Bataille Navale," 153.

37. Testimony by *Finch*'s seamen, Hicks' Letter to Court-Martial Board, and Hicks to Pring, 12 September 1814, Wood, *Select British Documents* 3:442–56, 486–93, 495–97; TM to John Rodgers, 6 May 1815, Subject File NI, RG 45, NA.

38. The quote from an 1815 issue of the *Naval Chronicle* is reprinted in Fitz-Enz, *Final Invasion*, 236.

39. Fitz-Enz, *Final Invasion*, 154–55.

40. TM to Jones, 11 September 1814, LR, RG 45, NA.

41. 24 September 1814, Smith, *Republic of Letters* 3:1744.

42. The diplomatic history of the end of this conflict is examined in detail in Perkins, *Castlereagh and Adams*, 81–127, and Engleman, *Peace of Christmas Eve*.

43. On the war's impact on the nation, see such studies as Stagg, *Mr. Madison's*

War; McKee, *Gentlemanly and Honorable Profession;* Skelton, *American Profession of Arms;* Steven Watts, *Republic Reborn;* Sellers, *Market Revolution;* Wood, *Radicalism of the American Revolution;* Watson, *Liberty and Power.*

44. Von Clausewitz, *On War,* 194.

Chapter 6. Life Ashore

1. Book of Common Prayer, sec. 24.

2. TM to Jones, 13 September 1814, Dudley and Crawford, *Naval War of 1812* 3:614–15.

3. Henley to TM, 12 September 1814, Private Collection of Royal D. Joslin, Philadelphia, copy in Early History Branch, NHC.

4. Henley to TM, 12 September 1814, *Naval Monument,* 144, 150.

5. *ASPNA* 1:311 (Purser George Beale's recapitulation of the return of killed and wounded has one extra killed and one extra wounded on the *Saratoga* who are not listed by name); Wood, *Select British Documents* 3:376, 429–38; Taché, "Bataille Navale" (offprint in the Special Collections, Bailey-Howe Library, Burlington), 153–54.

6. Henley to TM, 14 September, Israel Stoddard to TM, 16 September, Henley to TM, 17 September, Briggs to TM, 20 September 1814, War of 1812 Manuscripts; 18 September 1814, Log Book Kept . . . Sloop of War *Surprise,* NA.

7. Macdonough, *Life of Commodore Thomas Macdonough,* 30.

8. TM to T. Gamble, 14 September, TM to T. Stansbury, 18 September 1813, War of 1812 Manuscripts.

9. TM to Budd, 10 November 1814, Dudley and Crawford, *Naval War of 1812* 3:643–44.

10. TM to Bullus, 12 October 1814, War of 1812 Manuscripts.

11. Beale to TM, 21 December 1814, War of 1812 Manuscripts. Francis H. Penny to SecNav Benjamin W. Crowninshield, 18 April 1815, Subject File, Box 742, RG 45, NA; TM to Nathaniel Sanford, 8 May 1815, Thomas Macdonough Manuscripts, Franklin Delano Roosevelt Library; *ASPNA* 1:563–82; U.S. District Court for the Southern District of New York, 1812–1816, Cases 21, 26, and 44, Prize and Related Records for the War of 1812, NA; "An Act authorizing the purchase of the vessels captured on Lake Champlain," Peters, *Public Statutes* 3:229. McKee, *Gentlemanly and Honorable Profession,* 341–47, 494. See also *Rules of the District Court.*

12. R. H. J. Perry to Tazewell, 2 October 1814, powers of attorney, and accompanying copies of letters involved in the exchange, War of 1812 Manuscripts; *ASPNA* 1:582.

13. TM to Jones 20 August 1814, TM to Drury, 12 November 1814, Dudley and Crawford, *Naval War of 1812* 3:592–93. Lieutenant Drury perished when the USS *Epervier* went down with all hands in 1815.

14. Perry to TM, 28 November, Beale to TM, 21 December 1814, War of 1812 Manuscripts.

15. U.S. Congress, *Report of the Naval Committee;* Failor and Hayden, *Medals,* 210–11.

16. *New York Columbian,* 30 September 1814; *Burlington (Vt.) Northern Sentinel,* 18 November, 23 December 1814; TM to Rodney, 30 December 1815, Oliver Wolcott to TM, 4 September 1820, War of 1812 Manuscripts.

17. Reprinted in the *Plattsburgh (N.Y.) Republican,* 29 October 1814; *Burlington (Vt.) Northern Sentinel,* 18 November 1814.

18. *Naval Monument,* 156; much of the personal data here and elsewhere comes from Macdonough, *Life of Commodore Thomas Macdonough,* 211–17, 246–48.

19. Several letters, most of which are no longer extant, are reprinted in Muller, "Commodore and Mrs. Thomas Macdonough," 341–54; C. A. Rodney to TM, 7 July 1815, John McDonough to TM, 13 April 1816, War of 1812 Manuscripts. The Rev. B. G. Noble baptized Thomas N. Macdonough on 18 December 1814 and buried him on 23 June 1815. Parish Records, Christ Church, Church of the Holy Trinity, Middletown, Conn.

20. Tompkins to Decatur, 14 November, Fulton to Decatur, 15 November 1814, TM to Crowninshield, 6 February 1815, Dudley and Crawford, *Naval War of 1812* 3:641–42, 684–87.

21. Muller, "Commodore and Mrs. Thomas Macdonough," 350–52; TMPAB 1, 11, 21, 34, 43–44, 64; typescript copies, John McDonough to TM, 3 April 1816, 13 April 1817, David Smith to TM, 19 August 1821, John Thomas McDonough to TM, 20 January 1823, War of 1812 Manuscripts; Macdonough, *Life of Commodore Thomas Macdonough,* 222.

22. TM to James Monroe, 30 June, to John Rodgers, 23 August 1817, Letterbook, Thomas Macdonough Papers, LC (hereafter cited as Macdonough Letterbook); expenses relating to the house construction may be found in TMPAB, esp. pp. 19–20, 25, 34, 45.

23. Macdonough estate inventory, Middletown Probate Court, 1824–27, 13:342–46.

24. Muller, "Commodore and Mrs. Thomas Macdonough," 350–52; TMPAB, 34, 43–44, 64.

25. Estes, *Hall Jackson,* 100–101; McKee, *Gentlemanly and Honorable Profession,* 410–11, 572; Lloyd and Coulter, *Medicine and the Navy,* 348. On the Russian and Finnish sailors, see Lloyd, *Health of Seamen,* 107–10; Hinkkanen, "When the AB," 87–104.

26. William D. Johnson, "Tuberculosis," in *The Cambridge World History of Human Disease,* ed. Kenneth F. Kiple (Cambridge, Eng.: Cambridge University Press, 1993), 1059–68; Carl Muschenheim, "Tuberculosis," in Beeson and McDermott, *Cecil-Loeb Textook of Medicine,* 278–318.

27. TM to Crowninshield, 3 July 1815, Macdonough Letterbook.

28. TM to Crowninshield, 20 July, to Isaac Hull, 21 July, to Henry S. Langdon, 7 August, to Hull, 8 August, 12 August 1815, Macdonough Letterbook.

29. TM to Crowninshield, 26 November 1816, Henry L. Sheldon Scrapbook no. 10, Sheldon Museum.

30. Cornelius Bogert to TM, 11 July 1818, Henry Wheaton to TM, 5 May 1820, War of 1812 Manuscripts; TM to Bogert, [July 1818], Macdonough Letterbook.

31. TMPAB, 4. On the importance of the Lake Champlain defenses in the aftermath of the War of 1812, see Schweninger, "'Lingering War Must Be Prevented'"; Halleck, *Elements of Military Art and Science,* 210–34.

32. TMPAB, 33, 47.

33. Joseph Smith to TM, 2 August 1820, George Beale Jr. to TM, 23 September 1820, War of 1812 Manuscripts; Macdonough, *Life of Commodore Thomas Macdonough,* 38.

34. Richter, *Planting and Sustaining the Vine,* 32, 54; TMPAB, 33–34.

35. *Middlesex Gazette,* 5 December 1825.

36. Tingey to Chew, 20 June 1822, Historical Manuscripts, Navy Department Library; James Booth to TM, 22 February 1822, War of 1812 Manuscripts; TMPAB, 48.

37. TM to Sec/Nav, 22 January 1822, Macdonough Letterbook; TM to Sec/Nav, 20 September 1823, Macdonough, *Life of Commodore Thomas Macdonough,* 247.

38. *Middlesex Gazette,* 30 November 1825.

Chapter 7. Cruise of the *Guerrière*

1. TM to Crowninshield, 4 May 1818, Macdonough Letterbook; Crowninshield to TM, 12 May 1818, CL, Navy Department, M149, Roll 13, RG 45, NA.

2. Quoted in Macdonough, *Life of Commodore Thomas Macdonough,* 231–32. For her dimensions, see Journal of the U.S. Frigate *Guerrière* TMP (hereafter cited as *Guerrière* Journal).

3. TM to Crowninshield, 6 May, to same, 15 July 1818, Macdonough Letterbook; Morgan, *Autobiography of Rear Admiral Charles Wilkes,* 41; Homan to TM, 12 May, 4 July 1818, War of 1812 Manuscripts; Usher Parsons Journal, Rhode Island Historical Society.

4. TM to Deacon, 27 May, to Hull, 11 June, to Bainbridge, 9 July 1818, Macdonough Letterbook.

5. TM to midshipmen 17, 28, 30 June 1818, 9 July 1819, Macdonough Letterbook.

6. TM to Chase, 2 July 1819, Macdonough Letterbook; Rutledge, *Address,* 7. I am indebted to Philander D. Chase, editor in chief of the Papers of George Washington, University of Virginia, and Professor Reed Browning of Kenyon College, Gambier, Ohio, for leading me to material on the *Guerrière*'s chaplain.

7. TM to J. Smith, 29 June 1818, Macdonough Letterbook; see also order 17 December 1818, ibid.

8. Robbins to TM, 14 May 1818, Samuel Boyd to TM, 28 May 1818, Glaiser to TM, 10 July 1818, War of 1812 Manuscripts.

9. Macdonough estate inventory, 1824–27, 13:342–46, Middletown Probate Court.

10. Crowninshield to TM, 22 April, 30 June, Benjamin Homan to TM, 18 June, Campbell to TM, 18 June, TM to Homan, 22 July 1818, Homan to TM, 20 December 1821, typescript copies in Macdonough file, Operational Archives, Navy Department Library; TM to Homan, 24 April 1819, Macdonough Letterbook; Campbell to TM, 18 June 1818, War of 1812 Manuscripts; Morgan, *Wilkes*, 50.

11. Morgan, *Wilkes*, 51–52.

12. 24 July, 3, 19, 21 August 1818, *Guerrière* Journal; TM to Crowninshield, 22 August, TM to G. W. Campbell, 25 September 1818, Macdonough Letterbook; Journal of Philander Chase Jr., 12–13, Kenyon College Library (hereafter cited as Chase Journal).

13. Chase Journal, 18; 21, 25, 32, 30 August 1818, *Guerrière* Journal.

14. Chase Journal, 39, 41–59 on St. Petersburg; Morgan, *Wilkes*, 53–61; TM to Crowninshield, 2, 14 September 1818, Macdonough Letterbook.

15. Morgan, *Wilkes*, 60–61; 16 September–2 October 1818, *Guerrière* Journal.

16. TM to G. W. Campbell, 25 September 1818, Macdonough Letterbook.

17. TM to Crowninshield, 14 October 1818, copy of Crawly to TM, 23 April 1819, TM to Smith Thompson, 24 April 1819, Macdonough Letterbook; Morgan, *Wilkes*, 59–60. In the above letter to Secretary of the Navy Thompson, Macdonough also indicated that he subsequently learned that both men intended to leave the navy as soon as possible.

18. Ship Regulation, 14 November 1818, Macdonough Letterbook.

19. 14 October 1818, *Guerrière* Journal; Morgan, *Wilkes*, 61–62; Chase Journal, 66–68.

20. 16 October–6 December 1818, *Guerrière* Journal; TM to Crowninshield, 14 October, 12 November 1818, Macdonough Letterbook.

21. Morgan, *Wilkes*, 64–65.

22. Roosevelt, *Naval War of 1812*, 372–81; McKee, *Gentlemanly and Honorable Profession*, 189–90, 258–61; McKee, *Edward Preble*, 173–74, 226–27; Clowes, *Royal Navy* 6:169–73.

23. Case no. 163, Records of General Court Martial, M273, Reel 5, NA.

24. "Old Ironsides, No. II," 469–70.

25. 15 December 1818–13 April 1819, *Guerrière* Journal; Morgan, *Wilkes*, 68.

26. Morgan, *Wilkes*, 68–69; Chase Journal, 93–97.

27. TM to Stewart, 11 March, 7 April 1819, Macdonough Letterbook; Stewart to TM, 10 March, 12 April 1819, War of 1812 Manuscripts; Records of General Court Martial, NA.

28. Philander Chase Jr., Sermon Tenth, 4 April 1819, Chase Papers, Kenyon College Library.

29. Halsey to TM, 9 July 1819, War of 1812 Manuscripts.

30. Chase Journal, 210.

31. B. F. Bourne to TM, 29 April, TM to Stewart, 1 May 1819, Macdonough Letterbook. See also copy of Stewart to TM, ca. 19 February 1819, ibid.

32. 13 April–1 June 1819, *Guerrière* Journal; Case no. 348, M273, Roll 12; Case no. 62, M125, Roll 63; Case no. 66, M125, Roll 63, all in Records of General Court Martial, NA; Stewart to Thompson, 6 July 1819, CL, 1 June–29 July 1819, M125, Roll 63, RG 45, NA.

33. Case no. 330, Records of General Court Martial, NA; Ballard to Stewart, 4 March, Stewart to Ballard, 4, 5 March, Stockton to John Rodgers, 5 March 1819, Series 3A, vol. 2 (1814–1819), Box 31, Rodgers Family Papers, LC.

34. Stockton Court of Inquiry, Case no. 336, M273, Reel 12, Records of General Court Martial, NA; *Guerrière* General Order, 17 June, TM to Ballard and Gallagher, 19 June, to Don, 22 June 1819, Macdonough Letterbook; 21–26 June 1819, *Guerrière* Journal; Stewart to Don, 5 July 1819, M125, roll 63, no. 62 ff, RG 45, CL. See also Langley, "Robert F. Stockton," 80–81.

35. Case no. 348, Records of General Court Martial, NA; two letters TM to Stewart, 31 May 1819, Macdonough Letterbook; Morgan, *Wilkes*, 78–84. In his version of the affair, Midshipman Wilkes wrote that the court passed its sentence in Naples, but this is not what the transcript says.

36. Stewart to TM, 8, 9 July 1819, 239, War of 1812 Manuscripts; 8 July 1819, *Guerrière* Journal.

37. Stewart to Thompson, 6, 8 July 1819, M125, Roll 63, CL.

38. TM, Ballard, Gallagher, Page, Nicholson to Stewart, 10 July, TM to Thompson, 11 July 1819, Macdonough Letterbook; Stewart to TM et al., 13 July 1819, War of 1812 Manuscripts.

39. TM to *Guerrière* officers, 12 July 1819, Macdonough Letterbook; Morgan, *Wilkes*, 80–81; "Old Ironsides, No. II," 469–70.

40. TM to Tazewell, 10 July 1819, War of 1812 Manuscripts. On Tazewell's career, see the introduction to Heaton, "Littleton Weller Tazewell's Sketch," vi–xxxviii.

41. Stewart to TM, 9 July 1819, War of 1812 Manuscripts; 21 July–18 September 1819, *Guerrière* Journal; TMPAB, 29; Langley, "Robert F. Stockton," 82.

42. TM to Thompson, 16 February, 9 March 1820, Macdonough Letterbook; Thompson to TM, 22 February 1820, War of 1812 Manuscripts.

43. Copy, Thompson to TM, 10 March, TM to Thompson, 10 March 1820, Macdonough Letterbook; Callahan, *List of Officers*.

44. Bourne to Thomas Aspinwall, 22 August 1819, Naval History Manuscripts, Franklin D. Roosevelt Library; Russell Baldwin to TM, 25 April 1821, TM to Baldwin, 16 May 1821, Conover to TM, 22 June 1822, War of 1812 Manuscripts; Macdonough, *Life of Commodore Thomas Macdonough*, 245–46.

45. Knapp, *Thomas Macdonough*, 2–3.

46. Wolcott to TM, 8 February 1820, Thompson to TM, 10 February 1820, Smith to TM, 2 August 1820, War of 1812 Manuscripts.

47. *Biographical Sketch and Services,* 32–36.

48. William D. Shaler to TM, 20 May 1822, War of 1812 Manuscripts.

49. Guttridge and Smith, *Commodores,* 292–93.

Chapter 8. Life's Final Cruise

1. TM to Southard, 12 June, 2 August 1824, Macdonough Letterbook.

2. TM to Southard, 12 June, 9 July 1824, Macdonough Letterbook.

3. TM to Southard, 2, 4 August, 21 September, 8, 12, 27 October 1824, Macdonough Letterbook.

4. TM to Southard, 13 August, 2, 22 October 1824, Macdonough Letterbook.

5. TM to Barnhouse, 14 August 1824, TM to Southard, 16 August, 2, 20, 21 October 1824, Macdonough Letterbook; Southard to TM, 16 October 1824, M149, CL, RG 45, NA. Purser Timberlake merits a footnote in history as the first husband of Margaret "Peggy" O'Neale, who allegedly was having an affair with Senator John Eaton of Tennessee, an event that would eventually constitute a major scandal in the Andrew Jackson administration.

6. TM to Southard, 22 October 1824, Macdonough Letterbook.

7. TM to Rodgers, 19 June, 22 September, 1824, to Charles Morris, 29 September 1824, Macdonough Letterbook.

8. TM to Maj. Richard Smith, USMC, 25 August 1824, TM to Southard, 25 October 1824, Macdonough Letterbook.

9. Jones, *Sketches* 1:90. Jones boarded the *Constitution* as a schoolmaster shortly after Macdonough left the ship. Vallette remained as first lieutenant during Jones's tour. Most of the comments on shipboard life are based on Jones's *Sketches.*

10. For a description of a typical day, see Jones, *Sketches* 1:96–108, quotes, 104, 105.

11. For the typical Sunday, see Jones, *Sketches* 1:92–93, 108–9.

12. TM to Joseph Smith, 21 November 1818, Macdonough Letterbook.

13. A. H. Edwards, "U.S. Ship *Constitution* Watch and Quarter Bill," LC, lists the various gun crews. Gunnery exercises are discussed in Jones, *Sketches* 1:19–20.

14. For a description of burial at sea, see Jones, *Sketches* 1:36.

15. TM to Southard, 15 January 1825, CL, RG 45, NA; TM to Southard, 5 March, to David Deacon, 21 February, to Vail, 5 March, to Glentworth, 5 March 1825, to Morris, Mooers, and Swarthwout, 5 March, to J. O. Creighton, 14 May 1825, Macdonough Letterbook. In 1829 Bell would be court-martialed for "scandalous conduct" and sentenced to be cashiered from the service. President Andrew Jackson remitted the sentence. Bell died in 1833. See Records of General Court Martial, Case no. 471, 21 September 1829, RG 125, NA.

16. Southard to Rodgers, 15 January 1825, CL, RG 45, NA; Rodgers to Southard, n.d. May 1825, Rodgers Family Papers, LC; for Vail's case, see Records of General Court Martial, Case no. 429, 28 February 1825, RG 125, NA.

17. Rodgers to Southard, 2 July 1825, Rodgers Family Papers, LC.

18. Southard to Rodgers, 19 March 1825, Rodgers Family Papers, LC; Adams to

Rodgers, 7 February 1825, Diplomatic Instructions, Special Missions, 1:28, State Department, Records of General Court Martial, NA.

19. For Rodgers and his mission, see Paullin, *Commodore John Rodgers,* 327–39; Long, *Gold Braid and Foreign Relations,* 196–200; Finnie, *Pioneers East,* 26–28, 50–52, 57–63, 149–52, 247–61.

20. TM to Rodgers, 29 May 1825, Macdonough Letterbook; TM to Rodgers, 30 May 1825, Rodgers Family Papers, LC.

21. TM to Rodgers, 20, 21, 23 June, 6, 7 July, TM to Southard, 23 June 1825, Macdonough Letterbook.

22. Martin, *Most Fortunate Ship,* 224.

23. TM to Rodgers, 1 September 1825, Macdonough Letterbook.

24. TM to Rodgers, 30 August 1825, Macdonough Letterbook.

25. Muller, "Commodore and Mrs. Thomas Macdonough," 352–53.

26. *Middlesex Gazette,* 30 November 1825.

27. Jones, *Life and Services,* 30; TM to Rodgers, 24 September, 7, 12, 13 October 1825, Macdonough Letterbook.

28. Turk to Lucretia Ann Shaler, 24 November 1825, War of 1812 Manuscripts; Macdonough, *Life of Commodore Thomas Macdonough,* 250–55.

29. *Middlesex Gazette,* 5 December 1825. The funeral description and oration are published here.

30. Probate Court Records, Middletown Probate Court, 13:342–48, 455; 14:139; 15:94, 123, 340; 18:199, 274, 372, 387–93, 406–7, 421–42; Macdonough, *Macdonough-Hackstaff Ancestry,* 89–90.

31. For brief biographies of Macdonough's admirals, see Cogar, *Dictionary of Admirals* 1:15, 53–54, 95–96, 124–25, 172–73, 208–10.

32. Knapp, *Thomas Macdonough,* 6.

33. Roosevelt, *Naval War of 1812,* 356; Churchill, *History of the English Speaking People* 3:363; Bradford, "Macdonough, Thomas" 2:687; Mahan, *Sea Power* 2:381; Coles, *War of 1812,* 171; Horsman, *War of 1812,* 192; Dunne, "Battle of Lake Champlain," 103; Guttridge and Smith, *Commodores,* 262; Muller, *Proudest Day,* v–vi. See also Quimby, *U.S. Army* 2:622; Beach, *United States Navy,* 124–28; Hickey, *War of 1812,* 189–93; and Dudley, "War of 1812" 1:665. For the most part Canadian historians tend to blame Sir George Prevost for the defeat at Plattsburgh and do not give Macdonough much credit. See, for instance, Hitsman, *Incredible War of 1812,* 215–31; Stanley, *War of 1812,* 342–52; Turner, *British Generals,* 45–52.

34. Keithly and Tritten, "Charistmatic Dimension," 131–46, quotes 140. For a deeper understanding of the psychology of military leadership, consult several of the articles in Gal and Magelsdorff, *Handbook.*

35. Smith to H. Paulding, 10 February 1873, Paulding Papers, copy in Early History Branch, NHC.

36. Cooper, *History of the Navy,* 415–17.

37. Jones, *Sketches* 1:40.

Manuscripts

Archibald Stevens Alexander Library, Rutgers University, New Brunswick,
    New Jersey
    Paulding Papers in Francis Barton Stockton Papers
Bailey-Howe Library, University of Vermont, Burlington
    Isaac Clark Papers
    Thomas Macdonough Personal Account Book, 1813–1824
    Wilbur Collection
        Broadside. "Battle of Plattsburgh, and Victory on Lake Champlain"
Bixby Memorial Library, Vergennes, Vermont
    Monkton Iron Company Letterbook
Church of the Holy Trinity (formerly Christ Church), Middletown, Connecticut
    Parish Records
Clinton County Historical Society, Plattsburgh, New York
    Sailly Collection
Feinberg Library, State University of New York, Plattsburgh
    Bailey-Moore Collection
    Freligh Collection
Franklin Delano Roosevelt Library, Hyde Park, New York
    Naval History Manuscripts
    Thomas Macdonough Manuscripts
Historical Society of Delaware, Wilmington
    Macdonough Papers
    Muller Notes, MS 6100
    "New-Castle, June 2, 1775: At a Meeting of the Field-Officers of the County."
        Broadside. Box 32, Folder 1
    Rodney Collection
    Thomas Macdonough. "Journal Kept on Board the U.S. Frigate of 44 guns
        Constellation"
John Hay Library, Brown University, Providence, Rhode Island
    Broadside. "The Battle of Lake Champlain"
Kenyon College Library, Gambier, Ohio
    Journal of Philander Chase Jr.
    Philander Chase Jr. Sermons in Chase Papers

Library of Congress, Manuscripts Division, Washington, D.C.
   H. Edwards, "U.S. Ship *Constitution* Watch and Quarter Bill"
   James Madison Papers
   James Monroe Papers
   Rodgers Family Papers
   Thomas Macdonough Papers
      Journal of the U.S. Frigate *Guerrière*
      Letterbook, 1815–1825
Lilly Library, Indiana University, Bloomington
   Lucoes Goes Diary
   War of 1812 Manuscripts
Middletown Probate Court, Middletown, Connecticut
   Probate Court Records. Vols. 13–15
National Archives, Washington, D.C.
   Abstracts of Service Records of Naval Officers. RG 24
   Log Book Kept on the United States Sloop of War *Surprise [Eagle]*
   Naval Records Collection. RG 45
      Letters Received by the Secretary of the Navy: Miscellaneous
         Letters. M124
      Letters Received by the Secretary of the Navy: Captains' Letters. M125
      Letters Received by the Secretary of the Navy from Commanders. M147
      Letters Received by the Secretary of the Navy from Officers below the
         Rank of Commander. M148
      Letters Sent by the Secretary of the Navy to Captains. M149
      Letters Sent by the Secretary of the Navy to Officers. M149
      Miscellaneous Letters Sent by the Secretary of the Navy. M209
   Prize and Related Records for the War of 1812. U.S. District Court for the
      Southern District of New York, 1812–1816
   Records of General Court Martial and Courts of Inquiry of the Navy
      Department, 1799–1867. RG 125
   State Department. Diplomatic Instructions, Special Missions. Vol. 1, RG 59
   Treasury Department. 4th Auditors Accounts. RG 217
   War Department. Letters Received. RG 107
National Archives of Canada, Ottawa, Ontario
   RG 8, Ser. C
   Public Record Office. Kew, England (microfilm copies)
      Admiralty, 1/2737
      MG 11, CO 42
   Ruiter Papers
Naval Historical Center. Navy Department Library, Washington, D.C.
   Early History Branch
   Historical Manuscripts

Operational Archives
War of 1812 Manuscripts
Nimitz Library, U.S. Naval Academy, Annapolis, Maryland
Joel Abbot Family Papers
Pennsylvania Historical Society, Philadelphia
U. C. Smith Collection, William Jones Papers
Rhode Island Historical Society, Providence
Usher Parsons Journal
Russell Library, Middletown, Connecticut
Ephemeral Collection, Maps
Barratt, Joseph. *Plan of Main Street, Middletown, Showing the Buildings and Occupants from about 1770 to 1775* (1836)
Shelburne Museum, Shelburne, Vermont
Macdonough Papers
Sheldon Museum, Middlebury, Vermont
Henry L. Sheldon Scrapbook
State Historical Society of Wisconsin, Madison
Eleazer Wood Papers
Vermont Historical Society, Montpelier
David Sumner Papers
William L. Clements Library, University of Michigan, Ann Arbor
War of 1812 Papers
William R. Perkins Library, Duke University, Durham, North Carolina
Campbell Family Papers

Newspapers and Periodicals

Albany (N.Y.) Argus
Burlington (Vt.) Centinel
Burlington (Vt.) Northern Sentinel
Middlesex Gazette (Middletown, Conn.)
National Intelligencer (Washington, D.C.)
Naval Chronicle (London)
New York Columbian
Plattsburgh (N.Y.) Republican
Vermont Mirror (Middlebury, Conn.)
The War (New York)

Published Materials, Theses, and Dissertations

Adams, Charles Collard. *Middletown Upper Houses.* 1908. Reprint, Canaan, N.J.: Phoenix Publishing, 1983.
Adams, Henry. *History of the United States of America during the Second*

Administration of James Madison. Vol. 2. New York: Charles Scribner's Sons, 1891.

Alcock, Donald G. "The Best Defence Is . . . Smuggling? Vermonters During the War of 1812." *Canadian Review of American Studies* 25 (Winter 1995): 73–91.

American State Papers: Naval Affairs. 4 vols. Washington, D.C.: Gales and Seaton, 1834–61.

Bailey, Thomas A. *A Diplomatic History of the American People.* 6th ed. New York: Appleton-Century-Crofts, 1958.

Beach, Edward L. *The United States Navy, 200 Years.* New York: Henry Holt, 1986.

Beeson, Paul B., and Walsh McDermott, eds. *Cecil-Loeb Textbook of Medicine.* 11th ed. Philadelphia: W. B. Saunders, 1963.

Biographical Sketch and Services of Commodore Charles Stewart of the Navy of the United States. Philadelphia: J. Harding, 1838.

Bixby, George S., ed. *Peter Sailly (1754–1826): A Pioneer of the Champlain Valley with Extracts from His Diary and Letters.* New York State Library Bulletin 12. Albany: University of the State of New York, 1919.

Black, Jeremy. "Military Organisations and Military Change in Historical Perspective." *Journal of Military History* 62 (October 1998): 871–92.

Booth, James C. *Memoir of the Geological Survey of the State of Delaware.* Dover: S. Kimmey, 1841.

Bradford, James C. "Macdonough, Thomas." In *Dictionary of American Military Biography,* ed. Roger J. Spiller, 2:684–87. Westport, Conn.: Greenwood Press, 1984.

———. "The Navies of the American Revolution." In *In Peace and War: Interpretations of American Naval History, 1775–1978,* ed. Kenneth J. Hagan, 3–25. Westport, Conn.: Greenwood Press, 1978.

Brant, Irving. *James Madison: Commander in Chief, 1812–1836.* Indianapolis: Bobbs-Merrill, 1961.

Bushman, Claudia L., Harold B. Hancock, and Elizabeth Moyne Homsey, eds. *Proceedings of the Assembly of the Lower Counties on Delaware, 1770–1776, of the Constitutional Convention of 1776, and of the House of the Assembly of the Delaware State, 1776–1781.* Newark: University of Delaware Press, 1986.

Callahan, Edward. *List of Officers of the Navy of the United States and of the Marine Corps from 1775 to 1900.* 1901. Reprint, New York: Haskell House, 1969.

Chafee, Grace Irene. "Middletown." *Connecticut Quarterly* 4 (January 1898): 12–22.

Chambers, William. *Atlas of Lake Champlain, 1779–1780.* Bennington: Vermont Heritage Press and Vermont Historical Society, 1984.

Chapelle, Howard I. *The History of the American Sailing Navy: The Ships and Their Development.* New York: Bonanza Books, 1949.

Chapelle, Howard I., and Leon D. Polland. *The* Constellation *Question.* Washington, D.C.: Smithsonian Institution Press, 1970.

Churchill, Winston S. *A History of the English Speaking People.* 4 vols. New York: Dodd, Mead, 1956–58.

Clausewitz, Carl von. *On War.* Edited by Michael Howard and Peter Paret. Princeton, N.J.: Princeton University Press, 1976.

Clowes, William Laird. *The Royal Navy.* 7 vols. 1901. Reprint, London: Chatham Publishing, 1997.

Cogar, William B. *Dictionary of Admirals of the U.S. Navy.* Vol. 1. Annapolis: Naval Institute Press, 1989.

Coles, Harry L. *The War of 1812.* Chicago: University of Chicago Press, 1965.

Cooper, James Fenimore. *History of the Navy of the United States of America.* 2 vols. Philadelphia: Lea & Blanchard, 1839.

Crawford, Michael J. "The Navy's Campaign against the Licensed Trade in the War of 1812." *American Neptune* 46 (Summer 1986): 165–72.

Crisman, Kevin. *The* Eagle: *An American Brig on Lake Champlain during the War of 1812.* Shelburne, Vt.: New England Press, 1982.

———. *The History and Construction of the United States Schooner* Ticonderoga. Alexandria, Va.: Eyrie Publications, 1983.

Delaware: A Guide to the First State. New York: Viking Press, 1938.

Dudley, Wade G. *Splintering the Wooden Wall: The British Blockade of the United States, 1812–1815.* Annapolis: Naval Institute Press, 2002.

Dudley, William S. "War of 1812 and Postwar Expansion." In *Encyclopedia of the American Military,* ed. John E. Jessup, 1:629–76. New York: Charles Scribner's Sons, 1994.

Dudley, William S., and Michael J. Crawford, eds. *The Naval War of 1812: A Documentary History.* 3 vols. to date. Washington, D.C.: Naval Historical Center, Department of the Navy, 1985–.

Dull, Jonathan R. *The French Navy and American Independence: A Study of Arms and Diplomacy, 1774–1787.* Princeton, N.J.: Princeton University Press, 1975.

Dunne, W. M. P. "The Battle of Lake Champlain." In *Great American Naval Battles,* ed. Jack Sweetman, 85–106. Annapolis: Naval Institute Press, 1998.

———. "'The Frigate *Constellation* Clearly Was No More': Or Was She?" *American Neptune* 53 (Spring 1993): 77–97.

———. "An Inquiry into H. I. Chapelle's Research in Naval History." *American Neptune* 49 (Winter 1989): 39–55.

Elkins, Stanley, and Eric McKitrick. *The Age of Federalism: The Early American Republic, 1788–1800.* New York: Oxford University Press, 1993.

Engleman, Fred. *The Peace of Christmas Eve.* New York: Harcourt, Brace & World, 1962.

Estes, J. Worth. *Hall Jackson and the Purple Foxglove: Medical Practice and Research in Revolutionary America, 1760–1820.* Hanover, N.H.: University Press of New England, 1979.

Everest, Allan S. *Pliny Moore, North Country Pioneer of Champlain, New York.*
Plattsburgh, N.Y.: Clinton County Historical Association, 1990.
———. *The War of 1812 in the Champlain Valley.* Syracuse, N.Y.: Syracuse
University Press, 1981.
Failor, Kenneth M., and Eleonor Hayden. *Medals of the United States Mint.*
Washington, D.C.: GPO, 1969.
Ferguson, Eugene S. *Truxtun of the* Constellation: *The Life of Commodore Thomas
Truxtun, U.S. Navy, 1755–1822.* 1956. Reprint, Baltimore: Johns Hopkins
University Press, 2000.
Finnie, David H. *Pioneers East: The Early American Experience in the Middle East.*
Cambridge: Harvard University Press, 1967.
Fisher, Charles R. "Gun Drill in the Sailing Navy, 1797 to 1840." *American
Neptune* 41 (April 1981): 85–92.
Fitz-Enz, David G. *The Final Invasion: Plattsburgh, the War of 1812's Most Decisive
Battle.* New York: Cooper Square Press, 2001.
Folsom, William R. "The Battle of Plattsburgh." *Vermont Quarterly* 20 (October
1952): 235–59.
Fowler, William M., Jr. *Jack Tars and Commodores: The American Navy, 1783–1815.*
Boston: Houghton Mifflin, 1984.
———. *Rebels Under Sail: The American Navy during the Revolution.* New York:
Charles Scribner's Sons, 1976.
Fredriksen, John C., ed. "The Letters of Captain John Scott, 15th U.S. Infantry:
A New Jersey Officer in the War of 1812." *New Jersey History* 107
(Fall/Winter 1989): 61–81.
———. "The War of 1812 in Northern New York: General George Izard's
Journal of the Chateauguay Campaign." *New York History* 76 (April 1995):
173–200.
Gabaldon, Diana. *Dragonfly in Amber.* New York: Delacourt, 1992.
Gal, Reuven, and A. David Magelsdorff, eds. *Handbook of Military Psychology.*
New York: John Wiley, 1991.
Gardiner, Robert, ed. *The Line of Battle: The Sailing Warship, 1650–1840.* London:
Conway Maritime Press, 1992.
Garraty, John A., and Mark C. Carnes, eds. *American National Biography.* 24 vols.
New York: Oxford University Press, 1999.
Garrett, Carol. *New Castle County, Delaware, Land Records, 1749–1752.*
Westminster, Md.: Family Line Publications, 1998.
Garrison, J. Ritchie, Bernard L. Herman, and Barbara McLean Ward, eds. *After
Ratification: Material Life in Delaware, 1789–1820.* Newark: Museum
Studies Program, University of Delaware, 1988.
Goldwsky, Seebert J. *Yankee Surgeon: The Life and Times of Usher Parsons
(1788–1868).* Boston: Francis A. Countway Library of Medicine and Rhode
Island Publications Society, 1988.

Goodwin, Peter. *The 20-Gun Ship* Blandford. Annapolis: Naval Institute Press, 1988.

Graves, Donald E. *Field of Glory: The Battle of Crysler's Farm, 1813.* Toronto: Robin Bass Studio, 1999.

Grettler, David J. "Environmental Change and Conflict over Hogs in Early Nineteenth-Century Delaware." *Journal of the Early Republic* 19 (Summer 1999): 197–220.

Gruber, Ira D. "America's First Battle: Long Island, 27 August 1776." In *America's First Battles, 1776–1965,* ed. Charles E. Heller and William A. Stofft, 1–32. Lawrence: University Press of Kansas, 1986.

Gurwood, John, ed. *The Dispatches of Field Marshal the Duke of Wellington during his Various Campaigns...from 1799 to 1818.* 13 vols. London: John Murray, 1837–39.

Guttridge, Leonard F., and Jay D. Smith. *The Commodores.* Annapolis: Naval Institute Press, 1986.

Hagan, Kenneth J. *This People's Navy: The Making of American Sea Power.* New York: Free Press, 1991.

Hall, Peter. *Middletown: Streets, Commerce, and People, 1650–1981.* Wesleyan University Sesquicentennial Papers Number Eight. Middletown, Conn.: Wesleyan University Press, 1981.

Halleck, H. Wagner. *Elements of Military Art and Science.* New York: D. Appleton, 1846.

Heaton, Lynda Rees. "Littleton Weller Tazewell's Sketch of His Own Family... 1823: Transcribed and Edited." Master's thesis, College of William and Mary, 1967.

Hickey, Donald R. *The War of 1812: A Forgotten Conflict.* Urbana: University of Illinois Press, 1989.

———. "War of 1812: Still a Forgotten Conflict?" *Journal of Military History* 65 (July 2001): 741–71.

Hill, Ralph Nading. *Lake Champlain: Key to Liberty.* Woodstock, Vt.: Countryman Press, 1995.

Hinkkanen, Merja-Llisa. "When the AB was Able-Bodied No Longer; Accidents and Illness Among Finish Sailors in British Ports, 1882–1902." *International Journal of Maritime History* 8 (1996): 87–104.

Historical Society of Delaware. *Governor's Register, State of Delaware.* Wilmington, Del.: Star Publishing, 1926.

Hitsman, J. Mackay. *The Incredible War of 1812.* Toronto: University of Toronto Press, 1965.

Hoffman, Ronald. *A Spirit of Dissension: Economics, Politics, and the Revolution in Maryland.* Baltimore: Johns Hopkins University Press, 1973.

Horsman, Reginald. *The War of 1812.* New York: Knopf, 1969.

Hoxse, John. *The Yankee Tar: An Authentic Narrative of the Voyages and Hardships of John Hoxse.* Northampton, Mass.: John Metcalf, 1840.

Hughes, Richard L., Robert C. Ginnett, and Gordon J. Curphy. *Leadership: Enhancing the Lessons of Experience.* Homewood, Ill.: Irwin, 1993.

Izard, George. *Official Correspondence with the Department of War, Relative to the Military Operations of the Army under the Command of Major General Izard, on the Northern Frontier of the United States in the Years of 1814 and 1815.* Philadelphia: Thomas Dobson, William Fry, 1816.

James, William. *A Full and Correct Account of the Chief Naval Occurrences of the Late War between Great Britain and the United States of America.* London: T. Egerton, 1817.

———. *The Naval History of Great Britain, from the Declaration of War by France in 1793, to the Accession of George IV.* 6 vols. London: Harding, Lepard, 1826.

Jones, Charles C. *The Life and Services of Commodore Josiah Tattnall.* Savannah, Ga.: Morning News Steam Printing House, 1878.

Jones, George. *Sketches of Naval Life, with Notices of Men, Manners and Scenery, on the Shores of the Mediterranean, in a Series of Letters from the Brandywine and Constitution Frigates.* 2 vols. New Haven, Conn.: Hezekiah Howe, 1829.

Keegan, John. *The Mask of Command.* New York: Viking, 1987.

Keithly, David M., and James J. Tritten. "A Charismatic Dimension of Military Leadership?" *Journal of Political and Military Sociology* 25 (Summer 1997): 131–46.

Kemp, Peter, ed. *The Oxford Companion to Ships and the Sea.* New York: Oxford University Press, 1976.

Kiple, Kenneth, ed. *The Cambridge World History of Human Disease.* Cambridge: Cambridge University Press, 1993.

Knapp, Thomas L. *Thomas Macdonough, 1783–1825.* [New York: Monson Bancroft, 1834.]

Knox, Dudley W., ed. *Naval Documents Related to the Quasi-War between the United States and France.* 6 vols. Washington, D.C.: GPO, 1935–38.

———. *Naval Documents Related to the United States Wars with the Barbary Powers.* 6 vols. Washington, D.C.: GPO, 1939–44.

Langley, Harold D. "Robert F. Stockton: Naval Officer and Reformer." In *Quarterdeck and Bridge: Two Centuries of American Naval Leaders,* ed. James C. Bradford, 77–102. Annapolis: Naval Institute Press, 1997.

Lavery, Brian. *The Arming and Fitting of English Ships of War, 1600–1815.* London: Conway Maritime Press, 1987.

———. *Building the Wooden Walls: The Design and Construction of the 74-Gun Ship Valiant.* London: Conway Maritime Press, 1991.

———. *Nelson's Navy: The Ships, Men and Organisation, 1793–1815.* Annapolis: Naval Institute Press, 1997.

Leiner, Frederick C. "Decatur and Naval Leadership." *Naval History* 15 (October 2001): 30–34.

Letter from the Secretary of the Navy to the Chairman of the Naval Committee, Transmitting Sundry Documents from Captain Macdonough, Relating to the Capture of the British Fleet on Lake Champlain. Washington, D.C.: Roger C. Weightman, 1814.

Lewis, Dennis M. *British Naval Activity on Lake Champlain during the War of 1812.* Plattsburgh, N.Y.: Clinton County Historical Association, 1994.

Lewis, James. *The Last Campaign of the American Revolution: Rise and Fall of the Spanish Bahamas.* Columbia: University of South Carolina Press, 1991.

Lincoln, Charles Z., ed. *State of New York: Messages from the Governors.* Vol. 2, *1777–1822.* Albany: J. B. Lyon, 1909.

Lindstrom, Diane. *Economic Development in the Philadelphia Region, 1810–1850.* New York: Columbia University Press, 1978.

Lloyd, Christopher, ed. *The Health of Seamen: Selections from the Works of Dr. James Lind, Sir Gilbert Blane and Dr. Thomas Trotter.* London: Naval Records Society, 1965.

Lloyd, Christopher, and Jack L. S. Coulter. *Medicine and the Navy, 1200–1900.* Vol. 3, *1714–1815.* Edinburgh and London: E. & S. Livingstone, 1961.

Long, David F. *Gold Braid and Foreign Relations: Diplomatic Activities of U. S. Naval Officers, 1798–1883.* Annapolis: Naval Institute Press, 1988.

Longridge, C. Nepean. *The Anatomy of Nelson's Ships.* Annapolis: Naval Institute Press, 1961.

Lossing, Benson J. *The Pictorial Field-Book of the War of 1812.* New York: Harper & Brothers, 1869.

Macdonough, Rodney. *Life of Commodore Thomas Macdonough, U.S. Navy.* Boston: Fort Hill Press, 1909.

———. *The Macdonough-Hackstaff Ancestry.* Boston: Samuel Usher, 1901.

———. "A Paper on Commodore Thomas Macdonough, United States Navy." *Papers of the Historical Society of Delaware* 18 (1897): 15–20.

Mackesy, Piers. *The War for America, 1775–1783.* Cambridge: Harvard University Press, 1965.

Mackintosh, W. A. "Canada and Vermont: A Study in Historical Geography." *Canadian Historical Review* 8 (March 1937): 9–30.

Mahan, Alfred T. *Sea Power in Its Relations to the War of 1812.* 2 vols. Boston: Little, Brown, 1904.

Mahon, John K. *The War of 1812.* Gainesville: University of Florida Press, 1972.

"Maine Troops on Lake Champlain and the Loss of the *Eagle* and *Growler*, May–July 1813." *Moorsfield Antiquarian* 2 (May 1938): 34–42.

Malcomson, Robert. *Lords of the Lake: The Naval War on Lake Ontario, 1812–1814.* Toronto: Robin Bass Studio, 1998.

———. *Warships of the Great Lakes, 1754–1834.* Annapolis: Naval Institute Press, 2001.

Maloney, Linda. "The War of 1812: What Role for Sea Power?" In *In Peace and War: Interpretations of American Naval History, 1775–1978,* ed. Kenneth J. Hagan, 46–62. Westport, Conn.: Greenwood Press, 1978.

Martin, Tyrone G. *A Most Fortunate Ship: A Narrative History of Old Ironsides.* Rev. ed. Annapolis: Naval Institute Press, 1997.

McConaughy, James L. "Maritime Middletown." In *A Pamphlet Containing Two Articles on Middletown and the Connecticut River,* ed. Frank K. Hallock and James L. McConaughy. Middletown, Conn.: Tercentenary Celebration of the Founding of Middletown, 1950.

McKee, Christopher. *Edward Preble: A Naval Biography, 1761–1807.* Annapolis: Naval Institute Press, 1972.

———. *A Gentlemanly and Honorable Profession: The Creation of the U.S. Naval Officer Corps, 1794–1815.* Annapolis: Naval Institute Press, 1991.

McNeill, John R. "The Ecological Basis of Warfare in the Caribbean, 1700–1804." In *Adapting to Conditions: War and Society in the Eighteenth Century,* ed. Maarten Ultee, 26–42. Tuscaloosa: University of Alabama Press, 1986.

Merman, Bernard L. *Architecture and Rural Life in Central Delaware, 1799–1900.* Knoxville: University of Tennessee Press, 1987.

Millett, Allan R. *Military Professionalism and Officership in America.* Columbus: Mershon Center of Ohio State University, 1977.

———. *Semper Fidelis: The History of the United States Marine Corps.* Rev. ed. New York: Free Press, 1991.

Millman, Thomas. *The Life of Charles James Stewart.* St. Thomas, Ont.: Sutherland Press, 1953.

Morgan, William James, ed. *Autobiography of Rear Admiral Charles Wilkes, U.S. Navy, 1798–1877.* Washington, D.C.: Navy History Division, 1978.

Muller, Charles G. "Commodore and Mrs. Thomas Macdonough: Some Lights on Their Family Life." *Delaware History* 9 (October 1961): 341–54.

———. *Hero of Two Seas: The Story of Midshipman Thomas Macdonough.* New York: McKay, 1968.

———. *The Proudest Day: Macdonough on Lake Champlain.* New York: John Day, 1960.

Muller, H. N., III. "A 'Traitorous and Diabolical Traffic': The Commerce of the Champlain-Richelieu Corridor during the War of 1812." *Vermont History* 44 (Spring 1976): 78–96.

Munroe, John A. *Federalist Delaware, 1775–1815.* New Brunswick, N.J.: Rutgers University Press, 1954.

The Naval Monument. Boston: A. Bowen, 1816.

Naval Regulations Issued by Command of the President of the United States of America, January 25, 1802. [Washington, D.C.: Way & Groff, 1802.]

Noble, Henry H. "The Battle of the Boquet River." In *20th Annual Report of the American Scenic and Historic Society*, 591–92. Albany, N.Y.: American Scenic and Historic Society, 1915.

Nuxoll, Elizabeth M. "The American Navy, the 'War of Finance' and the Quest for Specie." In *New Interpretations in Naval History: Selected Papers from the Eighth Naval History Symposium*, ed. William B. Cogar, 28–44. Annapolis: Naval Institute Press, 1989.

O'Brian, Patrick. *Men-of-War: Life in Nelson's Navy*. New York: Norton, 1974.

———. *The Unknown Shore*. New York: W. W. Norton, 1995.

"Old Ironsides, No. II." *Hours at Home* 10 (March 1870): 468–77.

Pack, James. *The Man Who Burned the White House: Admiral Sir George Cockburn, 1772–1853*. Annapolis: Naval Institute Press, 1987.

Palmer, Michael A. *Stoddert's War: Naval Operations during the Quasi-War with France, 1798–1801*. Columbia: University of South Carolina Press, 1981.

Palmer, Peter S. *History of Lake Champlain, 1609–1814*. C. 1886. Reprint, Fleischmanns, N.Y.: Purple Mountain Press, 1992.

Parker, Wilmond W., ed. "Letters of the War of 1812 in the Champlain Valley." *Vermont Quarterly* 12 (April 1994): 105–24.

Paullin, Charles Oscar. *Commodore John Rodgers: Captain, Commodore, and Senior Officer of the American Navy, 1773–1838*. Cleveland: Arthur H. Clark, 1910.

Perkins, Bradford. *Castlereagh and Adams: England and the United States, 1812–1823*. Berkeley and Los Angeles: University of California Press, 1964.

Peters, Richard, ed. *The Public Statutes at Large of the United States of America*. Vol. 3. Boston: Little, Brown, 1861.

Powers, Stephen T. "Decline and Extinction of American Naval Power." Ph.D. diss., University of Notre Dame, 1965.

Pratt, Fletcher. *Preble's Boys: Commodore Preble and the Birth of American Sea Power*. New York: William Sloane, 1950.

Quimby, Robert S. *The U.S. Army in the War of 1812: An Operational and Command Study*. 2 vols. East Lansing: Michigan State University Press, 1997.

Register of the Commission and Warrant Officers of the Navy of the United States. Washington, D.C.: Davis and Force, 1822.

Richards, George H. *Memoir of Alexander Macomb*. New York: McElrath, Bangs, & Company, 1833.

Richter, Alice Bridge. *Planting and Sustaining the Vine: History of the Church of the Holy Trinity, Middletown, Connecticut*. [Middletown, Conn.: Church,] 1963.

Rightmyer, Nelson W. *The Anglican Church in Delaware*. Philadelphia: Church Historical Society, 1947.

Robinson, David S. *Conservation of a War of 1812 Anchor from Plattsburgh Bay, Clinton County, New York*. Vergennes, Vt.: Lake Champlain Maritime Museum, 2001.

Rodger, N. A. M. *The Wooden World: An Anatomy of the Georgian Navy.* London: William Collins, 1986.

Roosevelt, Theodore. *The Naval War of 1812.* 1882. Reprint, Annapolis: Naval Institute Press, 1987.

Rules of the District Court of the United States, for the District of New-York, in Prize Causes. New York: Pelsue and Gould, 1812.

Rutland, Robert A., and J. C. A. Stagg, eds. *The Papers of James Madison, Presidential Series.* 3 vols. to date. Charlottesville: University Press of Virginia, 1984–.

Rutledge, Edward. *An Address Delivered at the Internment of the Rev. Philander Chase, Jun.* Charleston, S.C.: C. C. Sebring, 1824.

Schweninger, Joseph M. "'A Lingering War Must Be Prevented': The Defense of the Northern Frontier, 1812–1871." Ph.D. diss., Ohio State University, 1998.

Seelye, John, ed. *Yankee Drover: Being the Unpretending Life of Asa Sheldon, Farmer, Trader, and Working Man, 1788–1870.* Hanover, N.H.: University Press of New England, 1988.

Seiken, Jeff. "'To Obtain Command of the Lakes': The United States and the Contest for Lakes Erie and Ontario, 1812–1815." In *The Sixty Years' War for the Great Lakes, 1754–1814,* ed. David Curtis Skaggs and Larry L. Nelson, 353–71. East Lansing: Michigan State University Press, 2001.

———. "'To Strike a Blow in the World that Shall Resound through the Universe': American Naval Operations and Options at the Start of the War of 1812." In *New Interpretations in Naval History: Selected Papers from the Fourteenth Naval History Symposium,* ed. Randy Carol Balano and Craig L. Symonds, 131–46. Annapolis: Naval Institute Press, 2001.

Sellers, Charles. *The Market Revolution: Jacksonian America, 1815–1846.* New York: Oxford University Press, 1991.

Skaggs, David Curtis, and Gerard T. Altoff. *A Signal Victory: The Lake Erie Campaign, 1812–1813.* Annapolis: Naval Institute Press, 1997.

Skelton, William B. *An American Profession of Arms: The Army Officer Corps, 1784–1861.* Lawrence: University Press of Kansas, 1992.

———. "Professionalization of the U.S. Army Officer Corps during the Age of Jackson." *Armed Forces and Society* 1 (August 1975): 443–71.

Smelser, Marshall. *Congress Founds a Navy, 1787–1798.* Notre Dame, Ind.: University of Notre Dame Press, 1959.

Smith, Gene A. *"For the Purposes of Defense": The Politics of the Jeffersonian Gunboat Program.* Newark: University of Delaware Press, 1995.

Smith, James Morton, ed. *The Republic of Letters: The Correspondence between Thomas Jefferson and James Madison, 1776–1826.* 3 vols. New York: W. W. Norton, 1995.

"Smuggling in 1813–1814: A Personal Reminiscence." *Vermont History* 38 (Winter 1970): 2–26.

Sprout, Harold, and Margaret Sprout. *The Rise of American Naval Power.* Princeton, N.J.: Princeton University Press, 1946.

Stagg, J. C. A. *Mr. Madison's War: Politics, Diplomacy, and Warfare in the Early American Republic, 1783–1830.* Princeton, N.J.: Princeton University Press, 1983.

Stanley, George F. G. *The War of 1812: Land Operations.* Toronto: Macmillan of Canada, 1983.

Symonds, Craig L. *Navalists and Antinavalists: The Naval Policy Debate in the United States, 1785–1827.* Newark: University of Delaware Press, 1980.

———. "William S. Bainbridge: Bad Luck or Fatal Flaw?" In *Command Under Sail: Makers of the American Naval Tradition, 1775–1850,* ed. James C. Bradford, 97–125. Annapolis: Naval Institute Press, 1985.

Taché, Étienne-Paschal. "Bataille Navale du Lac Champlain." In *Ordo[nna]nces de Mr. Paul de Chomedey, sieur de Maisonneuve, premier gouverneur de Montréal.* Montréal, [1859?]

Tucker, Spencer. *Arming the Fleet: U.S. Navy Ordnance in the Muzzle-Loading Era.* Annapolis: Naval Institute Press, 1989.

———. *The Jeffersonian Gunboat Navy.* Columbia: University of South Carolina Press, 1993.

Tunstall, Brian. *Naval Warfare in the Age of Sail: The Evolution of Fighting Tactics, 1650–1815.* Annapolis: Naval Institute Press, 1990.

Turner, Wesley B. *British Generals in the War of 1812: High Command in the Canadas.* Montreal & Kingston: McGill-Queen's University Press, 1999.

U.S. Army. Combined Arms Center. *Military Leadership.* FM 22-100. Washington, D.C.: Department of the Army, 1973.

U.S. Congress. Senate. *Report of the Naval Committee, Expressive of the Gallant Conduct of Cap. Macdonough, and the Officers, Seamen, Marines, &c. in the capturing of the British squadron on lake Champlain, on 11th September, 1814.* Washington, D.C.: Roger C. Weightman, 1814.

U.S. Naval Academy. Department of Leadership and Law. *Fundamentals of Naval Leadership.* Annapolis: Naval Institute Press, 1984.

Vandegrift, Lewis C. "Memoir of Commodore Thomas Macdonough." *Papers of the Historical Society of Delaware* 12 (1895): 5–13.

"Vermont Letters." *Vermont Historical Society Proceedings* 6 (March 1938): 15–20.

Ward, Christopher L. *The Delaware Continentals.* Wilmington: Historical Society of Delaware, 1941.

Watson, Harry L. *Liberty and Power: The Politics of Jacksonian America.* New York: Noonday Press, 1990.

Watts, Steven. *The Republic Reborn: War and the Making of Liberal America, 1790–1820.* Baltimore: Johns Hopkins University Press, 1987.

Wegner, Dana M. "The Frigate Strikes Her Colors." *American Neptune* 55 (Summer 1995): 243–58.

Wegner, Dana M., Colan Ratliff, and Kevin Lynaugh. *Fouled Anchors: The* Constellation *Question Answered.* Washington, D.C.: GPO, 1991.

Weigley, Russell F. *The American Way of War.* Bloomington: Indiana University Press, 1973.

Whipple, A. B. C. *To the Shores of Tripoli: The Birth of the U.S. Navy and Marines.* New York: William Morrow, 1991.

Whitehorne, Joseph A. *The Battle for Baltimore, 1814.* Baltimore: Naval and Aviation Publishing, 1997.

Wood, Gordon S. *The Radicalism of the American Revolution.* New York: A. A. Knopf, 1992.

Wood, William, ed. *Select British Documents of the Canadian War of 1812 (Publica-tions of the Champlain Society).* 3 vols. Toronto: Champlain Society, 1923.

THE ONLY full-length biography of the commodore is that written by his grandson Rodney Macdonough, *Life of Commodore Thomas Macdonough*. It is an admiring, uncritical study incorporating lengthy quotations from official and family documents, some of which are no longer available. He also published therein the commodore's autobiographical essay, the manuscript copy of which is owned by Thomas Macdonough Russell III of Mystic, Connecticut. Half a century later popular writer Charles G. Muller wrote a somewhat fictionalized narrative study of Macdonough's early career and of the battle of Lake Champlain titled *Proudest Day*. Shortly thereafter he published a number of letters in "Commodore and Mrs. Thomas Macdonough." Some of these manuscripts were lost after the death of their owner, Thomas Macdonough Russell Jr. Many of Muller's typescript copies of Macdonough materials are in the Delaware Historical Society, Wilmington. Muller also wrote a fictionalized children's biography of Macdonough's early life titled *Hero of Two Seas*. Some interesting contemporary comments appear in a virtually unknown pamphlet by Knapp titled *Thomas Macdonough*. Two short essays on Macdonough are worth consulting—Fletcher Pratt's chapter titled "Leadership" in Pratt, *Preble's Boys*, and Bradford's sketch, "Macdonough, Thomas."

Probably because his wife predeceased him and none of his four sons remained in Middletown, Connecticut, the Macdonough correspondence and records became scattered and lost. His daughter, Charlotte Rosella, lived in Middletown and maintained a small Macdonough collection that survived with her Russell family descendants. Thus there is no great corpus of Macdonough papers similar to the collections of the Perry, Rodgers, and Shaw naval clans. Over the years various Macdonough materials came into public archives at the Delaware Historical Society, Wilmington, the Lilly Library, Indiana University, Bloomington, the Franklin Delano Roosevelt Library, Hyde Park, New York, the Bailey-Howe Library, University of Vermont, Burlington, and the Manuscripts Division, Library of Congress, Washington, D.C. Of these, perhaps the most important are his journal of the *Constellation* cruise at the Delaware Historical Society, the Personal Account Book, 1813–1824 at the University of Vermont, and the *Guerrière* journal and his 1815–1825 letterbook at the Library of Congress. There are a host of official documents relating to Macdonough's career in the Naval Records Collection, RG 45, at the National Archives, plus the most useful estate records at the Middletown Probate Court. The Naval Historical Center has published three collections that relate to Macdonough's career: Knox, *Naval Documents Related to the Quasi-War;* Knox, *Naval Documents Related to the United States Wars;* and Dudley and Crawford, *Naval War of 1812.*

No study of the professionalization of the officer corps can avoid consulting McKee's authoritative *Gentlemanly and Honorable Profession.* Other important works include Hagan, *This People's Navy;* Palmer, *Stoddert's War;* Fowler, *Jack Tars and Commodores;* Symonds, *Navalists and Antinavalists;* Tucker, *Jeffersonian Gunboat Navy;* and Smith, *"For the Purposes of Defense."*

Any study of the second war with Great Britain should begin with Stagg's *Mr. Madison's War.* A solid survey of the conflict is Hickey, *War of 1812,* which should be supplemented by his bibliographic update titled "War of 1812: Still a Forgotten Conflict?"

On the naval aspects of the War of 1812, still useful are the three classic studies of Cooper, *History of the Navy;* Roosevelt, *Naval War of 1812;* and Mahan, *Sea Power.* A U.S. naval overview is found in Maloney, "War of 1812."

For a highly partisan, pro-British viewpoint, see James, *Full and Correct Account.* After James most Britons forgot the war ever took place. The Canadian perspective appears in Hitsman, *Incredible War of 1812,* and in Turner, *British Generals.*

Still the best study of the conflict along the "Mahican Channel" is Everest's *War of 1812,* which should be cautiously supplemented by Fitz-Enz, *Final Invasion.* Of high quality is Dunne, "Battle of Lake Champlain." On shipbuilding, see Chapelle, *History of the American Sailing Navy;* Crisman, *Eagle;* Crisman, *History and Construction;* and Malcomson, *Warships of the Great Lakes.*

The characteristics of naval command outlined in this volume are those developed in the text of the U.S. Naval Academy Department of Leadership and Law titled *Fundamentals of Naval Leadership.* Highly useful despite its focus on military rather than naval leadership attributes are several essays in Gal and Magelsdorff, *Handbook of Military Psychology.* These should be complemented by McKee's *Gentlemanly and Honorable Profession,* cited previously, and by Keithly and Tritten's provocative "Charismatic Dimension of Military Leadership?"

INDEX

David Curtis Skaggs is a well-known authority on military and naval operations during the North American wars from the colonial through the early national periods of United States and Canadian history. He has written and edited many books and scholarly articles on this period, including *A Signal Victory: The Lake Erie Campaign, 1812–1813*; *The Old Northwest in the American Revolution: An Anthology*; *War on the Great Lakes*; and *The Sixty Years' War for the Great Lakes, 1754–1814*. He is currently writing a biography of Commo. Oliver Hazard Perry.

The Naval Institute Press is the book-publishing arm of the U.S. Naval Institute, a private, nonprofit, membership society for sea service professionals and others who share an interest in naval and maritime affairs. Established in 1873 at the U.S. Naval Academy in Annapolis, Maryland, where its offices remain today, the Naval Institute has members worldwide.

Members of the Naval Institute support the education programs of the society and receive the influential monthly magazine *Proceedings* and discounts on fine nautical prints and on ship and aircraft photos. They also have access to the transcripts of the Institute's Oral History Program and get discounted admission to any of the Institute-sponsored seminars offered around the country.

The Naval Institute also publishes *Naval History* magazine. This colorful bimonthly is filled with entertaining and thought-provoking articles, first-person reminiscences, and dramatic art and photography. Members receive a discount on *Naval History* subscriptions.

The Naval Institute's book-publishing program, begun in 1898 with basic guides to naval practices, has broadened its scope to include books of more general interest. Now the Naval Institute Press publishes about one hundred titles each year, ranging from how-to books on boating and navigation to battle histories, biographies, ship and aircraft guides, and novels. Institute members receive significant discounts on the Press's more than eight hundred books in print.

Full-time students are eligible for special half-price membership rates. Life memberships are also available.

For a free catalog describing Naval Institute Press books currently available, and for further information about subscribing to *Naval History* magazine or about joining the U.S. Naval Institute, please write to:

Membership Department
U.S. Naval Institute
291 Wood Road
Annapolis, MD 21402-5034
Telephone: (800) 233-8764
Fax: (410) 269-7940
Web address: www.navalinstitute.org

/